"Scholar and professor Matthew D. Kim offers a theologically rich, biblically astute, culturally attuned, spiritually rooted, and communicationally aware introduction to homiletics. It will make you ready to preach but also, perhaps more importantly, ready to worship the triune God. More than an introduction to preaching, it is an introduction to how preaching is ultimately doxology. Read these pages and you will be ushered into prayer and praise: 'Glory be to the Father, and to the Son, and to the Holy Ghost.'"

—**Luke A. Powery**, Duke University Chapel, Duke University

"The world of preaching is ready and waiting for *Ready to Preach*! Kim's book fills a gap in homiletics literature by focusing on five forms of preparedness: theological, biblical, cultural, spiritual, and communicational. His theological framework is distinct from other preaching texts because it presses into a trinitarian foundation for preaching. A leader in the area of homiletics and culture, Kim gets us culturally ready to preach God's Word. This work is replete with biblical references, anecdotes, and practical wisdom. With depth and breadth, warmth and wisdom, he draws on the scholarship of those who have gone before him while pushing us all forward into thoughtful consideration about today's listeners, the Bible, and theology. Most importantly, his authorial voice is filled with grace, humility, and confidence in the God of the Bible and what God has called preachers to do each Sunday. I am delighted to add *Ready to Preach* to my preaching syllabus."

—**Patricia Batten**, Gordon-Conwell Theological Seminary

"Many introductory homiletics textbooks are very similar in content, style, and approach. They have a basic outline to move someone from the text to the sermon. But Matthew Kim's *Ready to Preach* breaks that mold. Coming from a seasoned academic and practitioner, this work is trinitarian-focused, is sensitive to cultural concepts related to gender and ethnicity, and demonstrates the centrality of preaching to all the other aspects of developing disciples within a local congregation. Those who labor weekly to preach the text of Scripture with faithfulness, depth, and clarity will welcome this work."

—**Eric C. Redmond**, Center for Compelling Biblical Preaching,
Moody Theological Seminary

"Those familiar with Matthew Kim's work have come to expect his remarkable ability to translate profound concepts into practical preaching wisdom—and this volume delivers. An experienced preacher and respected teacher of preaching, he brings that same tested insight to the page, guiding readers with probing questions and rich examples. Those who learn from him will find their preaching more deeply grounded in theological conviction and more thoughtfully crafted."

—**Ahmi Lee**, speaker, consultant, and author of *Preaching God's Grand Drama*

READY TO PREACH

READY TO PREACH

AN INTRODUCTION TO HOMILETICS

MATTHEW D. KIM

Baker Academic
a division of Baker Publishing Group
Grand Rapids, Michigan

Published by Baker Academic
a division of Baker Publishing Group
Grand Rapids, Michigan
BakerAcademic.com

Printed in the United States of America

Library of Congress Cataloging-in-Publication Data
Names: Kim, Matthew D., 1977– author
Title: Ready to preach : an introduction to homiletics / Matthew D. Kim.
Description: Grand Rapids, Michigan : Baker Academic, [2026] | Includes bibliographical references and index.
Identifiers: LCCN 2026007719 | ISBN 9781540968432 cloth | ISBN 9781493456666 ebook | ISBN 9781493456673 pdf
Subjects: LCSH: Preaching
Classification: LCC BV4211.3 .K555 2026
LC record available at https://lccn.loc.gov/2026007719

Any italics in Scripture quotations have been added for emphasis.

Cover design by Laura Powell

Baker Publishing Group publications use paper produced from sustainable forestry practices and postconsumer waste whenever possible.

26 27 28 29 30 31 32 7 6 5 4 3 2 1

To colleagues in homiletics—
thanks for journeying together in our common task
in teaching preachers to the glory of our triune God.

To students of homiletics—
thanks for answering God's call to preach the Word.
May your preaching ministry be faithful and fruitful
to the glory of our triune God.

CONTENTS

ACKNOWLEDGMENTS

What a truly unexpected email I received when executive editor Robert N. Hosack and his team at Baker Academic invited me to write this introductory preaching textbook. Thank you so much for the joy and honor to help train pastors and preachers through this volume. Thank you, Bob, for your constant support, encouragement, and belief over these many years in serving as a Baker author. I'm profoundly grateful to you. Thanks so much to the entire Baker Academic team for guiding me through the publication process: Kara Day, Anna English, Paula Gibson, Lydia Gustafson, Olivia Mason, Eric Salo, Elizabeth Sible, Mason Slater, and Jeremy Wells.

Over twenty-five years ago, God blessed me as a seminary student in meeting Scott M. Gibson at Gordon-Conwell Theological Seminary. I thought I was on my way to do doctoral studies in New Testament and become a professor of biblical studies. It was Dr. Gibson who redirected my course to study homiletics. Thank you, Scott, for your countless hours of investing in my life as a mentor, teacher, colleague, and friend. As you read this book, you'll quickly see that your homiletical legacy and fingerprints are scattered throughout. This book could only be written because you once said to me: "God loves you and I have a wonderful plan for your life."

The administrators of Baylor's Truett Seminary deserve a special word of gratitude. Thank you to Dean Todd Still and Associate Dean Angela Reed for their constant support and provision of ample space in the schedule for scholarship. I'm especially grateful to them and to President Linda Livingstone, Provost Nancy Brickhouse, and Vice Provost for Faculty Affairs DeAnna Toten Beard at Baylor University for granting me a research leave during the fall semester of 2025, enabling me to complete the manuscript. I appreciate my colleagues at Truett Seminary, including Jared Alcántara, Julie Covington,

Tyshawn Gardner, and Larry Parsley, who held down the preaching fort during my leave. Thanks also to Hannah Brown, my former graduate assistant at Truett Seminary, for compiling a solid bibliography upon which I drew some resources to write this project. In addition, I want to offer my deepest gratitude to the PhD in preaching students and MDiv students at Truett Seminary whom I have had the privilege of teaching and learning from.

The members of the Evangelical Homiletics Society have been like a second family to me. At the annual conference each year, I learn new things about the art and craft of preaching, for which I am truly thankful. While I cannot name every person who's made an impact on my life and homiletical thinking, here are friends in the world of preaching from the current and previous generations who have encouraged and invited me in myriad forms of gospel ministry: Shawn Allen, Kent Anderson, Jeff Arthurs, Eric Bargerhuff, Kris Barnett, Casey Barton, Patricia Batten, Wayne Baxter, Austin Carty, Sam Chan, Bryan Chapell, Calvin Choi, Bernie Cueto, Dave Currie, Charlie Dates, Michael Duduit, John Durham, Bob Eby, Lee Eclov, Andrew Finch, Nick Gatzke, Joel Gregory, Sarah Han, Paul Hoffman, Mary Hulst, Pablo Jiménez, Julius Kim, Abraham Kuruvilla, Ken Langley, Tara Beth Leach, Ahmi Lee, Endel Lee, Alyce McKenzie, David and Jennifer McNutt, Jolyon Mitchell, Winfred Neely, Jesse Nelson, Rob O'Lynn, Daniel Overdorf, Glenn Packiam, Rodney Palmer, Dennis Phelps, Luke Powery, Eric Redmond, the late Haddon Robinson, Greg Scharf, Rochelle Scheuermann, the late Jim Shaddix, William Storrar, Don Sunukjian, Al Tizon, John Tornfelt, Rich Villodas, Paul Scott Wilson, Daniel Wong, Matt Woodley, and Heather Joy Zimmerman. Thank you all for being my colleagues, teachers, and friends.

I'm also indebted to the Center for Pastor Theologians St. John Fellowship, including Tom Greggs, Gerald Hiestand, Joel Lawrence, Doug Sweeney, Zach Wagner, Todd Wilson, among others, to whom I presented the initial outline of this book at the June 2024 symposium. Thank you, CPT fellows and friends, for providing excellent feedback and suggestions. I especially want to thank Jason Meyer, Michael LeFebvre, and John Woods for reviewing a portion of the manuscript and offering their helpful and constructive wisdom on improving it.

I would be remiss not to take this opportunity to thank my family: Sarah, Ryan, Evan, and Aidan, who understand that a significant part of my work is research and writing. They are always gracious and supportive in giving me space to be productive for the church and the academy. My parents, Ki Wang Kim and Taek Hee Kim, as well as my in-laws, Chung Hyun Oh and Jung Sook Oh, have continually prayed for me, especially in writing this textbook. I couldn't have done this project without their collective prayer support. My brother, Dennis D. Kim, has always championed me and my work, for which I will always be grateful.

Last, but not least, I give praise, glory, honor, and thanks to our great and glorious triune God—Father, Son, and Spirit—for calling me to preach and for equipping me to become a preacher and teacher of preachers. Everything I do is an offering to you!

TEN SERMONIC STEPS

Step 1: Choose your **text**	(chapter 5)
Step 2: Know your **purpose**	(chapter 5)
Step 3: Appreciate your **genre**	(chapter 6)
Step 4: Understand your **context**	(chapter 7)
Step 5: **Study** your passage	(chapter 8)
Step 6: Establish your **point**	(chapter 9)
Step 7: **Outline** your passage	(chapter 10)
Step 8: **Write** your manuscript	(chapter 11)
Step 9: Point to the **Trinity**	(chapters 4 and 11)
Step 10: **Communicate** your message	(chapter 20)

INTRODUCTION

Why Preach?

The word of the Lord endures forever.

—1 Peter 1:25

Isn't it amazing that preachers speak on God's behalf? Just sit with this reality for a moment. The God who created the entire universe and spoke the world into existence allows us to communicate for him. Regardless of our opinion on sermons, preaching didn't happen by accident. It was God's idea for people of long ago, as human vessels, to gather in worship and to hear the very words he spoke. His words remain timeless, true, and applicable today. While the world has changed and continues to shift, God's Word never changes or expires. Peter the apostle puts it this way: "The word of the Lord endures forever" (1 Peter 1:25).

For this reason, sermons shouldn't be taken lightly or taken for granted. Preaching is not simply a polite activity to occupy space during a worship gathering. It's not a comedy act for those in search of a good laugh. And it's not a monologue offering self-improvement or cultural commentary.

Rather, a biblical sermon is a precious gift given by God for the people of God. The Bible is God's expression of love for his beautiful and exquisite church, the people of God, with an invitation to know him and experience an abundant life in the Trinity, beginning with God the Father, God the Son—Jesus Christ—and through the power of God the Holy Spirit. It is God's weekly sustenance for hungry souls. Scripture is God's blueprint for a meaningful life, informing and transforming our todays and culminating in a heavenly address for our tomorrows. The sermon is a medicinal story for a broken world—a word of hope that heals and transforms.

Those who feed others these weekly morsels of spiritual nourishment are called preachers. Preachers are called by God to share the words of God with the people of God. Many have tried to run from preaching, but it is an irresistible calling. God called people in the past, he calls them now, and he will call them in the future. Think of famous Bible characters scattered across Scripture who unsuccessfully attempted to run from God's calling to preach. We may try to flee on a weather-beaten sailboat, like Jonah, or rehearse a list of canned excuses, like Moses, or believe we are too insignificant, like Mary, the mother of Jesus. We may tell God and others that we are too young, too old, too shy, too weak, too scared, too fill-in-the-blank, but those whom God calls will ultimately surrender to his will. I've never seen God lose an arm-wrestling match. The question is whether those called to preach will thrive, find enjoyment, and be faithful in this eternally significant work of preaching the Word of God to the people of God.

In 1874, P. P. Bliss penned the memorable hymn "Words of Life," still sung in many congregations over one hundred fifty years later. The pleasant, melodic refrain goes, "Beautiful words, wonderful words, wonderful words of life." If you know this hymn, can you hear the tune ringing softly in your ears? Words are powerful. Words are meaningful. Words can be encouraging. Words can be harmful. Words can bring life.

As we commence this textbook on preaching, we ask the fitting question: Why preach? Why do we reserve this time every week in a worship service to hear someone speak from the pulpit? Why do preachers spend a good chunk of their working week preparing a sermon? What's the point?

The preacher brings these "wonderful words of life" to a specific congregation while always considering the time in history, the particular place and location, and hopefully the intention or purpose. But what is that purpose? In Colossians 1:28–29, the apostle Paul reminds preachers of our chief goal and responsibility: "We proclaim [Jesus Christ], admonishing and teaching everyone with all wisdom, so that we may present everyone fully mature in Christ. To this end I strenuously contend with all the energy Christ so powerfully works in me." Our homiletical aspiration, then, is to "present everyone fully mature in Christ." Since preaching concerns transformative discipleship, the sheer weight of preaching cannot be understated. As Julius J. Kim opens his book *Preaching the Whole Counsel of God*, "Preaching is a glorious calling. But it isn't easy."[1]

1. Julius J. Kim, *Preaching the Whole Counsel of God: Design and Deliver Gospel-Centered Sermons* (Zondervan, 2015), 19.

This work rests on the shoulders of many homileticians and their widely used homiletics textbooks who, in authoring them, have carefully navigated and disseminated their ground-breaking ideas on the art, science, and praxis of preaching.[2] Over the years, I have plucked and gathered wisdom from these homiletical giants. In fact, in this volume, there are hermeneutical, homiletical, pastoral, and theological insights, both explicit and implicit, that can be traced back to them. While I concur with Solomon's adage that "there is nothing new under the sun" (Eccles. 1:9), preaching is still contemporaneous with what people need to hear from the pulpit today, and how sermons are communicated by preachers does need to adapt to the times. By no means do I believe this volume is the definitive, be-all and end-all, last word on homiletics to be read by every student and seasoned preacher, in perpetuity. That would be utter foolishness and arrogance. Rather, my passion and aim for writing a homiletics textbook is much more modest.

Like notable homileticians Scott M. Gibson, who reminds us that "preaching is discipleship,"[3] or Abraham Kuruvilla, who says preaching "plays a key role in the spiritual formation of God's people,"[4] my aspiration in writing this book is to help pastors, preachers, and teachers consider the sermon as a form of cultivating Christian maturity in themselves and in their congregations. Keeping this in view, I define "preaching" as *communicating the triune God's Word to God's people for the purpose of life transformation and Christlikeness through explaining, envisioning, equipping, encouraging, and empowering preachers and listeners to become obedient to Scripture and to live more like Christ Jesus in every part of life.*

Using this definition, I've written this book attempting to answer many of the questions I had when I first started out in the call to preach.[5] Not that every single one of my questions will be reflected in your thinking, but

2. For instance, the following homiletics textbooks have been used widely for decades and even centuries: Charles Haddon Spurgeon, *Lectures to My Students* (1875; repr., Hendrickson, 2010); John A. Broadus, *On the Preparation and Delivery of Sermons*, 4th ed. (HarperCollins, 1979); H. Grady Davis, *Design for Preaching* (Fortress, 1958); D. Martyn Lloyd-Jones, *Preaching and Preachers*, 40th anniv. ed. (Zondervan, 2011); Haddon W. Robinson, *Biblical Preaching: The Development and Delivery of Expository Messages*, 4th ed. (Baker Academic, 2025); and Bryan Chapell, *Christ-Centered Preaching: Redeeming the Expository Sermon*, 3rd ed. (Baker Academic, 2018). Additional preaching textbooks can be found in the Further Reading section at the end of the book.

3. Scott M. Gibson, *Preaching with a Plan: Sermon Strategies for Growing Mature Believers* (Baker Books, 2012), 17.

4. Abraham Kuruvilla, *A Vision for Preaching: Understanding the Heart of Pastoral Ministry* (Baker Academic, 2015), 12.

5. See also Matthew D. Kim, *A Little Book for New Preachers: Why and How to Study Homiletics* (IVP Academic, 2020).

hopefully many of them will be. In short, what does a new or seasoned preacher need to know as one prepares for a lifelong preaching ministry?

Two other primary questions advanced in this book form bookends as you begin your preaching ministry: What do you want your preaching ministry to be known for? At the end of your time on earth, what will God say about your sermons? Here are some additional questions to ponder:

- What kinds of words fill our sermons?
- Are they the words of God or primarily our own thoughts and opinions?
- Are we speaking the words of God by allowing Scripture to saturate the minds and hearts of God's people?
- Are we conveying what God is saying in this text?
- Are we filling homilies and homiletical moments with more of God, the stories of God, and the plans of God?
- Are we the hero or main character of every sermon?
- Are listeners leaving the worship gathering overwhelmed by God's presence, purposes, and praise?
- Do listeners leave hearing the sermon with clear instructions, encouragement, and conviction to live out scriptural truths?

Before we get too far afield, it's important to acknowledge the sobering situation ahead of us. I echo the concern that preaching has been in jeopardy for decades. Haddon W. Robinson opens his homiletics textbook with these dour words: "This is a book about expository preaching, but it may have been written for a depressed market. . . . The word is out in some circles that preaching should be abandoned."[6] In many cases, preaching has been floundering without a clear direction and purpose. We are living in a time where preaching is often considered antiquated or accusatory by listeners, and a growing number of preachers are viewed with suspicion. The precarity of preaching is not because preachers don't preach. They do. Rather, for too long, the homiletical trend is that preachers have been minimizing use of the Scriptures in their sermons, in both duration and depth.

Instead of exegeting the text and applying the Word of God to the people of God, effective preachers are synonymous today with gifted storytellers, belly-shaking comedians, celebrity wordsmiths, or cultural commentators. Many have wielded precious sermonic seconds for personal gain, abusing

6. Haddon W. Robinson, *Biblical Preaching: The Development and Delivery of Expository Messages*, 4th ed. (Baker Academic, 2025), 1.

pastoral authority or encouraging listeners to elevate them to a celebrity status of sorts. Sermons today speak too little of the Scriptures and make too much of ourselves. As a result, listeners in the pews are left biblically malnourished. They need to hear more about God and about the Scriptures in our sermons. This diminution and mishandling of God's Word in the pulpit have led to feeble congregations and frenetic and fear-filled disciples. Would you agree?

While this book cannot solve all the pulpit concerns across the planet, it is an attempt to offer an introductory homiletics textbook for a new day. I envision the act of preaching as five major forms of readiness, including: theological, biblical, cultural, spiritual, and communicational. Effective biblical sermons involve careful consideration of each of these emphases. In other words, a sermon is the very compilation of time invested in understanding and interpreting theology, the Bible, the culture, the spiritual, and tailored communication.

This book seeks to restore the centrality of the Bible to its rightful place in the pulpit, where preachers and the Scriptures speak. Seeking to be comprehensive and still compact, this book differentiates itself from other influential and widely used textbooks, many which adorn our bookshelves, by emphasizing theology and a trinitarian approach for homiletics as well as providing extensive readiness for the cultural, spiritual, pastoral, and communicational aspects of preaching. I would encourage novice preachers to read the book sequentially. For more experienced preachers, you may be interested in reading specific parts and chapters to freshen up your craft. At the end of each chapter, starting in part 2, you will find questions for reflection and practice exercises to work on the chapter's contents. I'm hopeful that each part and chapter will have fresh insights for your sermonic imaginations, one and all.

The world is changing at light speed. I don't have to tell you that. We feel it every day, every moment, every second. It seems like the rapid advances in technological innovation and imagination are mind-boggling, stimulating, and yet alarming. Yet God promises that his Word will last forever. Those treasured words are tethered to every sermon we preach. Preaching is not as complicated as we make it out to be. As I often heard a preaching colleague say, "Preaching is just telling them what God says!"[7]

We are hoping to move ourselves and our listeners in that direction every week. And I believe our best preaching days are ahead, as we deliver trinitarian, gospel-rich, grace-filled, love-saturated, vision-inspired, application-personalized, correction-when-needed, disciple-oriented, fruit-produced,

7. A comment frequently made by my former preaching colleague Jeffrey D. Arthurs at Gordon-Conwell Theological Seminary.

kingdom-focused, and God-exalted sermons. To accomplish this, we will need to band together and make much about the Scriptures and less of ourselves in the pulpit. Will we courageously and lovingly proclaim God's truth to an anemic, malnourished, capitulating-to-culture Christian church?

The world is waiting to hear something markedly different in our sermons: a Scripture-imbued message. Christians in the pews are too. Listeners come to church expecting to hear life-transforming sermons. We have, as preachers of the Word, this amazing opportunity, every time we deliver a biblical message, to cast a vision for how our beloved listeners will live in such an attractive, countercultural way that others looking in will want to follow Jesus. Let's not squander this God-given opportunity rehearsing anecdotes about what we learned while waiting in the grocery line or using psychological, self-help placebos as substitution for scriptural substance.

While these narratives are appropriate at times, people need more than just another feel-good story, a clever joke, a little-known fact, or a tear-jerking testimony or two. Preach with an eye on eternity. People are dying, physically and spiritually, every day. Souls are at stake. Those who have not put their faith in Christ will be eternally separated from God. Sunday might be the only time they crack open their Bibles or see Scripture verses on a screen.

People need to hear the good news of Jesus Christ for the first time and on a regular basis. They need to hear repeatedly about the love of God. They need to know that there is a better way to live this short time on earth. They need to be reminded of God's love and faithfulness. They need to be confronted with God's holiness, righteousness, glory, and majesty. They need to know that forgiveness is possible even for the "worst of sinners." They need to encounter Jesus, who can transform their lives, their families, and their futures. They need to be empowered to live a Christ-honoring lifestyle. They need the Holy Spirit's direction and sage counsel, especially for difficult and desperate circumstances. They need to hear more about God. They need their lives to be transformed by the power of God's Word.

How can this occur? One way is through the faithful proclamation of Holy Scripture. Preaching was God's choice, not ours. Unlike quickly vanishing fashion trends, the writing and delivering of sermons will not go away. So, let's make the best of it. No matter our experience level, let's keep improving our homiletical craft. Show your listeners that Scripture is not dull, dated, or dead. It is alive! Give them a compelling vision for how exciting and rewarding it is to pursue hard after God.

Before we venture on, a brief word about me: Why am I qualified to write this textbook on preaching? Taking my first preaching class in seminary, I bombed. How's that for starters? While this story might not sound promising or give you, the reader, much confidence, it should give you a sense of where I've been. Please keep reading! It was an experience I would much rather forget. But I can't, and perhaps that's a good thing. Halfway through preaching my first sermon in class (fifteen minutes, without notes), my mind blanked. I couldn't remember a single word, phrase, or idea that came next. After standing frozen in silence for what felt like an hour, I said, with shame and a flushed face: "In conclusion . . ." and made something up on the spot. Then I disgracefully took my seat.

Preaching is hard, and it has never come naturally to me. To give myself some grace, preaching is hard for everyone because it should be. Like any beginning athlete, artist, musician, or skilled professional (name your discipline), I've been a preacher who, in God's providence, has learned more frequently from failure only to become more effective, through God's assistance, prayer, determination, hard work, and repetition.[8] For this reason, I come to you not as a preaching whiz or guru, but with a humility that comes from homiletical humiliation. In fact, those who are naturally talented at a sport or a profession, I believe, often have more difficulty in helping others improve. At least, that's what I've experienced and witnessed.

Yet, over the years, I've honed my sermonic craft and developed my voice to become a competent preacher. And I believe I can help you to do the same. Over the course of many years, I have trained well over a thousand aspiring preachers who've come with varying levels of skill, commitment, and confidence. With the power of the Holy Spirit, practical instruction, and increasing repetitions, however, all of my students have improved. We can become more effective preachers no matter how naturally gifted we may be. Say it with me: "God can help me and use me to be a faithful preacher in my generation!"

It's not going to be easy, but there can be a resurgence of Scripture-centered preachers who, like in the days of old, say, "Thus saith the Lord," in a winsome and irenic way, while keeping the ever-fluid contexts, hot-topic parleys, and culture wars in their view. We've been given an extraordinary gift in the act and service of preaching and in being called to the preaching ministry. Let's not squander this opportunity but steward this gift well. Since preaching is about God, we'll begin with theological readiness in part 1.

Let's first explore theology and become prepared theologically by asking: Who is this God about whom we preach, what does the Trinity mean for preaching, and why should preaching aim to be trinitarian?

8. See my primer on preaching, Matthew D. Kim, *A Little Book for New Preachers: Why and How to Study Homiletics* (IVP Academic, 2020).

PART 1

Theologically Ready

Much debate has ensued for centuries concerning whether sermonic priority should be given to centralizing or elevating one member of the Trinity above another—that is, God the Father, Son, or Spirit. Due to this standardization of centering one member of the Godhead, preachers tend to hold theological and hermeneutical presuppositions that often become exegetical blinders. I recognize that, by advocating a trinitarian framework for preaching, my proposition may fly in the face of centuries-long debates and that there will be some who will not agree in either theory or practice with what this book envisions and espouses. By no means do I want to stir up controversy or trigger undue hurt feelings with my pulpit allies. I respect that we will not always agree on every theological, hermeneutical, or homiletical minutiae of the sermonic process.

Yet, since you've consciously picked up this book, I want to advocate, in this opening part, for a more fulsome theological consideration, whereby preachers deliberate how each member of the Trinity in some shape or form aids us in living the Christian life and show listeners how each member of the Trinity intersects with, empowers, and even superintends over their daily lives (the preacher included). In these chapters, we will intentionally strive to embed the work of sermon preparation and proclamation in the trinitarian God rather than elevating one member of the triune God or falling into binitarian preaching or emphasizing two members of the Godhead.

1

DOCTRINE

What Does This Text Say About God?

> Be still, and know that I am God;
> I will be exalted among the nations,
> I will be exalted in the earth.
>
> —Psalm 46:10

The Bible is the story of God and the story about God. Unlike most movie scripts or books, where people are the central focus, in the Scriptures, the triune God—*Father, Son, and Spirit*—is the subject, protagonist, hero, and primary agent. Since this is a true statement, and since our messages are intended and expected to be biblical, sermons will be principally about God, the character of God, God's plan for the world, and God's will for the universe.

To get to the heart of the biblical narrative, we can't escape the subject matter of history. The concept of history that we know of as "his-tory" should more accurately be called "God-story" or "His-tory." That is, contrary to popular belief and even popular sermons, we are not the heroes of any biblical sermon—neither the preacher nor the people. The Bible is not anthropological. It's not a story mainly about humanity. Rather, it's about God. Yet, while preaching is known to be historical, effective preaching does not leave listeners in the past. We become and are part of God's grand narrative.

The emphasis in every sermon is that there is a basic pecking order to preaching: It is theologically and fundamentally about God, first, and people, second. Not the other way around! Sermons are not about our opinions or our reactions to what we think God's Word says. Rather, sermons are about what God's Word says and how we are to submit to, follow, and obey his Word, as his created beings in order to increase our discipleship and expand God's kingdom.

In every Scripture text, then, the preacher answers that critical question on behalf of the listeners: What does this text teach us about God? Only later in the sermonic process will we consider the corollary question: What does this text teach us about ourselves (see chapter 9)? As we consider the nature and doctrine of God to begin this book, let's put on our theological hats and remember that every preacher is a theologian.

Every Preacher Is a Theologian

In the book of James, he warns, "Not many of you should become teachers, my fellow believers, because you know that we who teach will be judged more strictly" (James 3:1). Teachers have a tall responsibility, since Bible teachers and preachers speak on God's behalf about God. In other words, they learn and speak theology. I confess my disinterest in Systematic Theology courses when I was in seminary. We had to read lengthy, often dense theological tomes and treatises. As students of divinity, it felt like we were always spinning in circles trying to fit God futilely into four corners of a cardboard box—an impossible task indeed. But theology is much more contoured and critical to the task of preaching than my original understanding of it.

Whether we care for the subject of theology or not, every preacher is a theologian by default just as Luther's notion of the "priesthood of all believers" conveys similarly that "every one of us is a minister of the gospel."[1] Preaching cannot be accomplished devoid of studying theology and experiencing divinity. In fact, as Chase R. Kuhn and Paul Grimmond point out in *Theology Is for Preaching*, "the intention of preaching is a clearer and more faithful theology."[2] A faithful preacher-theologian is, put simply, one who studies God, teaches about God, and hopefully knows and experiences God and leads others to do the same.

We know that God's Word demonstrates the "person of God" as the first and primary actor starting from the very first verse of the Bible: "In the

1. Michael Cooper-White, "Luther and Ministry 'in Crisis,'" Living Lutheran, June 28, 2017, https://www.livinglutheran.org/2017/06/23712.

2. Chase R. Kuhn and Paul Grimmond, eds., *Theology Is for Preaching: Biblical Foundations, Method, and Practice* (Lexham, 2021), xx.

beginning God created the heavens and the earth" (Gen. 1:1). It does not commence with "In the beginning, humans joined the heavens and the earth." So, what are we doing as preacher-theologians in the task of sermon writing and communicating? We are pointing people to God in three ways: toward his character, toward his actions, and toward his will.

Preaching Is Knowing God's Character

In J. I. Packer's classic theological work, *Knowing God*, he describes the nature and character of God and how we can know him. Packer opens the book by telling a story about a preacher at New Park Street Chapel, in Southwark, England, who on January 7, 1855, began his sermon to start the new year in this way:

> It has been said by someone that "the proper study of mankind is man." I will not oppose the idea, but I believe it is equally true that the proper study of God's elect is God; the proper study of a Christian is the Godhead. The highest science, the loftiest speculation, the mightiest philosophy, which can ever engage the attention of a child of God, is the name, the nature, the person, the work, the doings, and the existence of the great God whom he calls his Father.[3]

Said rightly, then, the task of preaching theologically is a matter of communicating to our listeners a clearer picture of God. What does a preacher need to know about God from Scripture, a book that primarily testifies about God? Let's begin with a discussion on the nature of God, particularly, his character. We come to know God better by knowing his character. Who is this God of whom the Bible speaks?

Listeners come to the worship gathering with all kinds of spiritual attitudes, conditions, experiences, and moods. They also have varied opinions and experiences of God: One moment they may love God, other moments they may hate him, and everything in between. Some may question the existence of God. Others remain distant from him—like a prodigal child running away from home—due to unrepentant sins, hardships, or circumstances. Some come with disappointment. Others come with hope, anticipation, and expectation. In every church, some listeners are waiting with giddy, bated breath for their weekly power nap. Yes, I speak as a preacher who has witnessed such sweet slumber every Sunday!

So, preachers indeed communicate the sermon to a mixed bag of listeners who are either engaged or disengaged, interested or disinterested. Two big

3. J. I. Packer, *Knowing God*, 50th anniv. ed. (IVP, 2023), 17.

underlying questions for our people include: What has God done for me lately? And why would God allow this to happen in my life or in someone else's life?

In some tangible and meaningful way, preachers inform their listeners who God is in the sermon based on the Scripture text read for the given worship gathering. Here is a list of characteristics or attributes of God that any given Bible text may bring to the surface, either explicitly or implicitly: God's comfort, compassion, forgiveness, generosity, holiness, justice, kindness, love, mercy, permission of evil, power, sovereignty, or wrath. Of course, there are others.

How are these characteristics of God presented in the Scriptures? Sometimes, God directly speaks for himself. We might refer to them as the "I am" passages where God makes absolute, truthful claims about who he is. This is communicated in first-person speech. For instance, God says, "I AM WHO I AM" to Moses in Exodus 3:14 to broadcast his résumé as the God of the universe who needs no introduction and no credit check. In Hebrew, YHWH or Yahweh, the name of God, can be translated as "I will be what I will be" and can be found over six thousand times in Scripture. We see it in English versions styled as LORD.[4]

God also refers to himself in the first person when he says in Leviticus 19:2, "Speak to all the congregation of the people of Israel and say to them, 'You shall be holy, for I the LORD your God am holy'" (ESV). In Exodus 3:6, God speaks to Moses in a face-to-face conversation, "'I am the God of your father, the God of Abraham, the God of Isaac and the God of Jacob.' At this, Moses hid his face, because he was afraid to look at God."

Notice, Jesus takes his turn, as well, in the Gospels. Explore the absolute "I am" statements found in John 6:20; 8:24, 28, 58; or 18:5.[5] The *ESV Global Study Bible* provides the following metaphorical "I am" statements:

"I am the bread of life." (John 6:35, 48; cf. 6:51)
"I am the light of the world." (8:12; 9:5)
"I am the door of the sheep." (10:7, 9)
"I am the good shepherd." (10:11, 14)
"I am the resurrection and the life." (11:25)
"I am the way, and the truth, and the life." (14:6)
"I am the true vine." (15:1)

4. Bethany Verrett, "Why Does God Call Himself 'I Am Who I Am'?," February 22, 2023, https://www.biblestudytools.com/bible-study/topical-studies/why-does-god-call-himself-i-am-that-i-am.html.

5. "The 'I Am' Statements of Jesus," in *ESV Global Study Bible* (Crossway, 2018), 1495.

It's difficult to talk about someone (in our case a divine someone) without naming what they're like and without sharing specific qualities, characteristics, or attributes. I might tell someone about my wife: My wife is beautiful, intelligent, clever, creative, patient, loving, kind, talented, and so on. I wouldn't just describe my wife as "my wife" without mentioning tangible characteristics. I would need to name some concrete descriptors for someone else to get a picture of what she's like. Similarly, the sermon does that regarding God. We tell God's people who God is by telling them what God is like. But there's more to a sermon than that.

Preaching Is Knowing What God Has Done and What He Will Do

In the third century, Novatian wrote: "The conception of God as He is can only be grasped in one way . . . by thinking of Him as a Being Whose attributes and greatness are beyond our powers of understanding, or even of thought."[6] And yet, it would be foolish to never attempt to know this God who is all-present, all-powerful, and all-knowing.

Without being overly reductionistic, the power in Scripture comes from describing the ordinary and extraordinary wonders of what God has done in history and by using various prepositions to describe his interactions with his people: for instance, in, among, to, with, alongside, and through his people. While we cannot be comprehensive, of course, let's start with some of the major biblical examples that showcase God's actions through biblical witness and testimony. Between the bookends of Scripture, from Genesis to Revelation, God has revealed his past and future actions. The text will provide you with specific "this is what God has done" moments to mention in your sermon. It won't take much exegetical digging to know what those past and future actions are.

So, how can we wow our listeners as we give them weekly meals from Scripture? How can we help them know that this God actively desires a true and lasting relationship/fellowship with them? How can we turn our listeners' eyes, ears, energies, affections, and even resources to growing in relationship with this God? By giving them regular glimpses of the majesty, wonder, affections, and glory of God!

To begin this process theologically, write down answers to the following:

1. What is God doing in my Scripture text? List all the actions of God mentioned in your passage.

6. Novatian, *On the Trinity* 1.2, in *The Treatise of Novatian on the Trinity*, trans. Herbert Moore (Macmillan, 1919), 27, available at https://ia801308.us.archive.org/4/items/cu31924096083344/cu31924096083344.pdf.

2. What are God's names and their meanings in this text?
3. What will God do? Has God made a promise, either explicitly or implicitly?

1. What Has God Done? (What Actions of God Are Described in Your Bible Text?)

Every text in some manner paints a picture or tells a story of what God has done. Consider the following:

- God spoke the heavens and the universe into existence (Gen. 1:1).
- God enjoyed creating all things, living and nonliving, and above all, people (Adam and Eve) (Gen. 1–2).
- God delivered the Israelites from slavery in Egypt (Exod. 14:30–31).
- God delighted in us, his people (Ps. 149:4–5).
- God forgave our sins: past, present, and future (Jer. 31:34).
- God sent his Son into the world to save us from sin and condemnation (John 3:16).
- God sent his promised Holy Spirit to live and dwell in us and to comfort/guide us (John 14:16).
- God granted us his peace (John 14:27).
- God won the victory over sin and death (1 Cor. 15:57).

2. What Are God's Names? (How Can We Know God's Character Based on His Names?)

For example, see the following names of God:

- Elohim: The Sovereign, Mighty Creator
- Jehovah: The Unchangeable, Intimate God
- El Shaddai: The All-Sufficient One
- Adonai: Lord and Master
- Jehovah Jireh: The Lord My Provider
- Jehovah M'Kaddesh: The Lord My Sanctifier
- Jehovah Nissi: The Lord My Banner of Victory
- Jehovah Rophe: The Lord My Health
- Jehovah Shalom: The Lord My Peace and Wholeness
- Jehovah Tsidkenu: The Lord My Righteousness
- Jehovah Rohi: The Lord My Shepherd

- Jehovah Shammah: God Is There
- El Elyon: God Most High
- Jehovah Tsebaoth: The Lord of Hosts
- Jehovah Makkeh: The Lord Who Molds Me
- Jehovah Gmolah: The Lord Who Rewards
- Jehovah Elohay: The Lord My God[7]

3. What Will God Do? (What Promise Has God Made in Your Scripture Passage?)

Another truth of Scripture is that God keeps his promises. Many of these promises relate to God's presence, comfort, peace, freedom, provision, and protection, which ensure confidence to trust him more.

- God will destroy the evil one (2 Thess. 2:8).
- God will judge the sins of the nations, the world, and us (Joel 3:1–21; Matt. 25:32).
- God will set the captives and prisoners free (Isa. 61:1).
- God will provide for his children (Matt. 6:31–32).
- God will grant ultimate peace (Phil. 4:6–7).
- God will never leave us or forsake us (Heb. 13:5).
- God will separate "the sheep" from "the goats" (Matt. 25:31–46).
- God will wipe away every tear from our eyes (Rev. 21:4).
- God will create a new heaven and a new earth (Rev. 21:1).

Having general knowledge of the promises of God gives the preacher and listeners confidence in God's Word and in what he instructs us to do. We have assurance that God is faithful and will fulfill his promises in every part of Scripture.

Preaching Is Knowing God's Will

If we were to summarize Scripture, it's safe to say that God's will is for all people on earth to worship and praise him. The fancy term for praise is doxology. We may come from traditions that sing the doxology: "Praise God from whom all blessings flow, Praise Him all creatures here below, Praise Him above ye heavenly hosts, Praise Father, Son, and Holy Ghost, Amen."

7. Marilyn Hickey, *The Names of God* (Whitaker House, 2009).

Where in Scripture does it refer to God's will? Specific mention of the "will of God," the "desires of God," and even the "expectations of God" are found in both the Old and New Testaments. If Jesus, the Son of God, cared about doing his Father's will, who are we to do otherwise?

Below is a sampling of verses concerning God's will, listed from general to specific:

> "Teach me to do your will, for you are my God!" (Ps. 143:10)

> "He has shown you, O mortal, what is good.
> And what does the Lord require of you?
> To act justly and to love mercy
> and to walk humbly with your God." (Mic. 6:8)

> "Your kingdom come, your will be done, on earth as it is in heaven." (Matt. 6:10)

> "Whoever does God's will is my brother and sister and mother." (Mark 3:35)

> "Father, if you are willing, take this cup from me; yet not my will, but yours, be done." (Luke 22:42)

> "For my Father's will is that everyone who looks to the Son and believes in him should have eternal life, and I will raise them up on the last day." (John 6:40)

> "Therefore do not be foolish, but understand what the Lord's will is." (Eph. 5:17)

> "Do not conform to the pattern of this world, but be transformed by the renewing of your mind. Then you will be able to test and approve what God's will is—his good, pleasing and perfect will." (Rom. 12:2)

> "Give thanks in all circumstances; for this is God's will for you in Christ Jesus." (1 Thess. 5:18)

> "For it is God's will, that by doing good you should silence the ignorant talk of foolish people." (1 Pet. 2:15)

> "The Lord is not slow in keeping his promise, as some understand slowness. Instead he is patient with you, not wanting [willing] anyone to perish, but everyone to come to repentance." (2 Pet. 3:9)

> "Instead you ought to say, 'If it is the Lord's will, we will live and do this or that.'" (James 4:15)

God's will is found in his Word. People often ask, "What does God want from me?" or "What does God want me to do?" The pattern we observe in Scripture is that usually we cannot know God's will apart from knowing his Word. God's will can also be discerned through prayer, in seeking his will, and in obedience to his instructions and commands. As people called by God to serve as his messengers and guides for Christian living, preachers openly share the will of God with God's people. In some cases, our listeners will reject God's will because God's will is often seen as being antithetical to our will. And yet, God has called preachers to give our people a holistic understanding of who God is, what he has done and will do, and what his will is for us and his created world.

In a Christian society that is often biblically illiterate, preachers have a divine opportunity to help their congregants stay connected to God by keeping their noses in Scripture. Preaching that is transformational happens when we help people know and experience this awesome God. Preaching is, therefore, consequential business. In fact, preaching is, in the memorable words of James Earl Massey, our "burdensome joy"[8] "to provide the means of transformation ordained by a sovereign God that will affect the lives and destinies of eternal souls committed to a preacher's spiritual care."[9] If we desire to know God, God has revealed himself through the Bible. It is the Bible that we preach as we teach our people how to become theologians for themselves: those who study, those who teach, and those who know/experience the Lord.

The next part of our theological readiness is to reflect personally on what theological, exegetical, or doctrinal blinders we might be seeing the biblical text through.

QUESTIONS

1. Which doctrines have been most important to you in your understanding of theology? Why?
2. What are three to five characteristics of God that your congregation needs to know and experience in this season?
3. In what ways has it been a struggle for you to experientially know God? Are there characteristics of God for which you have a disconnect?
4. What are three to five of the greatest challenges for you when preaching to your congregation about who God is?

8. James Earl Massey, *The Burdensome Joy of Preaching* (Abingdon, 1998).
9. Bryan Chapell, *Christ-Centered Preaching: Redeeming the Expository Sermon*, 3rd ed. (Baker Academic, 2018), 3.

2

PRESUPPOSITIONS

What Theological Presuppositions Do We Read into a Text?

> Now the Berean Jews were of more noble character than those in Thessalonica, for they received the message with great eagerness and examined the Scriptures every day to see if what Paul said was true.
>
> —Acts 17:11

Nobody interprets the Bible in a vacuum. Since Christians encounter and experience God differently, the interpretive process happens amid the complexity of what it means to be human, with embodied perspectives that are situated within a culture(s), denomination, ethnicity, family, gender, personhood, and so on. These learned perspectives influence how we read the Bible, view God, understand Christian doctrine, and listen to/obey God's instructions. Two questions many people wrestle with are, "Where is God now?" and "Where is he when we need him most?" Some sitting in the worship space today may feel like God is silent. Consider as well that how we view God often informs how we preach about God. Similarly, how we view the world can influence how we read, interpret, and preach a particular biblical text or theme.

In this second chapter, I alert us to some preunderstandings or presuppositions (things we presuppose/prethink/preconsider) that may cloud our vision when reading and interpreting a particular Scripture passage. Presupposition can also be viewed as placing or inserting meaning on top of the text where it doesn't belong—preventing the original biblical author's intention from being objectively understood.

This chapter seeks to answer the question in the subtitle: What theological presuppositions do we read into a text? Going further: Why does this matter for preaching? And how can we minimize our suppositions to allow God's voice and the biblical authors to be read and heard more clearly?

Imagine receiving a physical letter in the mail, to your surprise, from a former teacher who has had a profound influence on your life. In this letter, she praises you for the type of person you were when you were a student in her classroom and tells you how proud she is of who you have now become decades later. But that's not all. In this letter, your teacher shifts her focus and asks how your family is doing. She commends you and your spouse for how you've raised your children (whose names and even ages she still remembers). The letter then goes on to tell about her life and what's been taking place over the last several months. She shares touching details about her own family (particularly her grandchildren and great-grandchild), about how they are enjoying life together across the generations. It's a beautiful, heartfelt, and personal letter. It's something you'll always cherish.

When opening and reading such a letter, we don't simply read words on a page. We pick up on its meaning, tone, and message. This particular letter wasn't written to express frustration or disappointment about something that took place in the past. Rather, it's a jovial correspondence brimming with love, appreciation, and kind words. The one who penned the letter, this teacher, had a clear meaning behind the letter. Why was the letter written: to express her gratitude and to share her life with you. My role, as the recipient, is to receive the letter, read it, interpret its meaning and message, and ultimately appreciate it and the person who sent it. When necessary, it may involve some type of corresponding action in response.

A powerful way to read a letter is to read it aloud (especially if we can hear in our minds the author's audible voice). Words have power, feelings, and emotions behind them. As we hear the spirit of the letter through the writer's voice, it may become clearer what their tone and intentions are. The letter makes more sense because we know the person who wrote it.

The issue for preachers is that we are not the direct, original recipients of a particular Bible book or epistle. So there can be a notable disconnect. Since we don't have past experiences with the biblical author (e.g., Moses, the prophets, or the apostle Paul), it's hard to imagine the communication as being directed at us or toward us who are living in a distant time and a faraway place. As such, it can become easy to distance ourselves from the biblical author and therefore it becomes an easy temptation to read into the text something that the original author did not mean. Why does this occur?

We have cultural differences as well as chronological differences from the biblical author, world, and times. In our finiteness, the book is just a foreign person writing a foreign book/letter with a foreign meaning. The danger becomes presupposing or allowing what some have called "preunderstanding" of what we believe the author intended based on *our* limited knowledge, *our* worldview, and *our* sense of morality and ethics. And thus, we place meaning on the text that wasn't *ours* to make.

"Did God Really Say . . . ?"

A primary battle preachers face surrounding correct biblical interpretation is with our commitment to the trustworthiness of Scripture. As Jason C. Meyer notes, a foundational question all preachers must wrestle with comes straight from a pivotal moment in the garden of Eden. Meyer observes, "The first temptation was a focused attack on God's word. Satan successfully sowed seeds of doubt in Eve's heart concerning what God had clearly spoken. Our ancient foe hates true preaching and has set his sights on scrambling the clear signals of Scripture concerning it."[1] Similarly, John Durham shares an insight from his sermon that can apply to our interpretation of Scripture: "The question is not what feels right according to you, it is what is right according to Jesus!"[2] We might say it this way: The question is not, Does this feel like the right interpretation according to you? The question is, What is the right interpretation according to Jesus? In other words, we, through our own understanding, can—and do—cloud God's original meaning of his Word. We want to pray, seek, and ask the triune God to reveal God's meaning of the text and not our own. We are standing in the pulpit and declaring with humility and love, "Yes, God really did say _______!" Therefore, we don't have jurisdiction or permission to alter what God says and what he means.

To guide us toward a proper interpretation of Scripture, Anthony C. Thiselton asks two foundational questions regarding biblical interpretation: "Can the Bible mean anything we want it to mean?" and "How can we agree about norms or criteria for the responsible or valid interpretation of Scripture?"[3] Taking a similar approach, J. Todd Billings invites us to answer a true or

1. Jason C. Meyer, *Preaching: A Biblical Theology* (Crossway, 2013), 13.

2. John Durham, "Way, Truth, Life," sermon, March 2, 2025, Highland Baptist Church, Waco, Texas, available at https://youtu.be/A9X04loS77w.

3. Anthony C. Thiselton, *Hermeneutics: An Introduction* (Eerdmans, 2009), 2.

false quiz: "(1) Since all interpretation of Scripture is culturally conditioned (descriptive), then all interpretation of Scripture must be equally valid (normative). (2) Since all interpretation of Scripture is culturally conditioned (descriptive), then one culture never has the right to criticize another culture's interpretation of Scripture (normative)."[4] For students of Scripture (that includes all of us), how would you answer these questions?

Adding to Thiselton's questions, here are a couple of thoughts: (1) No, the Bible cannot mean anything we want. (2) It's more complicated than we think. To Billings's true or false test, I would respond: (1) No, all interpretations are not equally valid. (2) While we ought not to criticize another culture's interpretation, we can disagree. Well, then, you might ask: Who's right and who's wrong? The more pressing matter in this chapter goes back to our presuppositions. The most important supposition we can have is whether we believe God's Word is trustworthy and authoritative over our lives. This is the hinge point on which all interpretive decisions rest: trust in God's Word and in God's authority.

In what remains, I'd like to explore definitions of "preunderstanding" and "presuppositions" concretely (since they affect everyone's interpretation of the Bible) and then have us consider both theological and hermeneutical presuppositions we might be inserting or placing on a particular Bible text (which shouldn't be there) and why this practice can be a slippery slope in interpreting Scripture for preaching. We'll begin by defining some terms.

What Is Preunderstanding?

Everyone reads Scripture with some kind of preunderstanding or presupposition.[5] It's impossible not to do so because we are human. Let's drill down on what each term means. First, preunderstanding, according to J. Scott Duvall and J. Daniel Hays, is explained as follows: "One major influence that can skew our interpretive process and lead us away from the real meaning in the text is what we call *preunderstanding*. Preunderstanding refers to all of our preconceived notions and understandings that we bring to the text, which have been formulated, both consciously or subconsciously, *before* we actually study the text in detail."[6] What determines our preunderstanding

4. J. Todd Billings, *The Word of God for the People of God: An Entryway to the Theological Interpretation of Scripture* (Eerdmans, 2010), 106.

5. Thomas A. Howe, "Preunderstanding, Presuppositions and Biblical Interpretation," *Religions* 13, no. 12 (2022): 1.

6. J. Scott Duvall and J. Daniel Hays, *Grasping God's Word: A Hands-On Approach to Reading, Interpreting, and Applying the Bible*, 4th ed. (Zondervan Academic, 2020), 139–40.

is who we are, our identity, our experiences, and our prior learning on a given topic—for instance, family, gender, age, ethnicity/race, culture, denomination and church background, education, marital status, profession, economic class or income bracket, social location (urban, suburban, rural), the teaching of former or current pastors/teachers/others, and additional factors.[7]

Some have described preunderstanding as the glasses we wear that "color" our interpretation of the Bible. As missionary Paul Hiebert reminds us, "Theologizing must also affirm the priesthood of all believers and recognizes that they must and will take the universal message of the Bible and apply it to their own lives and settings. It must recognize that different people ask different questions when they read the Scriptures, and that their cultural and historical frameworks will color their interpretations."[8]

The primary emphasis here is not about whether we have a preunderstanding or not. We all do. But I do need to ask myself: Do I recognize my preunderstandings? How strictly or loosely do I hold on to my preunderstanding of a particular Scripture text? Am I willing to explore the interpretive world through the lens of another person who will likely have a prescription different from my own? As Richard L. Schultz asks, "What theological presuppositions and convictions do we hold? And are we willing to listen to the 'other side'?"[9] Sometimes our preunderstanding becomes a sticking point on which we are unwilling to listen to, and especially yield to, others and their views (particularly if a change of perspective is necessary). Granted, some biblical perspectives were never meant to be altered or swayed.

So, what does one's preunderstanding look like in real time? Let's provide a Bible text for our preunderstanding exercise. Envision someone reading the Beatitudes in Matthew 5:3–12:

> Blessed are the poor in spirit, for theirs is the kingdom of heaven.
>
> Blessed are those who mourn, for they shall be comforted.
>
> Blessed are the meek, for they shall inherit the earth.
>
> Blessed are those who hunger and thirst for righteousness, for they shall be satisfied.
>
> Blessed are the merciful, for they shall receive mercy.

7. To this list, we can include Eastern or Western mindset (worldview, beliefs, values), individualist faith vs. collectivist faith, cultural lenses (racial, ethnic, cultural, national), political identification, and so on.

8. Paul G. Hiebert, *Missiological Implications of Epistemological Shifts: Affirming Truth in a Modern/Postmodern World* (Trinity, 1999), 101–2.

9. Richard L. Schultz, *Out of Context: How to Avoid Misinterpreting the Bible* (Baker Books, 2012), 25.

> Blessed are the pure in heart, for they shall see God.
>
> Blessed are the peacemakers, for they shall be called sons [and daughters] of God.
>
> Blessed are those who are persecuted for righteousness' sake, for theirs is the kingdom of heaven.
>
> Blessed are you when others revile you and persecute you and utter all kinds of evil against you falsely on my account. Rejoice and be glad, for your reward is great in heaven, for so they persecuted the prophets who were before you. (ESV)

Now think of some real-life examples of people who live in quite different places and contexts with very dissimilar backgrounds and experiences. For instance, J. Todd Billings asks,

> How does God speak through Scripture to a Latin American Christian living under an oppressive political regime? How does God speak through Scripture to a first-generation Christian convert from Islam in east Africa? How does God speak through Scripture to a white Methodist parishioner in Nebraska? Questions such as these presuppose that God speaks through the instrument of Scripture. . . . But that leaves open the question of how the interpreter's contextual location impacts the event of God's speaking through Scripture.[10]

Who Jesus refers to as being blessed in these markedly different situations and places will be informed by our preunderstanding. Again, preunderstanding encompasses "all of our preconceived notions and understandings that we bring to the text, which have been formulated, both consciously and subconsciously, *before* we actually study the text in detail."[11]

Write down some ideas of how each person above (we can think of them as three different case studies) might preunderstand the first type of person Jesus mentions in the Beatitudes, "Blessed are the poor in spirit, for theirs is the kingdom of heaven" (Matt. 5:3). Then take a moment to consider your own preunderstandings. What preunderstanding do you bring to the interpretive process as a fill-in-the-blank person? Ask yourself these questions:

- Which cultural lens (or lenses) most dominantly impacts how we interpret the Bible?
- How does my gender influence my interpretation of Scripture?
- How does my race/ethnicity influence my understanding of Scripture?

10. Billings, *Word of God for the People of God*, 105.
11. Duvall and Hays, *Grasping God's Word*, 140.

- How does my upbringing/family influence my interpretation of Scripture?
- How does my church experience or denomination's doctrines influence my interpretation of Scripture?

What Is a Presupposition?

A more common term that is synonymous to preunderstanding is "presupposition." A presupposition refers to the following: "When we presume to explain the meaning of the Bible, we do so with a set of preconceived ideas or presuppositions. These presuppositions may be examined and stated, simply embraced unconsciously, or in some combination. But anyone who claims to have no presuppositions and who studies the Bible objectively and inductively is either deceived or naïve. We argue that interpreters should discover, state, and consciously adopt those assumptions they agree with and can defend, or else they will uncritically retain those they already have, whether or not they are adequate and valid."[12] Another way of explaining presupposition is literally being something I "presuppose," "prethink," or "preassume" about a person, place, topic, or issue, and so on.

Oftentimes, when a preacher or teacher of the Bible brings up the topic of culture, gender, ethnicity, and other "social" factors, we are told "just preach the Bible" or "just preach the gospel," as if the Bible and the gospel have no trace of culture or social elements embedded within them. Kevin J. Vanhoozer writes, "When I began my seminary teaching, few people talked about culture, and when it was mentioned, it was always *foreign*: something *they* had, over *there*. Much has changed since then."[13] Sadly, however, I, as an ethnic minority person, believe that much has remained the same regarding centering and normalizing the interpretations of dominant, majority cultures, without hearing from members of minority communities. Like the adage says, "It's like describing water to a fish"; we cannot see our own cultural blind spots. We assume everyone reads, thinks, and interprets as we do. And, if you don't, you should and you must.

For this reason, it's helpful to approach Scripture with a healthy level of personal and cultural suspicion about our own interpretations. As Paul drills home in Romans 12:3, "For by the grace given me I say to every one of you: Do not think of yourself more highly than you ought, but rather

12. William W. Klein, Craig L. Blomberg, and Robert L. Hubbard Jr., *Introduction to Biblical Interpretation*, 3rd ed. (Zondervan, 2017), 210–11.

13. Kevin J. Vanhoozer, foreword to Justin Ariel Bailey, *Interpreting Your World: Five Lenses for Engaging Theology and Culture* (Baker Academic, 2022), xi.

think of yourself with sober judgment, in accordance with the faith God has distributed to each of you." Humility is essential when attempting to understand the Scriptures. I need to recognize my own preunderstanding and presuppositions when reading and interpreting a text just as much as I also need to become aware of my own sins and cultural idols that have a clear impact on how I interpret Scripture. Consider the ways in which we are self-serving and read the text with a tendency to benefit ourselves, our families, and our situations. People are self-protecting, self-serving, and self-promoting by nature. To say differently is an unrealistic manner of approaching the Bible. We read the Bible with some measure of self-benefit and self-service. We will go into a bit more detail regarding cultural awareness and sins in a moment.

Theological Presuppositions

I hope by now we can agree that everyone reads, interprets, and views the world through their presuppositions. And so we can now ask, What might be some theological presuppositions we read into a Scripture text that may not be intended or warranted? Again, how we view God often shapes how we understand what the Bible teaches about him.

Here are some common theological presuppositions (sometimes doctrinal) that I may read into a particular Scripture passage: an emphasis on one person of the Trinity (Christ-centered, Spirit-centered, Theo-centered), election and salvation (Calvinist vs. Arminian), atonement (universal vs. limited), eschatology (premillennial, postmillennial, amillennial), baptism (paedo vs. believer), spiritual gifts (cessationists vs. continuationists), women's and men's roles in ministry (egalitarian vs. complementarian), and many others.

Let's return to the original questions we set out to answer at the beginning of the chapter. (1) Why do theological presuppositions matter for preaching? (2) And how can we minimize our suppositions to allow God's voice and the voices of biblical authors to be read and heard more clearly?

Theological Presuppositions and Preaching

How preachers view certain doctrines or ministry philosophies can cloud or redefine their reading and interpretation of texts. For example, I need to be able to determine and confirm my doctrinal belief—for instance, regarding the world of spiritual gifts, whether one is a cessationist (meaning spiritual gifts and miracles ceased at the end of the apostolic age) or a continuationist (spiritual gifts and miracles continue today). When I read a text that seems to support or deny the evidence of miracles, my presupposition determines how I preach a given passage.

We've all been indoctrinated (not always a pejorative term) to believe certain truths about God and the Bible that are not easily amenable to disagreement. According to Thiselton, presuppositions in our theology are "the impression of rooted beliefs and doctrines which are not only cognitive and conceptual, but which also can only be changed and revised with pain, or at least with difficulty."[14] Not that I must change my view on every presupposition, but is there humility in my spirit to learn and grow from another believer?

To do so, we must acknowledge that it is necessary to factor cultural and personal sins into our interpretation. There are positive, God-given elements in culture as well as destructive, sinful elements in any culture. We cannot blindly assume that a cultural reading or interpretation of Scripture is accurate or correct because the text may be read with cultural sin obstructing the readers' view.

Hearing the Voices/Interpretations of Others

What will help us recognize our theological presuppositions? Two foundational ways to stretch our thinking regard having a posture of listening and a posture of charity.

A Theological Posture of Listening

A steady posture of listening is encouraged throughout Scripture. James 1:19 reads, "My dear brothers and sisters, take note of this: Everyone should be quick to listen, slow to speak and slow to become angry." This eagerness to listen extends to the biblical interpretation enterprise as well. One of the reasons why I appreciate the "preaching teams" approach, where a handful of church members from different genders, educational backgrounds, ethnicities, occupations, and life experiences will come together presermon to discuss a given Scripture text to guide the pastor, is that it automatically creates an opportunity to learn from others about how they read and interpret the Bible. Oftentimes, a person will walk away from such a gathering and say,

14. Anthony C. Thiselton, *New Horizons in Hermeneutics: The Theory and Practice of Transforming Biblical Reading* (Zondervan, 1992), 45.

"That was eye-opening. I never considered some of the things people shared tonight about this Scripture text." Listening to the experiences and interpretations of others can offer a wealth of wisdom in the sermon process. There have been countless times in my ministry where I've appreciated hearing the interpretation of others and even marveled at how another's interpretation made so much sense.

A Theological Posture of Charity

The King James Version renders 1 Timothy 4:12 as, "Let no man despise thy youth; but be thou an example of the believers, in word, in conversation, in charity, in spirit, in faith, in purity." Charity can also be translated as "in love." Listening to others is in its most basic form an act of love. Listening to others gives us the ability to be charitable toward someone who's had a different experience than we have. Charity, to be clear, is not blind acceptance. Yet, charity offers us the ability to sit, listen, ponder, reflect, and authenticate another person and what they have gone through in their lives. A person who is economically struggling (for instance, living in low-income housing) and a financially thriving person (for instance, living in a gated community) are not going to read the Bible, and particularly any passages about money, in the same way. We would hope that some measure of charity could be given in either direction. When we take a posture of charity, we will not automatically discredit or discard another's interpretation and experiences. Hearing another's voice allows me as the preacher to extend grace to someone who's experienced life much differently from me.

CONCLUSION

In this chapter, we have provided a definition for "preunderstandings/presuppositions" that influence how we read and interpret a biblical passage (for preaching). We have also established that every person has a penchant toward certain preunderstandings/presuppositions that shapes how we preach the Scriptures. As we journey forward to our next chapter, we will consider how theological presuppositions affect our preaching perspectives on the Trinity.

QUESTIONS

1. What preunderstandings/presuppositions guide your reading and interpretation of Scripture? Can you name them?
2. How might your preunderstandings/presuppositions be obscuring your hermeneutical process?
3. Are there any preunderstandings that you feel strongly need to be maintained? Why or why not?
4. Which presuppositions are you willing to let go of in your interpretive process?

3

TRINITY

Do We Centralize All Three Persons of the Trinity (or Just One)?

May the grace of the Lord Jesus Christ, and the love of God, and the fellowship of the Holy Spirit be with you all.

—2 Corinthians 13:14

Did you know that "Trinity" can be a fighting word?

I was attending a paper presentation at an academic conference in a room full of pastors, preaching professors, and seminarians. The speaker argued for a God-centered or theocentric preaching model contending that our sermons should emphasize God the Father.[1] Later, the conversation dialed up a few degrees and erupted into a near physical altercation over whether preachers should centralize the second member of the Trinity, God the Son, in the person of Jesus Christ, or God the Father, in one's preaching. Those in the Christ-centered preaching camp became visibly upset (some even turning purple in the face and pounding the table). A shouting match broke out where those in the Christ-centered group contested that any sermon not centralizing Christ was antithetical to the preaching task and Christian ministry. They teetered on calling non-Christocentric preachers heretics.

1. Ken Langley, "When Christ Replaces God at the Center of Preaching," paper, presented at Evangelical Homiletics Society Conference, Beeson Divinity School, Birmingham, Alabama, 2008.

How do you feel about preaching and the Trinity? Do you have strong beliefs on this topic? Preaching on the triune God—Father, Son, and Spirit—can trigger polarizing emotions. The Trinity is a theological doctrine unlike any other to explain clearly. We often sing hymns and songs about the triune nature of God, being one yet three persons. Due to the Trinity's mysteriousness, preachers have a daunting task of trying to communicate the doctrine of the Trinity in a stand-alone sermon, let alone trying to create a trinitarian hermeneutical and homiletical paradigm for all sermons. And yet, in this book, that is what I am calling us to do as a faithful theological response—to preach biblically and theologically about our trinitarian God.

As we begin this chapter, and if I may be so bold, remember this: Failing to help our listeners in every sermon understand how the triune God acts and empowers them impoverishes God's people, who desperately need to taste and experience how this triune God speaks and encourages them in every part of their lives.

Imagine being a personal chef for each member of the congregation. Not preaching trinitarian sermons is like offering our listeners a lifetime of meals without a major source of nutrients, like protein. Over time our listeners become increasingly malnourished and protein deficient. Our physical bodies need protein just as our spiritual bodies need the Trinity. Whether congregants realize it or not, they need to know and regularly encounter God the Father, God the Son, and God the Spirit! This triune God is always working; therefore, we want to emphasize sermonically what that means for us and our hearers.

Before we envision and articulate a trinitarian sermonic model in the next chapter, let's first take a moment to consider a theological presupposition that may creep into our understanding of the doctrine of the Trinity. Depending on our church backgrounds and experiences, do we tend to centralize one member of the Trinity: God the Father, God the Son, or God the Holy Spirit, or does our preaching emphasize (as equally as possible) all three?

In the first part of this chapter, we will understand what it looks like to only preach one member of the Trinity at a time based on our theological presuppositions. Then, in the latter part, I will contend for a trinitarian emphasis in sermons and why it is necessary and impactful for our preaching ministry.

Theological Presuppositions: Centralizing Only One Member?

Each denomination or preaching tradition tends to hold tightly to or prioritize one or more members of the Trinity. Whether this has been modeled by previous pastors or is simply a theological conviction we have landed on, there are some who preach by centralizing only a single member of the Trinity as a theological, hermeneutical, and homiletical commitment. Stated differently, our sermons default to centralizing God the Father, God the Son, or God the Spirit. What does centralizing one person of God look like?

Centralizing God the Father

At the beginning of chapter 1, I made the point that Scripture is the story of God and the story about God. Between then and now, nothing has changed in my mind. Preaching, if done rightly, is fundamentally theological, and God is the main subject. To centralize God the Father in one's preaching is the first hermeneutical and homiletical course one might choose to adopt.

Kenneth J. Langley proposes a theocentric view of preaching: "Preaching should be God centered because God is God centered and wants us to be God centered in everything we do. . . . Preaching is all about God and all for God."[2] Langley continues, "The God-centeredness of the Bible's own preaching and that of Jesus himself is reason enough to be God centered in preaching."[3] A biblical passage used to showcase a potential God-centered preaching model might be Philippians 2:9–11, in the Christ-hymn, where Paul gives final glory to Father God: "Therefore God exalted him to the highest place and gave him the name that is above every name, that at the name of Jesus every knee should bow, in heaven and on earth and under the earth, and every tongue acknowledge that Jesus Christ is Lord, *to the glory of God the Father*." As we read and interpret a biblical text such as this one, we may hold tightly to a God-centered theological presupposition.

Centralizing God the Son

More than the "God the Father" theological camp, anecdotally I believe there are more who espouse a Christ-centered or Son-centered approach to preaching. Again, when one endorses a particular member of the Trinity over another, it is not exclusive to the point where there is no mention of God the Father or God the Spirit. Here are some well-known advocates for such a Christ-centered, or sometimes called a "redemptive-historic," hermeneutic and homiletic. Charles Haddon Spurgeon recounts the story, in one sermon, of a young Welsh minister, Jonathan George, who once said, "I have never yet found a text that had not got a road to Christ in it, and if I ever do find

2. Kenneth J. Langley, "Theocentric View," in *Homiletics and Hermeneutics: Four Views on Preaching Today*, ed. Scott M. Gibson and Matthew D. Kim (Baker Academic, 2018), 81–82.

3. Langley, "Theocentric View," 88.

one that has not a road to Christ in it, I will make one; I will go over hedge and ditch but I would get at my Master, for the sermon cannot do any good unless there is a savour of Christ in it."[4] This became a way of saying that Christian sermons ought to get to Christ and the cross quickly regardless of the primary thrust in the preacher's Scripture passage.[5]

In more recent history, an early proponent of the Christ-centered preaching philosophy was Sidney Greidanus, who maintained: "Redemptive-historical interpretation seeks to understand an Old Testament passage first in its own historical-cultural context. Only after we have heard a passage the way Israel heard it can we move on to understand this message in the broad contexts of the whole canon and the whole of redemptive history. It is at this point that the questions concerning Jesus Christ, the center, emerge."[6] He continues to provide more definitional language: "Preaching Christ is good news for people, and preaching Christ is as broad as preaching the gospel of the kingdom—as long as this kingdom is related to its King, Jesus. More specifically, to preach Christ is to proclaim some facet of the person, work, or teaching of Jesus of Nazareth so that people may believe him, trust him, love him, and obey him."[7] Here is where Greidanus becomes emphatic: "Committed Christians as well as non-Christians will benefit from explicitly Christ-centered preaching today."[8]

To combat what Bryan Chapell calls the "fallen condition focus," or the sinful nature prevalent in every person, he contends that "all Scripture is redemptive revelation that is inspired to address humanity's fallen condition (or incompleteness) with divine provision. Uncovering aspects of this provision is the focus of Christ-centered preaching."[9] Thus, in every sermon, Chapell asserts that "God's redemptive work is integral to every biblical passage's proper exposition."[10] This redemptive work is found in the person and salvific work of Christ. As Chapell makes aware, "Many times I have been questioned about whether this understanding requires the preacher to mention

4. Charles Haddon Spurgeon, "Christ Precious to Believers," sermon, March 13, 1859, available at https://www.ccel.org/ccel/spurgeon/sermons05.xix.html.

5. Interestingly, Thomas Breimaier notes, "In referring to his method of biblical interpretation, Spurgeon was said to insist, 'I take my text and make a beeline to the cross.' The quotation, which certainly resonates with Spurgeon's general approach to Scripture, is problematic in that I have not found it within Spurgeon's sermons or books." See Thomas Breimaier, *Tethered to the Cross: The Life and Preaching of C. H. Spurgeon* (IVP Academic, 2020), 3.

6. Sidney Greidanus, *Preaching Christ from the Old Testament: A Contemporary Hermeneutical Method* (Eerdmans, 1999), 228.

7. Greidanus, *Preaching Christ from the Old Testament*, 8.

8. Greidanus, *Preaching Christ from the Old Testament*, 14.

9. Bryan Chapell, *Christ-Centered Preaching: Redeeming the Expository Sermon* (Baker Academic, 2018), 257.

10. Chapell, *Christ-Centered Preaching*, 258.

Jesus in every sermon. I have great respect for those who ask because they are conscience-bound that a Christ-centered approach should not force them to impose on Scripture what it does not say. Conscientious expositors should want to explain only what the text truly means. So I consistently respond, 'No, I do not think there is a biblical mandate to name Jesus in every sermon.' Then I quickly add, 'But why wouldn't you?'"[11] This tongue-in-cheek retort is another way for Chapell to say, "Yes, Jesus must be integrated into every sermon" that is worthy of being a redemptive message.

Timothy J. Keller wrote in his homiletics book, *Preaching*, "To reach people gospel preachers must challenge the culture's story at points of confrontation and finally retell the culture's story, as it were, revealing how its deepest aspirations for good can be fulfilled only in Christ."[12] He expounds on his preaching philosophy: "We have a balance to strike—not to preach Christ without preaching the text, and not to preach the text without preaching Christ."[13] Going further, if one were to suggest a Christ-centered method to Keller's approach, this would be the prescription in Keller's own words: "To preach the gospel every time is to preach Christ every time, from every passage."[14]

Finally, David M. King commences his book *Your Old Testament Sermon Needs to Get Saved* with the following prickly questions: "What thickheaded preacher would fail to observe Jesus's own Christ-centered approach to the Scriptures? What obtuse interpreter would overlook how the apostles virtually fastened themselves to the Bible in proclaiming Jesus as the Christ?"[15] While he quickly admits that that preacher was himself, he then quips quite matter-of-factly: "If a preacher fails to interpret and apply the Old Testament in light of Christ, his Old Testament preaching will inevitably be sub-Christian."[16] Another emphatic point he makes is this: "No matter how many true things are said about the text, a sermon is lost until the Lord Jesus Christ stands in the middle of it."[17]

While there are several biblical texts offered as evidence for a Christocentric preaching lens, Luke 24:27 is a preacher's oft-used ammunition, where Jesus says to the two apostles walking on the road to Emmaus: "And beginning with Moses and all the Prophets, he interpreted to them in all the Scriptures

11. Chapell, *Christ-Centered Preaching*, 260.

12. Timothy J. Keller, *Preaching: Communicating Faith in an Age of Skepticism* (Penguin, 2016), 20.

13. Keller, *Preaching*, 67.

14. Keller, *Preaching*, 56–57.

15. David M. King, *Your Old Testament Sermon Needs to Get Saved: A Handbook for Preaching Christ from the Old Testament* (Moody, 2021), 9.

16. King, *Your Old Testament Sermon Needs to Get Saved*, 10.

17. King, *Your Old Testament Sermon Needs to Get Saved*, 20.

the things concerning himself" (ESV). Christ-centered preaching is a second monotheological lens that a preacher can ascribe to and employ as a hermeneutical and homiletical method.

Centralizing God the Spirit

A third way to centralize one member of the Godhead is Spirit-centered preaching. There is a noticeable lacuna of writings on this specific topic, where sermonic emphasis is placed on the Holy Spirit. Here's a possible explanation: During my time in pastoral ministry, Francis Chan's *Forgotten God: Reversing Our Tragic Neglect of the Holy Spirit* became a perspective-altering book. Chan laments:

> From my perspective, the Holy Spirit is tragically neglected and, for all practical purposes, forgotten. While no evangelical would deny His existence, I'm willing to bet there are millions of churchgoers across America who cannot confidently say they have experienced His presence or action in their lives over the past year. And many of them do not believe they can.[18]

When I think back on the sermons I've heard and preached over the years, the Holy Spirit does seem to get snubbed. Unless the text specifically mentions the Spirit, the third member of the Trinity is often omitted or rarely gets invited to the party. What a tragedy! On the contrary, the Holy Spirit is not a tangential member of the worship gathering. As Robertson McQuilkin observes, "The person of the Holy Spirit is the provision of the triune God for living godly in an ungodly world."[19] In other words, we cannot pursue a godly Christian life apart from the indwelling and powerful work of the Spirit. The Christian life does not work devoid of him.

In John 14, Jesus comforts the disciples whom he has just informed he would soon be leaving. He makes his promise that he would not abandon them completely. Rather, Jesus foretells in John 14:16–17, "And I will ask the Father, and he will give you another advocate to help you and be with you forever—the Spirit of truth." In this very passage, we see God's explicit triune nature. Each member of the Trinity is present. Isn't Jesus's promise a compelling enough reason to integrate and maximize the Holy Spirit's involvement

18. Francis Chan, *Forgotten God: Reversing Our Tragic Neglect of the Holy Spirit* (David C. Cook, 2009), 15.

19. Robertson McQuilkin, "Spiritual Formation Through Preaching: Three Components of Bible-Based Preaching," Preaching Today, accessed December 2, 2025, https://www.preachingtoday.com/books/art-and-craft-of-biblical-preaching/high-call-of-preaching/spiritual-formation-through-preaching.html.

in every sermon? The apostle Paul invites us to be filled with the Spirit in Ephesians 5:18 and other passages. Why? As Bill Bright in *A Handbook for Christian Maturity* exhorts us, "A desire to serve Him and help others find Him should be your motive for being filled with the Holy Spirit."[20]

Now that we've done a quick survey of preaching that places a specific member of the Trinity at its center, stop here and ponder with me which member of the Trinity you may be centralizing in your sermons. Is there one person in the Trinity that you tend to favor, accentuate, or feel you must include in your messages? Are there members of the triune God that you don't feel so strongly about? If so, why is that the case? How strongly do you feel that centralizing one member of the Godhead is necessary? Are you willing to consider another perspective?

Preaching Binitarian Sermons

Sometimes, we can lock ourselves into binitarian thinking by focusing on two members of the Trinity rather than only one. Binitarianism is the belief in the deity of two members of the Trinity: typically, God the Father and God the Son. Historically, binitarianism has not affirmed the Holy Spirit as God. My hope is that each member of the Trinity enters our message on some level.

The problem, however, is sermonically centralizing and granting supremacy to any one person in the Trinity to the omission and diminishment of others. The Bible is trinitarian in nature and in expression. As Scott R. Swain reminds us: "By his word, God reveals his triune name in Holy Scripture [as] the God-breathed Scriptures are the primary discourse of Trinitarian theology."[21] As students of the Scriptures, we stand corrected: It is not in our purview to dissect the Trinity. With a dose of humility, let's meditate on the fact that God is One in three persons and not One to the omission or de-emphasis of the others.

Who are we to demote or discard any member of the Godhead—not least the Holy Spirit? In your preparation, remember the "Forgotten God," the Third Person of the Trinity, the Holy Spirit. As Timothy C. Tennent entreats, "It is the Holy Spirit who is central in the work of discipling and maturing communities of believers."[22] It is not our place as created, human subjects to

20. Bill Bright, *A Handbook for Christian Maturity* (Campus Crusade for Christ International, 1992), 157.

21. Scott R. Swain, *The Trinity: An Introduction* (Crossway, 2020), 20.

22. Timothy C. Tennent, *Invitation to World Missions: A Trinitarian Missiology for the Twenty-First Century* (Kregel, 2010), 73.

prioritize or emphasize one member of the Trinity above or to the exclusion of another. So, what do I propose? What's the alternative?

Centering the Doctrine of the Trinity

In this textbook, my primary theological commitment is to encourage and weave a fulsome trinitarian approach to the task of the preaching ministry. I am not the first to propose such a homiletic. Namely, Michael Pasquarello III envisions a trinitarian theology that informs our homiletic in his book *Christian Preaching: A Trinitarian Theology of Proclamation*.[23] Yet, most modern homiletics textbooks, particularly those used in introductory courses, fail to give much intentional thought, detail, or application to trinitarianism as an interpretive and homiletic model. In fact, there's been a glaring omission of trinitarian witness across the spectrum of the homiletical enterprise spanning several decades.[24]

Any time we exegete a passage, we concentrate on the contents of the text, and rightfully so. If the said text discusses the singular operations of one member of the Trinity, naturally the exegesis we do on that passage is an exegesis and exposition of that person of the Godhead without consideration of the others. By injecting another member of the Trinity into the exegesis of such a passage, the preacher could be charged with the crime of eisegesis.

But our task as preachers goes beyond merely exegeting a Scripture verse or passage. While a seminary lecture on a passage might summarily exegete the passage, a sermon extends beyond a seminary lecture about the text. Though the sermon, like a lecture, includes and interweaves our exegesis and interpretation, it goes further. The next sermonic step is to tease out what the text means for the life of disciples by helping them to know God (who is triune) and know how God is asking them to participate in the world today in the wisdom and strength of the triune God.

The sermon thus functions as a bridge across cultures in ways that a lecture is not necessarily able to do. An instructor in the Christian Scriptures

23. Michael Pasquarello III, *Christian Preaching: A Trinitarian Theology of Proclamation* (Baker Academic, 2008).

24. In recent years, there's been an uptick in scholarship on the doctrine of the Trinity and worthy attempts at a trinitarian homiletic. See, e.g., D. Glenn Butner Jr., *Trinitarian Dogmatics: Exploring the Grammar of the Christian Doctrine of God* (Baker Academic, 2022); Brandon D. Smith, *The Biblical Trinity: Encountering the Father, Son, and Holy Spirit in Scripture* (Lexham, 2023); and Matthew Barrett, Ronni Kurtz, Samuel G. Parkison, and Joseph Lanier, *Proclaiming the Triune God: The Doctrine of the Trinity in the Life of the Church* (B&H, 2024). I owe a debt of gratitude to Barrett and company in this latter volume. They have sown trinitarian homiletical seeds as I refer to their work in part 1.

department seeks to help her students translate, explain, and interpret the passage at hand. For instance, in the story of Jacob and Esau in Genesis 25:19–34, a lecturer might explain the ancient Jewish customs, for instance, the significance of birthrights in the Jewish world and how Jacob stole Esau's birthright over a pot of stew, or even the differentiation between Esau's proclivity to hunt versus Jacob working in tents. A sermon, however, must deal with more than just the ancient rituals or the sequence of events of biblical characters. The next step is to help listeners in the pews cross the bridge into their own world. What does this ancient story have to do with me? What are the text's implications and applications for honoring God in our familial relationships in today's world?

Since the sermon situates the text in the life of the believer with a God who is triune, the sermon should make explicit and illuminate how the message of the text informs and transforms the listeners' relationship to all three members of the Godhead: Father, Son, and Spirit. All three members of the Trinity are actively at work in the process of our sanctification and discipleship. Therefore, though exegetically speaking the text might only mention one person (or sometimes even no members) of the Trinity, attention to the passage's implications and applications for the listeners' life with our triune God in totality is critical for preaching biblical sermons.

Put more strongly, it is mission critical that preachers highlight every passage of Scripture, implicitly or explicitly sharing about the active participation of God in three persons. Preaching the work and involvement of all three members of the Trinity is not an eisegetical add-on but a requirement for healthy, transformative preaching. It is not just a matter of the sermonic content we speak in the pulpit. The power of preaching is in naming what the triune God is doing in the sermon and postsermon to help us work out our sanctification and Christlikeness with fear and trembling (Phil. 2:12), regardless of whether the Scripture text mentions one, two, or three persons of the Trinity.

Michael Quicke similarly notes the magnitude of preachers' omission of trinitarian sermons: "Theology is *speaking meaningfully about God*. Everyone who expresses ideas about God has a theology, whether they admit it or not! What matters is whether theology is scripturally sound or not—whether it is about the Christian God! Christian theology is *speaking meaningfully about God in three persons*. Sadly, too much current preaching and worship speaks of God in *less* than three persons."[25]

25. Michael Quicke, "Thinking as Trinitarians," Preaching.com, accessed January 6, 2025, https://www.preaching.com/articles/thinking-as-trinitarians.

Over the course of centuries of preaching, the concept of the Trinity has vacillated in terms of being a well-defined or well-integrated theological, biblical, and homiletical method and practice. Homiletically speaking, we have minored in the doctrinal majors and majored in the doctrinal minors. To my knowledge, there is no comprehensive homiletics textbook that envisions a trinitarian model for sermons. This book attempts such a comprehensive approach.

Even though the doctrine of the Trinity is mysteriously complex and a concept that simplistic Sunday school lessons cannot impart sufficiently, it is still vital that we explore and explain to God's people the centrality of the Trinity. People desperately need to understand God's triune nature, function, work, and power. One of the earliest teachings on inseparable operations is provided by Athanasius of Alexandria.[26] The Athanasian Creed helpfully attempts such an explanation: "For there is one person of the Father, another of the Son, and another of the Holy Spirit. But the Godhead of the Father, of the Son, and of the Holy Spirit is all one, the glory equal, the majesty coeternal."

In his book *Meditations on the Trinity*, A. W. Tozer says,

> We've suffered the loss of that high concept of God, and the concept of God handled by the average gospel church now is so low as to be unworthy of God and a disgrace to the church. . . . If we can restore again knowledge of God to [people], we can help in some small way to bring about a reformation that will restore God again to [people].[27]

He continues: "When I say God, I mean Jesus and the Father and the Holy Spirit. So when I talk about God, I do not split up the Godhead. You cannot divide the Godhead. . . . Wherever God is, God is all there, because you cannot divide the substance that is God. . . . So the blessed Trinity is here—He is all here, not partly but all here."[28]

In their book *Our Triune God*, Philip Ryken and Michael J. LeFebvre begin, "To know God is to know him as triune. There is one God in three Persons. Or to express the same truth in a different way, God is three Persons in one being—Father, Son, and Holy Spirit."[29] The concept itself is not overly arduous to comprehend: God is One divine being and yet three distinct, unified persons. The mystery is in understanding how they are distinct, what their

26. Matthew Y. Emerson and Brandon D. Smith, *Beholding the Triune God: The Inseparable Work of Father, Son, and Spirit* (Crossway, 2024), 4n1.

27. A. W. Tozer, *Meditations on the Trinity* (Moody, 2017), 238–39.

28. Tozer, *Meditations on the Trinity*, 266.

29. Philip Ryken and Michael J. LeFebvre, *Our Triune God: Living in the Love of the Three-in-One* (Crossway, 2011), 13.

specific roles and functions are, and that somehow they are inseparable. To augment my case for a trinitarian model of preaching, it would prove helpful to explain how the triune God is inseparable.

Inseparable Operations

My foundational argument for the critical importance of preaching in such a manner that all three members of the Godhead are involved is the doctrine or concept of inseparable operations. The doctrine of inseparable operations articulates that God in three persons is always working in conjunction and cooperation with each other: They are inseparable from each other and do not operate apart or in isolation from each other. Each works together to support the mission and ministry of God the Father.

Various scholars support the doctrine of inseparable operations, which is "the doctrine that affirms that since the Trinity is undivided, the external operations of the Trinity are also undivided."[30] For example, Adonis Vidu simplifies the origins and complexity of inseparable operations in *The Same God Who Works All Things* as follows: "It is Scripture that calls for a kind of reading that does not divide the actions of the triune persons. Such an indivisibility, however, is without equal in the finite world. For this reason, we cannot probe its depths, we cannot explain it; we lack the capacity for understanding it; we can only attest to it in faith."[31] It is not a cop-out to say that the inseparable nature of God is assumed and yet incomprehensible. Both are truthful statements.

Where do we see this omnipresence, interworking, and inseparability of God the Father, Son, and Spirit in Scripture? Surveying the canon, we see glimpses of the Trinity in both Testaments. The "pre-existent Son" and "pre-existent Spirit," though not explicitly named in Genesis, are not absent figures in the Old Testament. As Kevin J. Vanhoozer rightly maintains, "We can therefore say that YHWH always referred to the one God who is Father, Son, and Spirit, even if the authors of the Old Testament did not yet have a developed concept of the Trinity."[32]

We must stop to briefly note a couple of common misunderstandings about the doctrine of the Trinity. One erroneous view is *tritheism*, which believes that God is not one but rather three different gods.[33] Another major faulty

30. Barrett et al., *Proclaiming the Triune God*, 8.

31. Adonis Vidu, *The Same God Who Works All Things: Inseparable Operations in Trinitarian Theology* (Eerdmans, 2021), xiv.

32. Kevin J. Vanhoozer, *Mere Christian Hermeneutics: Transfiguring What It Means to Read the Bible Theologically* (Zondervan Academic, 2024), 309.

33. Mary Ann Fatula, *The Triune God of Christian Faith* (Liturgical, 1990), 12. See also Matthew Y. Emerson and Brandon D. Smith, who similarly acknowledge these erroneous

understanding is *modalism*, where God is believed to be one but has three different modes or expressions such as Father, Son, and Holy Spirit.[34] This book does not endorse either of these perspectives. Rather, I hold to a doctrinal definition that God is One divine, unified being with three distinct, divine persons (Father, Son, and Spirit) who perform unique and specific functions in the world and in the lives of believers.

Let's venture on. New Testament passages such as the baptism of Jesus showcase the Trinity's presence marking the introduction of Jesus's earthly ministry. The Gospel of Matthew records: "As soon as Jesus was baptized, he went up out of the water. At that moment heaven was opened, and he saw the Spirit of God descending like a dove and alighting on him. And a voice from heaven said, 'This is my Son, whom I love; with him I am well pleased'" (3:16–17). Here, it is evident that the "Spirit of God" is the Holy Spirit. The "voice from heaven" is God the Father. And Jesus is the One in whom the Father is well pleased.

In the Great Commission passage in Matthew 28:18–20, Jesus commands and empowers us in trinitarian fashion: "All authority in heaven and on earth has been given to me. Therefore go and make disciples of all nations, baptizing them in the name of the Father and of the Son and of the Holy Spirit, and teaching them to obey everything I have commanded you. And surely I am with you always, to the very end of the age."

For economy of space, Hebrews 9:14 is a final example of the Trinity working distinctly according to roles but also collectively to accomplish our salvation and sanctification: "How much more, then, will the blood of Christ, who through the eternal Spirit offered himself unblemished to God, cleanse our consciences from acts that lead to death, so that we may serve the living God!" Here's the point: The Bible is a trinitarian book, and it must therefore be preached in trinitarian fashion.

CONCLUSION

In this chapter, I have attempted to show that to omit any member of the Trinity in our preaching is no small faux pas. As Matthew Barrett, Ronni Kurtz, Samuel G. Parkison, and Joseph Lanier assert in *Proclaiming the Triune God*, "Without an orthodox doctrine of the Trinity, there is no Christianity."[35]

---

understandings in *Beholding the Triune God: The Inseparable Work of Father, Son, and Spirit* (Crossway, 2024), 2–3.

34. Fatula, *The Triune God of Christian Faith*, 12.

35. Barrett et al., *Proclaiming the Triune God*, 1.

Since God the Father, the Son, and the Spirit cannot be separated, why would our sermons miss the mark by omitting one or more members of the Trinity?

Since we trust that God is three members in One and since they work in concert with each other, then it is not a leap to claim that our preaching should aim in all cases to be trinitarian.[36] The next question then is, What does that exactly mean and how can that be administered without falling into the same presuppositional traps mentioned above? To construct a workable trinitarian hermeneutic and homiletic is the next part of our process.

QUESTIONS

1. What has been your philosophy or practice with centering each member of the Trinity?
2. Is there any member of the Trinity who has received less attention in your preaching and in your spiritual journey? Why?
3. Has your understanding of the Trinity changed after reading this chapter? If so, how?
4. What might it look like for you to center the Trinity in your reading and interpretation of Scripture?

36. Vidu, *The Same God Who Works All Things*, xiii.

4

TRINITARIAN SERMONS

How Do We Preach the Triune God?

> This is the one who came by water and blood—Jesus Christ. He did not come by water only, but by water and blood. And it is the Spirit who testifies, because the Spirit is the truth. For there are three that testify: the Spirit, the water and the blood; and the three are in agreement. We accept human testimony, but God's testimony is greater because it is the testimony of God, which he has given about his Son.
>
> —1 John 5:6–9

The previous chapter contended for a robust emphasis on the doctrine of the Trinity and why it is necessary to view the sermonic process through the lens of trinitarian theology. If God is One in three persons and inseparable in nature and function—which he is—how can we not preach sermons that demonstrate the presence and power of each trinitarian person? In fact, some have even said it this way: "The doctrine of God must be the bull's-eye on the preacher's dartboard, the center of our thinking, living, and preaching."[1] Without treating the Trinity as a gimmick or inserting each member of the Trinity in à la carte fashion where he does not necessarily belong, what might trinitarian sermons propose to be on a weekly basis?

Let's first define and then explore what a trinitarian homiletic aspires to be without falling prey to the same types of "tagging on" tendencies of

1. Robert Letham, "The Trinity," *Theology for Ministry: How Doctrine Affects Pastoral Life and Practice*, ed. William R. Edwards, John C. A. Ferguson, and Chad Van Dixhoorn (P&R, 2022), 32.

theocentric, Christocentric, and pneumacentric preaching approaches. How might the preacher centralize the entire triune God—Father, Son, and Spirit—into one's sermons without it feeling inauthentic or forced?

We will pursue this conversation by addressing three primary questions:

1. What do we mean by trinitarian preaching?
2. How is the triune God working inseparably in this passage?
3. How do we preach the presence, power, and performance of the triune God in this passage?

Let's consider each question and engage with relevant Bible passages to substantiate our answers.

What Do We Mean by Trinitarian Preaching?

Does trinitarian preaching mean that the Trinity is mentioned in every biblical text? The simple answer is, "No, rarely is that ever the case." Then what do we mean? Let's start with what we don't mean. In their book *Proclaiming the Triune God*, Matthew Barrett and his coauthors explain that there is a subtle temptation to formulate a simplistic understanding of the Trinity as "a mathematical calculation (passages about the Father + passages about the Son + passages about the Spirit = the doctrine of the Trinity)."[2] A similar temptation exists in our preaching to read into the biblical text who is there and who is not when it comes to the Trinity. Then, we fill the gap and insert into the text the missing divine person. That's not what we desire to do either.

Rather, since the Trinity (all three members of God) are omnipresent (in all places at all times), then our job as preachers is to determine how each trinitarian member works together in this preaching text and in our time. What, then, is trinitarian preaching? Trinitarian preaching, in my estimation, highlights the stated and unstated ways that our triune God—Father, Son, and Spirit—serves as an active agent in every sermon by naming the primary ways each member of the Godhead demonstrates his unique forms of presence, power, and performance to transform the lives of preachers and hearers of God's Word. Robert Smith Jr. puts it this way in describing doctrinal preaching as a whole: "Doctrinal preaching is the exegetical escorting of the hearers by the *Word of God* into the presence of Christ, the *Son of God*, through the power of the *Spirit of God* for the purpose of transformation. . . . Only

2. Matthew Barrett, Ronni Kurtz, Samuel G. Parkison, and Joseph Lanier, *Proclaiming the Triune God: The Doctrine of the Trinity in the Life of the Church* (B&H, 2024), 5.

the trinitarian God transforms!"[3] We, as God's children, are escorted by the living God into his purpose and into a transformative process that only this trinitarian God can perform in and through us.

How Is the Triune God Working Inseparably in This Passage?

Throughout the biblical canon, we find a triune God working simultaneously and tirelessly for God's good plan and purpose and for his glory. The oneness of God is a consistent theme in both Testaments. Deuteronomy 6:4, in what is known as the Shema, clearly sets out this principle of God's oneness in the Pentateuch: "Hear, O Israel: The Lord our God, the Lord is one." It was important that the Israelites hear repeatedly that God is One and that this truth be passed down to future generations.

Our God is a God of unity, inseparability, and indivisibility. In *Beholding the Triune God*, Matthew Y. Emerson and Brandon D. Smith explain: "Put simply: the doctrine of inseparable operations teaches that you cannot separate the acts of God between the persons of God. Every act of God is a singular act of Father, Son, and Spirit."[4] Emerson and Smith helpfully expound on this truth by way of the doctrine of appropriations. Since God is One in three persons, appropriations allows us to differentiate, or "attribute, particular acts of God to one of the persons of God . . . [and to say] that the act is uniquely associated with the mission of that one person."[5]

As a case in point, using God's work in an individual's journey toward salvation, Emerson and Smith present the following example: "The Father sends the Son, the Son is sent by the Father, and the Spirit is the agent through whom the Father sends the Son."[6] In and through their unity, the Father, Son, and Holy Spirit work in tandem to accomplish the overarching mission of God.

Drinking Deeply from the Trinitarian Well

The task of preaching is hard work and requires "deep thinking" or "deep drinking," at least when done properly and effectively. Shallow preaching

3. Robert Smith Jr., "Doctrinal Preaching," in *Handbook of Contemporary Preaching: A Wealth of Counsel for Creative and Effective Proclamation*, 2nd ed., ed. Michael Duduit (B&H Academic, 2024), 87.

4. Matthew Y. Emerson and Brandon D. Smith, *Beholding the Triune God: The Inseparable Work of Father, Son, and Spirit* (Crossway, 2024), 6.

5. Emerson and Smith, *Beholding the Triune God*, 7.

6. Emerson and Smith, *Beholding the Triune God*, 8.

leads to shallow living. Why do I bring this up? Our challenge is that it can take extra sermonic energy to determine how the Trinity works together in any given Scripture text. Therefore, it's easy to skip this process and only mention any individual member of the Trinity in a text that is low-hanging fruit. Our default mode is simply to bring up only the divine person(s) who are explicitly in the text. It's going to require extra brain cells and prayers for God's enlightened understanding as to how each member of the Trinity works inseparably in your preaching text for the week. Some passages are more obvious than others. However, we can make trinitarian thinking as we read and interpret Scripture a habit more than a nuisance. It might be helpful to describe this trinitarian mindset as an interpretive paradigm shift. In other words, think of every passage as a trinitarian text. How is each member of the Trinity involved and working in every passage?

Identifying Trinitarian Type Texts

In *The Trinity: An Introduction*, Scott R. Swain breaks down Scripture's examples of the Trinity into a helpful threefold type. We might similarly find this tool useful to help our listeners become aware of the different types of trinitarian passages. The first is what he calls "inner-trinitarian conversation texts," which allow readers to "overhear the persons of the Trinity speaking to and of each other." For instance, in the baptism of Christ in Matthew 3:16–17, "the Father speaking of/to the Son, 'This is my beloved Son, with whom I am well pleased.'"[7] The second type is "cosmic framework texts" that situate the Trinity in "the entirety of God's work in the cosmos." Colossians 1:15–20 is an example "that frames the entirety of God's work in the cosmos in creation, redemption, and consummation in relation to him."[8] The third is "redemptive mission texts" that "display the sending or 'mission' of the Son (and, sometimes, the sending of the Spirit) as the great divine acts whereby God fulfills his redemptive purpose."[9] We find a "redemptive mission" type text in Luke 4:18, where Jesus shares one of the Father's missions he has come to fulfill: "The Spirit of the Lord is on me, because he [the Father] has anointed me to proclaim good news to the poor."

Identifying the Trinity at Work

Having a basic rubric to understand the three main types of trinitarian texts, let's explore further what this inseparable work looks like when each

7. Scott R. Swain, *The Trinity: An Introduction* (Crossway, 2020), 39.
8. Swain, *The Trinity*, 45.
9. Swain, *The Trinity*, 38.

member of the Godhead is named in our sermon and credited for specific roles in our process of spiritual transformation. In his book *Invitation to World Missions*, Timothy C. Tennent notes: "It is one thing to see the Trinitarian basis for mission; it is entirely another to fail to see that the church has been ordained by God to reflect the Trinity through redemptive actions in the world."[10] How do we come to know which "redemptive actions" are required of us? Through preaching infused with, by, and through the three persons of the Trinity. Also, what happens when each member of the Trinity is or is not officially mentioned by name in the text? Both textual possibilities can be guided by remembering to intentionally identify and include each member of the Trinity in our sermons.

As you study a text, try to explore at least one question below and ask yourself how each person of the Trinity fits into this preaching text. Sometimes it is helpful to think in the present tense, so we can use the former questions. If God's activity is more easily interpreted using past tense, then go for it! This information will give you and your listeners a deeper understanding and appreciation of what the triune God has done and how this God continues to work toward your discipleship and Christlikeness. It will also enable you to guide your congregation through a weekly road map in actively considering all three persons in your pursuit of trinitarian preaching.

Question 1: What is God doing here/what has God done?

A. *What is the Father doing here/what has the Father done?*
B. *What is the Son doing here/what has the Son done?*
C. *What is the Spirit doing here/what has the Spirit done?*

Question 2: What is God asking of us here/what has God asked of us?

A. *What is the Father asking of us here/what has the Father asked of us?*
B. *What is the Son asking of us here/what has the Son asked of us?*
C. *What is the Spirit asking of us here/what has the Spirit asked of us?*

Question 3: How is God helping us here/how has God helped us?

A. *How is the Father helping us here/how has the Father helped us?*
B. *How is the Son helping us here/how has the Son helped us?*
C. *How is the Spirit helping us here/how has the Spirit helped us?*

What we're accomplishing by taking time to answer these questions is to name God's indicative (what God has done) (question 1) which leads to God's

10. Timothy C. Tennent, *Invitation to World Missions: A Trinitarian Missiology for the Twenty-First Century* (Kregel, 2010), 56.

imperative (what God asks of us) (question 2) and being encouraged through God's assistance (how God helps us) (question 3).

What's your sermon text for this coming Sunday? Some passages like Romans 8 are overtly trinitarian in nature. It doesn't require any trinitarian imagination to read the names of God—Father, Son, and Spirit—since they are found directly in the text. However, let's consider, as an example, Isaiah 12:1–6. There is nothing specifically trinitarian about this text. In fact, only the Lord is definitively mentioned. In many scriptural passages, "the Lord" refers mainly to God the Father.

As you read this text several times to get the point of the passage (see chap. 9), walk through these diagnostic questions and their subparts. Try to provide a biblical response from the text at hand for each subquestion with appropriate verse numbers (for easily identifiable reference later). You can paraphrase or quote the verses verbatim. Trace back your learning experiences from previous Bible classes, theology courses, or even your devotional life. Make this a fun weekly exercise. It might be a puzzle sometimes, but it doesn't have to be tedious.

> In that day you will say:
> "I will praise you, LORD.
> Although you were angry with me,
> your anger has turned away
> and you have comforted me.
> Surely God is my salvation;
> I will trust and not be afraid.
> The LORD, the LORD himself, is my strength and my defense;
> he has become my salvation."
> With joy you will draw water
> from the wells of salvation.
> In that day you will say:
> "Give praise to the LORD, proclaim his name;
> make known among the nations what he has done,
> and proclaim that his name is exalted.
> Sing to the LORD, for he has done glorious things;
> let this be known to all the world.
> Shout aloud and sing for joy, people of Zion,
> for great is the Holy One of Israel among you." (Isa. 12:1–6)

Question 1: What is God doing here/what has God done?

A. What is the Father doing here/what has the Father done? Make a list.

- God has turned his anger away. (v. 1)
- God has pursued us in his comfort. (v. 1)

- God has comforted. (v. 1)
- God is my salvation. (v. 2)
- God is my strength and my defense. (v. 2)
- God is described as "great is the Holy One of Israel." (v. 6)

Less clear in this passage is what the Son and Spirit are doing/have done. What do we do when this is the case in our given Scripture text? There is no need to panic. Let the immediate context and cross-references serve as your guide. As theologian Fred Sanders explains, "In the fullness of time, God did not give us facts about himself, but gave us himself in the person of the Father who sent, the Son who was sent, and the Holy Spirit who was poured out."[11] That means the Godhead is present and available to us in every iota of Scripture.

To answer questions B and C below, take this opportunity to acknowledge that "all theology ought to be doxology, but Trinitarian theology in particular is essentially a matter of praising God."[12] Giving praise to God, then, automatically invites us to praise both the Son and Spirit in conjunction with God the Father in this passage. God the Father is not acting independently from the Son and the Spirit. Include the Son and Spirit in your collective praise and worship. When we proclaim his name, first speak aloud each member of the Trinity.

B. What is the Son doing here/what has the Son done?

This might be a natural place to interject teaching on God's wrath. It's not a popular topic, but it is a necessary one. In verse 1, the psalmist teaches God's people how God has "turned away" his anger from the people. We know from hindsight that in the New Testament God the Father turned away his anger from the people and onto his Son, Jesus. The Second Person of the Trinity received God's wrath and paid our penalty. As we read in 1 Thessalonians 5:9, "For God did not appoint us to suffer wrath but to receive salvation through our Lord Jesus Christ." This wrath was placed on Jesus who provided a means for salvation. Likewise, we read in Romans 5:9, "Since we have now been justified by his blood, how much more shall we be saved from God's wrath through him."

C. What is the Spirit doing here/what has the Spirit done?

Like we just saw in section B, God comforts us in verse 1 through his Spirit. In John 14, we read that Jesus promised the Holy Spirit, the Comforter, who would comfort the disciples in their distress of missing Jesus who would soon

11. Fred Sanders, *The Triune God* (Zondervan, 2016), 40.
12. Sanders, *The Triune God*, 25.

leave them to go to the Father. It could be said that this act of God to "comfort me" (Isa. 12:1) is an allusion to John 14 and the sending of the Spirit. All members of the Trinity are included in some fashion in verse 1.

Question 2: What is God asking of us here/what has God asked of us?
A. What is the Father asking of us here/what has the Father asked of us?
Isaiah duly notes several instructions the Lord has for the people to respond to his faithfulness:

- "I will praise [sing to] you, LORD." (vv. 1, 4, 5, 6)
- "I will trust." (v. 2)
- "I will . . . not be afraid." (v. 2)
- "Proclaim his name." (v. 4)
- "Make known among the nations what he has done." (v. 4)

B. What is the Son asking of us here/what has the Son asked of us?
What are some similar texts where the Scriptures speak of the Son and of him telling the nations about God? Verse 4 appears to be a natural way to introduce the Great Commission text of Matthew 28:18–20 into this sermon. Jesus tells his disciples to spread the good news to the ends of the earth. Isaiah tells us to go and do the same.

C. What is the Spirit asking of us here/what has the Spirit asked of us?
One of the dominant commands of this text is to sing/praise God (as noted above in vv. 1, 4, 5, 6) for his mighty works and to testify and be witnesses to the nations of his actions. The Holy Spirit in Acts 1:8 equips believers in the following way: "But you will receive power when the Holy Spirit comes on you; and you will be my witnesses in Jerusalem, and in all Judea and Samaria, and to the ends of the earth." To proclaim the Lord and his deeds is what the Spirit asks of us, not in our own strength but with his power.

Question 3: How is God helping us here/how has God helped us?
A. How is the Father helping us here/how has the Father helped us?

- God has clearly applied "his strength and his defense" to us (v. 2).
- God has given us the ability to drink from the well of salvation (v. 3).
- God has done "glorious things" (v. 5). It is assumed that the people already knew all the wonderful things God had done for them. Therefore, the only response is to praise him and tell others of his wondrous works.

B. How is the Son helping us here/how has the Son helped us?
The word "salvation" (Hebrew, *Yeshua*) is found three times in this text. Where is salvation found? According to Acts 4:12, "Salvation is found in no one else, for there is no other name under heaven given to mankind by which we must be saved." Whose name? Yeshua is the name of Jesus, God's one and only Son. A clear play on words, we can find Yeshua (salvation) only through the name of Yeshua (Jesus). Yeshua is the only one who can help us.

C. How is the Spirit helping us here/how has the Spirit helped us?
Overcoming our fear in verse 2 might be a seamless way to invite the Spirit into this sermon. Fear is not the way of Christians. As 2 Timothy 1:7 similarly reminds us, "For God gave us a spirit not of fear but of power and love and self-control" (ESV). Who helps us to eliminate fear from our lives? The Holy Spirit gives us a spirit that is contrary to fear. Therefore, with the Spirit's empowerment, we can choose not to fear.

Now that we've sought to answer each of these questions concerning the Trinity, here's our final question to develop the Trinity in our preaching process.

How Do We Preach the Presence, Power, and Performance of the Triune God in Each Passage?

Think of any person in the world whose name you might have heard, but who you've never met or interacted with meaningfully. This is akin to how we perceive and relate to each person of the Trinity. If we have encountered and experienced God, Father, Son, or Spirit, we can share with others who they are and what they mean to us. If not, they are just another person we know about but don't know personally.

The central purpose of a trinitarian homiletic is to make the intangible tangible. The mystery or strangeness of the Trinity has made it easy for preachers to dismiss it as an "odd doctrine" lacking relevance for daily life. Rather, incorporating the triune God into our preaching makes the doctrine of the Trinity personal, meaningful, and transformative in the believer's life. We will begin to understand how each member of the Godhead is involved not only in the world but also in our personal lives and corporate lives as Christians who are embedded and actively worshiping and serving in a local church context.

In *The Triune God of Christian Faith*, Mary Ann Fatula expresses some universal thoughts regarding discussions on the Trinity: "Yes, we do confess faith in a triune God; but to put the question bluntly, so what? Isn't the Trinity an unnecessary complication, an interesting but dispensable addendum to our faith, an abstract idea in technical books written for theological experts? What possible relevance can faith in a triune God have for our real life and for the urgent problems of our world . . . ?"[13] This is not the type of distant thinking we want to continue among Christians. We don't want our preaching to be devoid of trinitarian presence, power, and performance, because we were meant to experience each member of the Trinity in a unique and powerful way.

Trinitarian Presence

In some shape or form, a trinitarian sermon will highlight the presence, power, and performance of each person of the Trinity. Let's start with presence. From the very beginning of Scripture, in Genesis 1:1, Moses pens these indelible words, "In the beginning God created the heavens and the earth." One might, at first glance, assume that God refers to the Father alone. While this argument is a safe one to make, is it permissible to also ask the question: Does God refer here also to Jesus and the Holy Spirit? Those who hold to a preexistent view of Jesus the Son, and a preexistent view of the Spirit, would present the case that "God" refers to the triune God and is not restricted to God the Father only, even in Genesis 1 in the creation account.

Another way to see this perspective is as follows: God the Son and God the Spirit were both present with God the Father at the creation of the world. God the Son and God the Spirit were not an afterthought. They have always existed, just like God the Father. They were not mere spectators at the inception of creation. They were active participants. God (the triune God) spoke the world into existence with the very words, "Let there be . . ."

Since before the creation of the world, then, God (Father, Son, and Spirit together) has been working to form the world into existence and carry out the plan of the Father from the inception of the world and its created order (including us).[14] If so, then God the Father, Son, and Spirit, from the very beginning, work together in creating everything in the cosmos, including human beings, and forming all people into their collective triune likeness.

13. Mary Ann Fatula, *The Triune God of Christian Faith* (Liturgical, 1990), 17.

14. Biblical scholars question whether Genesis 1:26 alludes to the entire Godhead being present at creation: "Then God said: 'Let *us* make mankind in our image, in our likeness, so that they may rule over the fish of the sea and the birds in the sky, over the livestock and all the wild animals, and over all the creatures that move along the ground.'" The translated word for "us" is cross-referenced with Gen. 3:5; 11:7; Ps. 100:3; and Isa. 6:8 in the NIV translation.

Family and the Persons of God: As Father, as Son, and as Spirit (All Persons Present)

Though an imperfect analogy, one way to consider the phrase "trinitarian presence" is to think of each person of the Godhead as members of the same family who are unique persons. They are present and active in every part of individual life and in the world. There is only one family name—God—but there are three persons in the family with individual family members' names being Father, Son, and Spirit.

Let's go a bit deeper into the John 14 text. Since John 14 is a trinitarian passage, it not only mentions each member of the Trinity by name, but it also emphasizes the intimate relationship we can have with each member of the Trinity. Here's the quick context: After sharing with his disciples of his imminent departure, Jesus comforts them with news of the Spirit's pending arrival. The disciples are disheartened and discouraged, but Jesus promises to send them aid.

Beginning in John 14:15, Jesus tells his disciples that for those who love him and keep his commands, he will ask the Father who "will give you another advocate to help you and be with you forever—the Spirit of truth" (vv. 16–17). Jesus says of this Spirit: "The world cannot accept him, because it neither sees him nor knows him. But you know him, for he lives with you and will be in you" (v. 17).

What does this mean for the disciples and for us? Jesus informs us that the Spirit is a (divine) person who can be known. But the knowing and being known doesn't stop there. In verse 20, Jesus says: "On that day you will realize that I am in my Father, and you are in me, and I am in you." The knowability of the Trinity is palpable here. We can know and be known by God: Father, Son, and Spirit.

In the same way, I suggest that we read the Bible, interpret, and communicate its truth in such a way that no trinitarian family member is left out. Scripture, implicitly and explicitly, invites the reader on a journey to witness and experience the triune God. Our job is to help identify how each member works powerfully in our sanctification process.

Trinitarian Power

Likewise, the Gospels are trinitarian in the way they showcase God the Father, Son, and Spirit through inseparable operations (which we described earlier). We might think of it as a mini doctrinal lesson concerning each member of the Trinity and what role they play in being God and in shaping our discipleship and transformation. It's a way to illustrate how powerful each member of the Trinity is and what that means for us today in living out God's Word.

Throughout the Scriptures, God's unique power is manifested clearly in biblical passages. Here is just a short sampling of such texts:

> **God the Father's Power**
> Ah, Lord God! It is you who have made the heavens and the earth by your great power and by your outstretched arm! Nothing is too hard for you. (Jer. 32:17 ESV)
>
> **God the Son's Power**
> Now to him [Jesus] who is able to do far more abundantly than all that we ask or think, according to the power at work within us . . . (Eph. 3:20 ESV)
>
> **God the Spirit's Power**
> May the God of hope fill you with all joy and peace in believing, so that by the power of the *Holy Spirit* you may abound in hope. (Rom. 15:13 ESV)

We serve a trinitarian God full of indescribable power. This same God can empower believers today to accomplish his will in our communities. The power of God expresses itself in the fact that God indwells his people (John 14:17; Rom. 8:7–9; 1 Cor. 6:19–20, and others). In each sermon, we can emphasize the power of God: Father, Son, and Spirit. Do not neglect this opportunity to help our listeners marvel at the powerful God we love and serve. Not only mention the power of God but remind your listeners of how each person of the Trinity performs a specific function in our very existence.

Trinitarian Performance

Finally, each member of the Trinity performs a unique role and function even as they work together and inseparably. In the New Testament letters, notice how Paul expresses gratitude toward the Ephesian believers in Ephesians 1:16–19: "I do not cease to give thanks for you, remembering you in my prayers, that the God of our Lord Jesus Christ, the Father of glory, may give you the Spirit of wisdom and of revelation in the knowledge of him, having the eyes of your hearts enlightened, that you may know what is the hope to which he has called you, what are the riches of his glorious inheritance in the saints, and what is the immeasurable greatness of his power toward us who believe" (ESV).

Here, the power of God, in three persons, shows up conspicuously in his opening remarks. Paul names the triune God: the God of our Lord Jesus

Christ, the Father of glory, [and] the Spirit of wisdom and of revelation. This God, Paul prays for the Ephesians, is the one who would enable them to "know what is the hope to which he has called you." The revelation of God, the "knowledge of him," "having the eyes of your hearts enlightened" are works that only God can do in and through our transformation and life change.

CONCLUSION

In this first part, I hope to have underscored how crucial it is that the triune God is the hero and central character of our sermons. In every sermonic moment, we point to this loving, gracious, holy, righteous, just, merciful, patient, faithful, all-powerful, all-knowing, all-present God who relentlessly pursues his children. We have laid out a clear pathway toward trinitarian preaching. While every single Bible text does not mention each member of the Trinity by name, every text of Scripture invites reflection on the Trinity. Prioritizing the Trinity in our weekly sermons and explaining how each triune person enters the biblical account provides our sermons with theological reflection and depth that is sorely missing in many messages today. As an antidote to anemic trinitarian contemplation, I have offered diagnostics here to work through each week so that we might centralize God the Father, the Son, and the Spirit in all our preaching. Incorporating theological rigor into our homiletical understanding and practice, we will now shift to the crux of our textbook, which is part 2, becoming biblically ready.

QUESTIONS

1. Do you feel that your preaching ministry has emphasized the Trinity or can be described as trinitarian? How?
2. What might it look like for you to preach more intentional trinitarian sermons?
3. How has this chapter guided your thinking about preaching trinitarian sermons?
4. If you are unconvinced, what will it take for you to desire preaching trinitarian sermons?

PART 2

Biblically Ready

Once we have a foundational understanding of theology and of the Trinity, preachers enter biblical preparation. Here, the preacher walks through steps to properly understand and apply the Scripture text. While various homiletics textbooks have helpfully guided their readers through the process from exegesis to sermon writing, this second part, on being biblically ready, builds on the foundation of other homileticians to continue this salient conversation regarding how much exegesis should be included and what is most effective for our listeners.

These ten steps below will challenge preachers to be objectively clear. Each chapter in part 2 provides deliberate exercises or practices in what has immediately been discussed to help you grow in your sermon preparation process. Please take some time during or after reading each chapter to work through the questions and exercises. While additional questions may arise, be patient with the sermonic process on offer, as it will be integrated in chapters 10 and 11.

Here are the ten sermonic steps:

Step 1: Choose your **text** (chapter 5)
Step 2: Know your **purpose** (chapter 5)
Step 3: Appreciate your **genre** (chapter 6)
Step 4: Understand your **context** (chapter 7)
Step 5: **Study** your passage (chapter 8)
Step 6: Establish your **point** (chapter 9)
Step 7: **Outline** your passage (chapter 10)
Step 8: **Write** your manuscript (chapter 11)
Step 9: Point to the **Trinity** (chapters 4 and 11)
Step 10: **Communicate** your message (chapter 20)

5

TEXT

Which Passage Will We Preach On?

> All Scripture is God-breathed and is useful for teaching, rebuking, correcting and training in righteousness, so that the servant of God may be thoroughly equipped for every good work.
>
> —2 Timothy 3:16–17

I was once talking "sermon shop" with an experienced preacher who shared his random sermon selection process with me. These were his words: "Every Monday morning I close my eyes, flip through the pages of the Bible, and then place my index finger on a page, any page. Wherever my finger lands is the launching pad of the passage for that Sunday."

Are you surprised?

What he was describing is what many pastors of a previous generation called the Rolodex method of text selection. The Rolodex was a filing system for your contact list written down on physical note cards that you could spin around for easy access. Thankfully, smartphones have solved that problem for us.

When I asked him why he chose this approach, his response was, you guessed it, the passage above: "All Scripture is God-breathed and is useful for teaching, rebuking, correcting and training in righteousness, so that the servant of God may be thoroughly equipped for every good work," quoting 2 Timothy 3:16–17. Fair enough. You will probably agree that any text of

Scripture is worth preaching and should be preached. However, I believe there is a more thoughtful, intentional, and Spirit-infused way to go about selecting a text and creating a sermon series.

Step 1: Choose Your Text

Since we preach the Scriptures, *step 1 in the process is to choose a text.* It might seem gratuitous to spend an entire chapter on selecting a preaching text. How difficult could it be? Like a magician doing a card trick, you might be saying to yourself, "Pick a text, any text!" The truth is that text selection is a critical first component to the sermonic process. Preachers have often compared individual sermons to the meals we eat. You don't eat anything and everything, do you? The same goes for preaching.

Visualize text selection as standing in line at an all-you-can-eat buffet restaurant. As your mouth waters, the choices before you are endless. But you can only fit so much on one plate. While it's easy to quickly dart toward your favorite entrée or dessert, it's probably wise to scan the entire spread to see what's available and even take an extra moment to ask yourself what your body needs most for nutritional value! The sermon represents one plate of food. You can always go back for seconds and thirds but not today. You can only fit a plate's worth of food in one sermon preached.

Since we believe a sermon is biblical and its foundational basis is a biblical text, the goal of this opening chapter in part 2 is to introduce how to select a sermon text or sermon series. What do we need to know and what are some useful practices to keep in mind as we start from the beginning in discerning which passage we will preach on? Like most things in the Christian life, we want to start with prayer.

Pray About Your Text Selection

Before we select any text to preach on, it's vital to stop and pray first. This is not a quick lunchtime prayer, "Thanks, God, for my peanut butter and jelly sandwich," but a moment to pray earnestly and ask God, Father, Son, and Spirit, for help and wisdom. I know that there are moments in pastoral ministry where I relied on basic logic in this first step, asking myself, "What does the church need to hear this week?" From there, I would simply go to a book of the Bible or biblical passage that I was familiar with or that I felt addressed the theme or topic (not that distant from the Rolodex example above).

From the moment we think about preaching any text, prayer is a good habit to form as a first response. Why pray? Preaching is not a human venture alone. Preachers rely not on their own understanding (Prov. 3:5–6). All preachers need God's help and wisdom!

In this prayer, we are asking the Lord, "What book of the Bible or passage do you want me to preach on? What do you want *me* to learn and apply from this specific passage? What is it that you want to teach and communicate to the congregation this week about yourself and how can we participate in your great plan and work?" As we pray, we listen to the Lord about what comes next. For most preaching traditions, this involves planning a sermon series in addition to perhaps some stand-alone or even topical sermons.

Plan Your Preaching Calendar

Depending on your church tradition or denomination, you will not be preaching fifty-two stand-alone sermons, meaning fifty-two individual sermons that are not connected to one another in a meaningful or purposeful way. Rather, as you think about the Christian calendar, there are two historically poignant Sundays where our listeners expect traditional sermons: Christmas and Resurrection Sunday (Easter). Do not skip over these two important dates and themes!

Your church tradition, if you follow a liturgical calendar and preach through selected readings from the lectionary,[1] may also create your preaching calendar based on specific seasons that are celebrated or remembered in Christian tradition, such as Epiphany, Lent, Easter, Pentecost, and culminating with Advent. Dianne Bergant and Richard N. Fragomeni explain, "The Lectionary is a unique genre of ecclesial literature. It is part of the liturgical canon, a collection of books that also includes the Sacramentary, the Ritual Books for Sacraments, the Book of Blessings, the Pontifical, and the Liturgy of the Hours, to name a few. . . . The Lectionary, while not identical to the Bible, is drawn from its contents, providing a kind of narrative infrastructure for celebration of the Liturgical Year."[2] These sermon series address annual Christian observances and celebrations with designated themes and texts to match them.

1. The lectionary is a selected group of readings that loosely follow a similar theme taken from an OT narrative, Psalm, Gospel, and Epistle. It is divided into three-year cycles designated as Year A, Year B, and Year C. See, e.g., Dianne Bergant and Richard N. Fragomeni, *Preaching the New Lectionary: Year A* (Liturgical, 2001).

2. See Bergant and Fragomeni, *Preaching the New Lectionary*, vii.

A helpful way to plan and track your preaching calendar would be to open a spreadsheet for easy entry, access, and alterations. See the sample preaching calendar at the end of this chapter. If you are a lead/senior/preaching pastor, you will want to take at least two weeks to pray about what the preaching calendar might look like for a given year. Which books of the Bible will you preach through from the Old and New Testaments? Are there topical sermon series that your congregation would benefit from hearing? Are there certain pastors/missionaries or others whom you would like to invite as guest preachers on occasion?

I've found it helpful to spend two consecutive weeks sometime in the fall of each year to plan out the next year's sermon series. Of course, this can and perhaps should be done in consultation with your pastoral staff and other lay leaders. Pray and ask the Spirit individually and collectively to help you discern what areas of discipleship are most needed in this next calendar year.

In *Preaching with a Plan*, Scott M. Gibson explains that our primary role as preachers is to be disciple makers. Viewing the task of preaching as discipleship concretizes our preaching ministry with a clear purpose rather than thinking of it loosely as a weekly "what do I want to preach about *this* week" exercise. It removes the burden of needing to come up with an original preaching series or text every single week. Once you've planned, you know where you're going. You have a clear road map.

As you prayerfully plan out the year's preaching schedule, ask the Spirit to lead you first in determining a yearly discipleship theme. Your church probably does this already. What's the overall vision for the church this year? How does God want your church to grow? Not that we cannot deviate from this overall theme when appropriate, but in general your sermon series or stand-alone sermons for the year should stay connected to this umbrella discipleship goal. Next, we're going to explore planning longer book series, shorter book series, and finally stand-alone or topical sermons.

Longer or Shorter Book Series

As a general preaching philosophy, consider preaching through entire books of the Bible rather than hopping around from book to book. One way to strategize would be to find at least one Old Testament book and one New Testament book that address your yearly theme. For example, let's say your church's theme for discipleship is "The Year of Prayer." Are there Old Testament books and New Testament counterparts that you could preach your way through to educate and edify the congregation about prayer?

Prayer is a central theme that runs through various books of the Bible. For example, you might preach through the book of Nehemiah in the Old Testament and later that year preach through a parallel New Testament book like 1 Thessalonians. Even though these books of the Bible present a wide variety of topics (no book of the Bible sticks to one theme only), the church will hear somewhat regularly about the overarching theme as you make your way through the sermon series week by week.

One of the key benefits of preaching through an entire book without skipping passages is that it validates 2 Timothy 3:16–17, mentioned at the beginning of the chapter. When God says that all Scripture is "useful for teaching, rebuking, correcting and training in righteousness," then we are putting this truth to the test by showing our listeners that we believe the apostle Paul's instructions. We're not going to skip any passage or verse of Scripture because we don't like what it says or it's arduous to explain.[3]

Stand-Alone and Topical Sermons

Sometimes the church will benefit from a stand-alone sermon or two (not connected to a series) or hearing about a specific topic (topical sermon series or topical sermons).[4] By this, I'm not saying that these sermons lack a biblical text as their anchor. They will still be rooted in a specific Scripture passage. However, if you're not a regular preacher, you'll be asked to prepare a sermon on a specific passage or topic that will not be part of an established sermon series.

If the text or topic is completely your choice, pray and ask the Holy Spirit what the congregation needs. You can also ask the pastor or person who invited you for input. The default posture for text selection is, "What do my listeners need to hear right now?" and not "What do I feel like preaching about?" If we focus on the former question and not the latter, I believe our listeners will benefit more from the sermon we preach. In other words, preaching is never self-focused or self-interested.

Guidelines for a Viable Preaching Text

Determining the parameters of a text involves a few primary considerations. We begin with knowing the purpose.

3. See Eric J. Bargerhuff and Matthew D. Kim, *What's God Saying Here? How to Navigate Awkward, Troubling, and Bizarre Passages We Would Rather Skip* (Zondervan Reflective, 2025).

4. See, e.g., Sam Chan and Malcolm Gill, *Topical Preaching in a Complex World: How to Proclaim Truth and Relevance at the Same Time* (Zondervan, 2021).

Step 2: Know Your Purpose

Step 2 in the sermonic process is to know your purpose. Why are you preaching this sermon series or sermon? For preachers, one of the most foundational considerations is to know your purpose or rationale. In other words, what are you trying to accomplish through this sermon? Why preach on this text or topic? Why do your listeners need to hear a message on this passage? While some might refer to this as the application (which we will consider later), the purpose of our preaching is not so much the application but the intentional goal or aim of our sermon or sermon series in its entirety. What do you hope will happen in your hearers/congregation because of preaching this message?

As an example of purpose, here is a sermon series that I preached when I served as a senior pastor in Colorado. Early on in my ministry there, I realized that some congregants did not fully understand Jesus or had an incomplete view of Jesus. They might have referred to Jesus as a good teacher or point out some other characteristic about him. As I prayed about various sermon series, the Holy Spirit brought me to the Gospel of Mark. I decided to preach a twelve-part sermon series titled "Who Is Jesus?," walking listeners through Mark not verse by verse but attribute by attribute.

The purpose of this sermon series was to introduce the church to Jesus and help them encounter Jesus as described by Mark, the Gospel writer, leaning into Jesus's range of characteristics. You can look at the twelve topics covered below.

Sample Sermon Series
"Who Is Jesus?" from the Gospel of Mark

Who Is Jesus?	Text
Jesus Prepares for Ministry	Mark 1:1–12
Jesus Calls the Disciples	Mark 1:14–20; 2:13–17
Jesus's Parables	Mark 4:1–34
Jesus's Power over Creation	Mark 4:35–41
Jesus's Power over Sickness	Mark 5
Jesus's Power over Hunger	Mark 6:30–56
Jesus, a Prophet Without Honor	Mark 6:1–6
Jesus the Teacher	Mark 7:1–20
Jesus Is the Christ	Mark 8:27–38
Who Is the Greatest According to Jesus?	Mark 9:33–37; 10:35–45
Jesus and the End Times	Mark 13
Jesus Defeats Sin and Death	Mark 16:1–8

In a different sermon series, I wanted to intentionally build toward a congregational sense of community with one another. A biblical book that appropriately discusses such themes is Nehemiah. For this reason, I created a sermon series going through the book of Nehemiah one chapter at a time (chapters 6 and 7 were combined into one sermon).

Sample Sermon Series
"Building Community" from the Book of Nehemiah

Building Community	Text
Checking Our Spiritual Pulse	Nehemiah 1
Godly Possibilities	Nehemiah 2
Every Little Bit Helps	Nehemiah 3
The God Who Fights	Nehemiah 4
God's Heart for Justice	Nehemiah 5
Don't Give Up	Nehemiah 6 and 7
Created for Worship	Nehemiah 8
The Israelites Confess Their Sins	Nehemiah 9
The Pledge of Obedience	Nehemiah 10
Reasons to Celebrate	Nehemiah 11
The Need for Recognition	Nehemiah 12
Becoming Christians with Purpose	Nehemiah 13

Having a clear purpose in mind is paramount to communicating a clear sermon and sermon series. A sermon without a purpose is a sermon without a destination. The sermon should lead your congregation toward some aspect of discipleship and transformational growth.

The definition of preaching I provided in the introduction is worth revisiting here. Earlier, I defined preaching as *communicating the triune God's Word to God's people for the purpose of life transformation and Christlikeness through explaining, envisioning, equipping, encouraging, and empowering preachers and listeners to become obedient to Scripture and to live more like Christ Jesus in every part of life.*

How does life transformation take place in a sermon *through* explaining, envisioning, equipping, encouraging, and empowering our listeners to become obedient to Scripture and to live more like Christ Jesus in every part of life? Let's expound briefly on each part separately and in that order.

Explain

A hefty portion of any biblical sermon involves explaining the passage to our people. In most cases, our listeners will not have spent as much time as we have learning about the sermon text. I'm reminded of the memorable story found in Acts 8:26–40 where the Ethiopian government official read through the prophet Isaiah while waiting in his chariot (v. 28). Philip, the disciple, heard from the Holy Spirit and ran to meet the official and asked him, "Do you understand what you are reading?" to which the official replied in verse 31, "How can I . . . unless someone *explains* it to me?" The prerequisite of explaining the Scriptures to our people is that we understand the text for ourselves and will help them do likewise. Flipping the story, we might ask ourselves, "How can I preach unless I can explain the text to myself and to others?" One central purpose of preaching is to explain the meaning of the passage.

Envision

A second tangible purpose in every sermon is to help our listeners envision what this text looks like to live out its meaning. What would it look like for my listeners and my congregation to embody and heed God's Word in every part of life? Paul writes in Ephesians 3:20–21, "Now to him who is able to do immeasurably more than all we ask or imagine, according to his power that is at work within us, to him be glory in the church and in Christ Jesus throughout all generations, for ever and ever! Amen." Without a daily, monthly, yearly, lifelong dream, congregants fail to visualize the "immeasurable" things God can do in their lives. While some might pejoratively call this daydreaming, the preacher's greatest opportunity is to help listeners dream the passage into existence and visualize the text as lived reality. Allow listeners to imagine and dream with you. Give listeners a lucid vision for how exciting a life with Christ and living for Christ can be!

Equip

Third, Ephesians 4:12 gives preachers a clear task: We are called "to equip [God's] people for works of service, so that the body of Christ may be built up." Equipping the saints is more than simply giving directives. To equip the saints effectively requires a relationship. Each person has a unique assignment and spiritual gifts given to them by God. Each congregation has a unique assignment as well. We are not called to reach all people in all places. That's an impossible ask! However, we can equip our saints for the individual and corporate work that God has invited us to participate in with him in his kingdom work. In each sermon, your purpose as the pastor/preacher is to equip the saints for their individual and collective ministries.

Encourage

While not formally in my job description as a pastor or a professor, one of my greatest joys in ministry is to act as "head cheerleader" of my congregation and of my classroom. You may not be well-versed in hearing or giving encouragement, but let me remind you that you also are your congregation's greatest cheerleader! Encouragement is sorely lacking in our world today. Your people need words of encouragement from their pastor. So much of preaching involves encouraging our listeners to follow Christ and not the world. Hebrews 10:24–25 exhorts: "Let us consider how we may spur one another on . . . not giving up meeting together, as some are in the habit of doing, but encouraging one another—and all the more as you see the Day approaching." In every sermon, encourage your listeners. Give them a pat on the back so they don't lose heart. One encouraging word from their pastor can do wonders for their pursuit of discipleship.

Empower

Finally, sometimes after hearing a sermon, we may leave the sanctuary discouraged and defeated. If I've been struggling to overcome a stubborn sin or lack motivation to obey God's Word, is it possible to change and live differently? Thankfully, empowerment is not manufactured by human determination. In Genesis 18:14, we are reminded of God's confidence in his abilities. When the Lord foretells of Sarah's pregnancy, she laughs. Then the Lord asks Abraham rhetorically about himself, "Is anything too hard for the Lord? I will return to you at the appointed time next year, and Sarah will have a son." Transformation can take place in our lives because God, through the Son and Spirit, empowers us to accomplish his will. Since his will is for our holiness and obedience, he can give us the supernatural ability to do what is humanly impossible. Yes, this takes motivation and determination on our part (human responsibility), but the promise remains that with God *anything* is possible (divine sovereignty).

Plan Enough Time for Unpacking

Have you ever taken a trip only to find that you've either overpacked or underpacked the amount of clothing you would need? Similarly, for your sermon, you can ask yourself, how much sermonic clothing do I need for this message? Practically speaking, ask yourself: How many minutes do I have to preach this sermon? While sermon lengths vary from fifteen to fifty-five minutes, depending on your church's tradition, you want to make the most out of that time.

Remember, your listeners' time is valuable, just as you value your personal time. Less is more when it comes to the preaching moment. You don't have to preach for forty-plus minutes for the sake of preaching a forty-minute sermon to feel validated that you've done your job. The most important thing is whether you feel confident that you've shared the appropriate Scripture and message that God has prepared in and through you. The average length of a Sunday sermon is twenty-five to thirty-five minutes. There's plenty that you can communicate in that time frame.

A brief word must be said about cultural and denominational expectations. Depending on your ethnic/racial/cultural background and denomination, the church has certain expectations on sermonic length. I once participated in a short-term mission trip to Kenya, where the preacher was expected to preach at least one hour per service. To preach less than an hour was insulting to the congregants, who often traveled over an hour by foot to join the worship gathering. While most of us do not come from such backgrounds or traditions, there may be preexisting expectations from the congregation or denomination on how long a sermon should be. Consult your church leaders and denominational leaders regarding sermon length, and keep to that allotted time.

Second, how much of this biblical text can we properly explain and apply in those minutes? I once visited a church in the city where I used to serve as a senior pastor. As the preacher was known for his effective preaching ministry, I listened eagerly and intently to the message. The preacher began the sermon with a very long, meandering personal story. The preaching professor in me wondered when he would talk about the passage at hand. I looked at my watch to see how long the introduction was. It was over twenty-five minutes long! The entire sermon was about thirty-five minutes in length. Toward the end of the sermon, the preacher said, rather nonchalantly, "I'm sorry we didn't get to talk about much of the text today. I didn't have time." Similarly, one of the common refrains I hear from students of preaching is, "I didn't have enough time to talk about the text or that part of the text." We do have time. We need to use it wisely.

Granted, I recognize that we will never be able to do justice to every single verse we read. However, if we don't talk about the Scripture text at all, minimally, or sporadically, we've missed a crucial underpinning for the ministry of preaching. As Paul tells Timothy in 2 Timothy 4:2, "Preach the Word!" Paul doesn't tell Timothy to preach ourselves or preach our culture or preach the stories of others. No, in resoundingly clear fashion, he says we are preachers of *the Word*. We explain and apply the Word to the best of our ability. As mentioned in chapter 2, we are not the subject or hero of the sermon. The triune God is.

As you prepare and write your sermon, determine how much text you can communicate about. Only read what you'll take time to explain and apply for your listeners. To read something that you don't talk about is a disservice to your congregation. (This is different from reading various passages using the lectionary on that date to increase Scripture reading and awareness of related texts.) In addition, sometimes we read too little of the chapter or passage and spend the rest of the time filling the sermon with supplemental passages and any number of stories and illustrations. This is an unhelpful practice. In the next chapter on genre, we will offer more genre-sensitive advice on how to discern the length of your sermon passage for the message.

Plan Your Series Length

Depending on your annual discipleship theme and the specific book of the Bible you've decided to preach on to address this theme, the next step is to determine the length of your sermon series. Is there an optimal number? While this is not a precise science, I would make an educated guess that most sermon series fall in the range of six to eight weeks (perhaps no longer than twelve weeks). This is not a rule by any means. However, the preacher and listeners may get tired or bored if the sermon series extends beyond that. If you follow this range, you'll want to break up your sermon texts into appropriate chapters and passages or pericopes. You'll find an example at the end of the chapter.

Lay Out Text Parameters: Remember, the Main Point Includes the Entire Pericope

It is futile to try to preach substantive sermons when we fail to properly give our passage boundaries. Laying out text parameters will enhance your ability to preach effectively on a given text. What do we mean by parameters of a text? Mark Mitchell offers helpful clues as we begin this section:

- Remember that there were no chapter or verse divisions in the original manuscripts of the Bible. Even the paragraph divisions included in most modern versions of the Bible were placed there by editors.
- Be mindful of the literary genre. In narrative literature, the writer will often change the subject by starting an entirely new story. In poetic literature, the subject will change with a new verse or stanza. In a letter, the subject will change with a new paragraph.[5]

5. See Mark Mitchell, "5 Steps to Get the Big Idea," Preaching Today, accessed December 2, 2025, https://www.preachingtoday.com/preaching-guides/finding-and-crafting-sermons-big-idea/5-steps-to-get-big-idea.html.

In addition to considering the sermon time and length of a series, we also don't want to shortchange the importance of getting the full main idea of the text. Many of us tend to divide sermon texts based on the English subheadings to determine what constitutes a complete passage. Sometimes referred to as a pericope, this is the specific biblical passage or set of verses on which we build our sermon or what Haddon Robinson calls a "unit of thought."[6] A unit of thought is the main point the author is making in each section of the biblical book. To determine a thought unit involves understanding the biblical author's line of reasoning. Therefore, the main point of the passage (and our sermon) may require us to preach a longer portion of the text (pericope) or even an entire chapter or two to get the full picture/point.

In his Sermon on the Mount in Matthew 6:1–18, for example, Jesus teaches the Pharisees and religious leaders the proper motivation by which we live out Christian piety. Jesus divides these motivations into three different types: praying, giving, and fasting. While we could choose to preach one section at a time, delving into praying, giving, and fasting each week, another way to approach the sermon would be to preach on the entirety of verses 1–18 as one unit of thought. The aggregate central idea is this: pray, give, and fast not as a public spectacle but in secret because our heavenly Father will reward us.

Sometimes a biblical passage has a peculiar ending that seems to derail the rest of its meaning. What happens at this point is that we start to panic and either skip or drop the last verse or two that make no sense to us. Let me provide such an example.

James 4:13–17 is a passage that instructs businesspeople on how they should focus on today rather than boasting about the future. The NIV subheading for this text is "Boasting About Tomorrow." At face value, the point James seems to be making is found in verse 15, "If it is the Lord's will, we will live and do this or that." The emphasis is on the businesspeople's lack of recognition that they are not in control over each day's affairs and outcomes and that it's foolish to boast in oneself and in one's successes. Notice, however, that in verses 16 and 17 there is a clear shift in James's tone. He says, "As it is, you boast in your arrogant schemes. All such boasting is evil." Now verse 17 highlights the twist: "If anyone, then, knows the good they ought to do and doesn't do it, it is sin for them."

Over the years, I have heard several sermons on this text from James 4:13–17. In those sermons, I have yet to hear a preacher exegete and speak about verse 17. The preacher conveniently leaves off verse 17, whether purposefully

6. Haddon W. Robinson, *Biblical Preaching: The Development and Delivery of Expository Messages*, 4th ed. (Baker Academic, 2025), 34.

or subconsciously. Sometimes verse 17 isn't even read aloud so as not to stir up end-of-the-sermon controversy. Why does this happen? James's calling out of sin appears strange and doesn't seem to fit with the rest of the text.

Let's take a moment to unpack this. James not only challenges his readers with the idea that self-dependence and boasting is evil (v. 16), but he goes a step further and warns them saying, "If anyone, then, knows the good they ought to do and doesn't do it, it is sin for them" (v. 17). What is the sin? "To continue down a path of worldliness and self-reliance instead of trusting God in our everyday choices is sin. We know what we should do, so we have no excuse not to do it."[7] Instead of skipping over the final verse in this passage, include it in the main point you're trying to make. That is taking the entire passage into consideration and not leaving out inconvenient or difficult sections of a passage because we don't want to stir the pot.

Other Considerations

Here are a few other factors or questions to consider when selecting a preaching series or sermon.

Listeners' Spiritual Condition

An important element in choosing a sermon series or sermon text is knowing the congregation and the spiritual condition of your people. Giving your listeners a vision for their lives and growth areas for discipleship is a requisite part of your preaching ministry. Imagine a preacher saying, "You're good enough. Don't worry about obedience to Christ!" Of course, we are mindful of discipleship areas in which we need to experience the transformational power of God. Yet, sometimes preachers have a blind spot to the spiritual condition of our hearers. How are they doing? Does this sermon series, topic, or text align with where the people are at in this stage of the discipleship journey?

Listeners' Emotional Condition

A second area of discernment for putting together our preaching calendar is addressing the emotional state of our listeners. Take time to pray, think about your recent pastoral visitations, and ask your pastoral staff and other church leaders how people are doing. Take time at the beginning of the sermon to read the emotional conditions represented in the room. Not that we

7. BibleRef, "What Does James 4:17 Mean?," accessed January 6, 2026, https://www.bibleref.com/James/4/James-4-17.html.

shy away from difficult books of the Bible or topics simply because people don't want to hear about them. Yet there is wisdom in understanding and anticipating how people will receive a sermon series or Scripture passage. This will guide you in delivering a biblical truth with pastoral love, patience, and care. Are people ready to hear about this subject matter? What are some pushbacks or warnings we might offer so that we are acknowledging the complex emotions of our people? We'll discuss this further in chapter 19, on being an empathetic preacher.

Listeners' Distracted Condition

Third, I don't have to tell you that we are living in an age of diminishing attention spans. In his book *Preaching in an Age of Distraction*, J. Ellsworth Kalas writes, "Many people who come to church on Sunday have just watched a sitcom the night before, with its changing scene every ten or fifteen seconds and its three or four commercials in the space of a minute. Can we expect people who experience life in such a fashion all through the week to give undivided attention to a sermon or a prayer when they're accustomed to living with several clamoring voices surrounding them at all times?"[8] In our world of social media clips and mindless flipping to the next screen, we've become a society preconditioned and conditioned to no longer stay focused on sermon listening.

Moreover, it seems that the ministry of preaching is not as celebrated as it once was but merely tolerated by Christians today. In *Proclaiming the Word*, David Jackman observes, "Preaching seems to be just another example of the church being out of touch, out of date, and out of steam."[9] While I was visiting with a group of pastors recently while delivering a preaching lectureship, some pastors in the room lamented the fact that their church leaders and parishioners scoffed at the fact that a sermon could be more than twenty or twenty-two minutes in length. The very idea of preaching a standard thirty-minute sermon was anathema to them. In their parishioners' words, "The sermon was just too long!"

Listeners are not only distracted about many things, but they've also become increasingly disinterested in hearing sermons. If we're honest, I imagine when you and I listen to a sermon, we're not totally engaged for the duration of the sermon either. Put yourself in your listeners' shoes! What's the antidote? We want our sermons to be as engaging, educational, and

8. J. Ellsworth Kalas, *Preaching in an Age of Distraction* (InterVarsity, 2014), 10.

9. David Jackman, *Proclaiming the Word: Principles and Practices for Expository Preaching* (Crossway, 2024), 1.

inspiring as possible. This doesn't mean we need to become a comedian or entertainer. Rather, we are expositors who make the Bible come to life for the congregation, with the help of the Holy Spirit. It's our job to make the Scriptures come alive! What are your people distracted by or anxious about today or over the last year? How can this sermon draw your people closer to the Lord?

CONCLUSION

Picking a Scripture text might seem to be a no-brainer. Just pick a text! Does it really matter? After reading this chapter, I hope you'll agree with me that it is significant and not as straightforward as it may seem. There are many considerations when selecting a sermon series/book of the Bible to preach through or even for a one-off sermon. Make it a habit to pray and consult the wisdom of others as you engage in this first step. Consider how much time you have to preach and how much text you can sufficiently exposit, illustrate, and apply for your listeners. After you select a text, you will want to learn about its genre. That is the next part of the sermonic process.

QUESTIONS

1. What has been your strategy for selecting sermon series or sermon texts to this point? Why is that your preferred method?
2. What do you need to know about your congregation to disciple them effectively from the pulpit?
3. Which current sermon series and sermons have you chosen to preach on this year? Why did you choose them?
4. After reading this chapter, what has God taught you about creating a preaching calendar?

PRACTICES

1. Review the sermon series and sermons you have preached over the last one or two years. What has your church been preaching about (Bible books, topics, themes, etc.)?

2. Make a spreadsheet and create a possible sermon series for one quarter of this year—three months. As you fill out the details, be concrete and specific. Title the series, choose specific books, passages, themes, and so on. Fill in the table below.

Theme for the year: ______________________________

Book of the Bible: ______________________________

Sermon Planning Calendar

Date	Sermon series	Text	Preacher

Date	Sermon series	Text	Preacher

3. Make a list of four to six discipleship areas that you would like to see your congregation grow in this year.

6

GENRE

What Is the Literary Genre of Our Text?

> For whatever was written in former days was written for our instruction, that through endurance and through the encouragement of the Scriptures we might have hope.
>
> —Romans 15:4 (ESV)

Readers, even from a young age, can differentiate between two primary literary forms: poetry and prose. If I'm being transparent, I've never been a fan of poetry. However, I have grown to appreciate it over the years because poetry teaches us about life in ways that prose cannot. When we read poetry, we are given clues based on visual and oral features such as paragraph structure (centered alignment on a page and not justified right or left), rhyme scheme, imagistic language, metaphors, similes, and other noticeable traits. Prose, on the other hand, is putting together basic, logical sentences one after the other. There is less intentional artistry and structure in prose than there is in poetry.

The Bible is composed of several different literary genres. Since God is creative and colorful, it's no surprise that the Bible is not one-dimensional, uniform, or even uni-genred (if I may take some liberty and make up a term). Understanding the literary genre of a Scripture passage is paramount to comprehension, explanation, and application for any biblical sermon. We want to develop skills in how to read these various types of books (or literary forms) in the Bible so that we can align the sermonic form and outline to that genre/form. Thomas G. Long says it this way: "The literary form and dynamics of a biblical text can and should be important factors in the preacher's navigation of the distance between text and sermon. . . . What is needed, then, is a process of sermon development sufficiently nuanced to recognize and employ these differences in the creation of the sermon itself."[1]

Since genre is critical to our interpretation and sermon preparation, we will spend the next moments identifying the major genres in Scripture and offer requisite tools to equip us to preach each genre according to its literary form. Each genre has a unique flow and purpose that God uses to communicate his truth. Let's begin by getting a wide-angle view of the literary landscape.

Step 3: Appreciate Your Genre

Step 3 in the sermon process is to appreciate the biblical genre. Do you have a favorite biblical genre or perhaps a least favorite? Think of literary genre like visiting your favorite bookstore. The store is laid out with shelves clustered together based on their literary genre: history, fiction, nonfiction, science fiction, poetry, religion, psychology, self-help, maps, children's books, educational aides, and more.[2] In the same way, the Bible contains roughly seven distinct shelves of Scripture (including the parables). These are collections of writings that have a similar style, function, and purpose. So, what are these literary/biblical genres? God has prepared Scripture via narrative texts, poetical books/wisdom literature, prophetical books, the Gospels, the Epistles/Letters, and apocalyptic literature. For our sermonic intentions, the parables of Jesus in the Gospels will constitute their own genre.

In the rest of this chapter, we will unpack each type of genre/form and explain how this genre informs and shapes the sermon going forward. Remember, a literary genre is determined not by individual, isolated portions of texts but taken as a whole. For example, you may have a poem embedded within a narrative book. That doesn't change the fact that the book is a narrative text. By the end, my hope is that you'll be able to identify a literary form and begin generating ideas on how you might approach preaching each of these

1. Thomas G. Long, *Preaching and the Literary Forms of the Bible* (Fortress, 1989), 11.

2. Mel Lawrenz, "The Many Genres of Scripture," *Bible Gateway Blog*, March 3, 2016, https://www.biblegateway.com/blog/2016/03/the-many-genres-of-scripture.

genres. For specifics on sermon construction and outlines, we will address these matters according to their literary genre in chapter 10.

Narrative Texts

Narrative texts are biblical passages that narrate or tell a story. The human and divine authors work together to weave contexts, situations, characters, events, conflicts, experiences, lessons, principles, or conundrums, serving as a guide for the reader. Most of the Bible contains narratival material. In fact, some estimates testify that more than 40 percent of the Bible is in story form.[3]

What's unique about story in terms of the preaching task and preaching moment? To our benefit, listeners from almost any generation will appreciate a good story. During my time as a senior pastor, we shared ministry and worship space in a building with an elderly congregation. Between the services, theirs and ours, I would often sit down in the church foyer next to the older members of the other church. Story after story would fly in my direction (often the very same ones) from people who wanted to share with me about their prior years and experiences. In the same way, story is the art form of communication among the younger generations. Thus, the ability to understand and communicate biblical stories effectively is crucial for ministry and preaching as discipleship.

We find narrative texts in both Testaments. From Genesis through the book of Acts, you will find numerous biblical books that relay a story with biblical principles and instructions for God's people to hear and to learn from. Recently, I read through the book of Genesis again. While there are some other elements included, such as the Table of Nations in Genesis 10, which is simply a list of names of people and places where they inhabited, almost the entirety of the book tells stories of the first couple, Adam and Eve, and the generations following them: Noah and his sons, Abraham and Sarah, Isaac and Ishmael, Jacob and Esau and their descendants, and finally Joseph and his brothers and their progeny.

The entire book of Genesis is a story of God's creation, the fall of Adam and Eve, the promise of God to make Abraham a great nation, the sinful nature of humanity, and the future generations of Israelites and what they encountered in Egypt during the time of Joseph. Narrative texts not only tell the story, although that is significant. They also recount essential truths about

3. "Literary Styles," episode 3 of "How to Read the Bible" video series, Bible Project, accessed January 19, 2026, https://bibleproject.com/videos/literary-styles-bible.

God and how he relates to the world, including human beings. The following is a list of biblical books that would be considered narratival texts (18 books): Genesis, Exodus, Leviticus, Numbers, Deuteronomy, Joshua, Judges, Ruth, 1 Samuel, 2 Samuel, 1 Kings, 2 Kings, 1 Chronicles, 2 Chronicles, Ezra, Nehemiah, Esther, and Acts.

As you read through these narratives, it's clear that the biblical and divine authors are telling a unique story filled with knowledge and wisdom about who God is, stories of biblical persons, their journeys and experiences, their stories of obedience and disobedience (including entire nations like Israel, Judah, or Edom), and morals/principles for righteous living that the original readers and we today will glean from them.

Poetical Books / Wisdom Literature

The Bible is generously furnished with poetry in both Testaments. However, those considered primarily poetical books include Job, Psalms, Proverbs, Ecclesiastes, Song of Songs, and Lamentations. What makes them poetical? Jeffrey Kranz explains: "These books are almost entirely made up of poems, songs, and wise sayings that the ancient Jews (and the Christians who followed) used to make wise decisions and worship God."[4] Most of us have probably heard and/or preached from these books of biblical poetry (perhaps Song of Songs and Lamentations less frequently). Many, if not all, of these books seek to lavish the reader with wisdom from the Lord through positive and negative examples. For this reason, I have merged the two categories into one, even as some specific differences will be named.

Here are two foundational questions that come to the surface regarding the genre of poetry: What are some central considerations for preaching on/through biblical poetry? How is preaching from poetical books different from other genres? Biblical poetry, from a preacher's vantage point, provides two main distinctions from other genres. First, when preaching on poetry, it's crucial to maintain the style or flow of the passage. Not that we will write an entire sermon that mimics the poetry in the text (with iambic pentameter), but it helps the listener understand what the author is communicating through their use of poetic language, imagery, comparison, illustration, and more. At least in ancient/biblical Hebrew, there are three primary forms of poetic meaning demonstrated through the use of parallelism: synonymous, antithetical, and synthetic. Here's what we mean by each.

4. See Jeffrey Kranz, "Poetry and Wisdom Books of the Bible: The Beginner's Guide," Overview Bible, March 4, 2020, https://overviewbible.com/poetry.

Synonymous parallelism is when the same thought is repeated using different words. Proverbs 22:1 says, "A good name is more desirable than great riches; to be esteemed is better than silver or gold." There are two lines here that convey the same truth about the value of a good name. "A good name is more desirable than great riches" is another way of saying "to be esteemed is better than silver or gold." In English, the semicolon gives it away that what has just been said is connected to or resembles the second part of the sentence. Both lines are synonymous, meaning both lines communicate that a good reputation is highly valuable.

Antithetical parallelism can be found when two or more themes are compared or more likely contrasted. An example of antithetical parallelism is found in Proverbs 1:7, which reads: "The fear of the Lord is the beginning of knowledge, but fools despise wisdom and instruction." The first part of the proverb explains where the beginning of knowledge can be found (in fearing the Lord), while the second line provides the opposite response to the beginning of knowledge, which is that fools will despise or reject the very wisdom and instruction that comes from the Lord. These two statements have contrasting meanings and are therefore antithetical.

Synthetic parallelism occurs when one idea builds upon or synthesizes (brings together) something that has been communicated earlier. For example, Proverbs 3:5–6 says, "Trust in the Lord with all your heart and lean not on your own understanding; in all your ways submit to him, and he will make your paths straight." Each of the basic instructions is twofold. In verse 5, the parallelism is synthetic because it builds on the previous statement: Trust in the Lord with all your heart and lean not on your own understanding. What does it mean to trust in the Lord with all your heart? It means to not lean on your own understanding or wisdom. Then, in verse 6, we read, "In all your ways submit to him," which has the following result, "and he will make your paths straight," which builds on the former statement.

In each of these types of parallelism, the poet is imparting wisdom to his readers. The poet, through language, images, metaphors, comparison, contrast, illustrations, examples, relationships, and so on, has a clear intention behind the flowery or iconic language highlighted in the text. Part of the beauty of the poetic genre is that we don't have to go very far to explain what the text means through providing additional illustrations. The examples are already embedded in the meaning of the passage in a literal and sometimes figurative way.

Poetry is also different from other genres because there is an added complexity in determining the meaning of the text. We must wade through the vivid imagery and connect the dots for ourselves and for our hearers. The meaning is not immediately deciphered in some lines of poetry. Like proverbs in other languages, there is a subtlety to poetry that requires a bit more time and pondering. Such is the case in the following African proverb: "When two elephants fight, it's the grass that gets hurt."[5] The meaning of this synthetic proverb doesn't fly off the page. We must grapple a moment with the meaning behind the meaning. It doesn't literally mean that the grass becomes hurt on account of the weight of the two elephants. Rather, the emphasis is on the heated exchange taking place between two elephants who are unyielding to the other, causing them to stand long and hard (on the grass) where they are. When preaching biblical poetry, we want to keep the language, imagery, and illustrations of the text and guide our listeners to the proper interpretation of the passage, which takes a minute or two longer than prose might.

Four Major Prophetical Books

Prophetical books are those in which God communicates messages of rebuke, repentance, and renewal to his people through selected prophets who serve as his mouthpieces. In the Old Testament, four books are considered major prophetical works based on their length and not according to their significance. These major prophetical works include Isaiah, Jeremiah, Ezekiel, and Daniel.[6]

Preaching chapter by chapter, verse by verse through the Major Prophets is a massive undertaking (there are 66 chapters in Isaiah, 52 in Jeremiah, 48 in Ezekiel, and 12 in Daniel). The sheer volume of chapters can make it daunting for any preacher. The prophets' repetitive call to repentance and renewal might feel like watching a television commercial stuck on repeat.

Yet, the Major Prophets can be divided into larger sermon series or broken into pericopal chunks. Preaching thematically might be the best approach when it comes to the Major Prophets. As Andrew C. Thompson suggests, "This [preaching major themes] might shorten a book like Isaiah to somewhere between ten and fifteen weeks,"[7] including the Lord's rebuke, repentance, renewal, idolatry, kings and kingdoms, covenant, oracles, the Messiah,

5. Patty Lane, *A Beginner's Guide to Cross Cultures* (InterVarsity, 2002), 117.

6. For helpful information on how to preach books of the Bible, see Matthew D. Kim and Scott M. Gibson, eds., *The Big Idea Companion for Preaching and Teaching: A Guide from Genesis to Revelation* (Baker Academic, 2021), which offers homiletical guidance on each of the sixty-six books of the Bible. See also Douglas Stuart and Gordon D. Fee, *How to Read the Bible Book by Book: A Guided Tour* (Zondervan, 2014).

7. Andrew C. Thompson, "Isaiah," in *The Big Idea Companion for Preaching and Teaching: A Guide from Genesis to Revelation*, ed. Matthew D. Kim and Scott M. Gibson (Baker Academic, 2021), 251.

Sabbath, holiness, and more. A similar sermon series might be appropriate for Jeremiah and Ezekiel, in particular. With a shorter book like Daniel, it's more reasonable to preach through the entire book without skipping a chapter or verse.

Twelve Minor Prophets (From Hosea to Malachi)

At least in recent memory, each year there is a popular list published showcasing baby names for boys and girls. Among the twelve minor prophetical books, I've yet to see one of these boy names making the cut. That doesn't make preaching the Minor Prophets any less significant than preaching through Matthew, Mark, Luke, or John. When selecting a sermon series or book series, the Minor Prophets are not immediately in our preaching purview. Each of the minor prophets is tailored for a specific readership and nation(s).[8] Like any of the major prophets mentioned above, the minor prophets communicate a clear message of rebuke, repentance, and renewal for targeted generations in Israel, Judah, and other nations.

Understanding the uniqueness of each minor prophet is a good place to start in considering whether we might dedicate an entire series to it. Hosea, Joel, Amos, Obadiah, Jonah, Micah, Nahum, Habakkuk, Zephaniah, Haggai, Zechariah, and Malachi tell a unique story about the unfaithfulness of God's people and the faithfulness of God. Take, for instance, the book of Hosea. In my many years of being a Christian, I have yet to hear an entire sermon series dedicated to Hosea. Yes, I've heard one-off sermons or perhaps two consecutive sermons on this minor prophet but never fourteen sermons through fourteen chapters. The book of Hosea is a mind-boggling journey into the life of God's prophet Hosea, who is commissioned or commanded by God to marry a prostitute named Gomer. Like Israel's unfaithfulness to God, Gomer is unfaithful to her husband Hosea. The ongoing saga of Gomer's betrayal is heart-wrenching, to say the least. And yet, Hosea accepts his mission and ministry to remain faithful to a faithless woman, which mirrors the Lord's relationship with Israel.

The twelve Minor Prophets could represent an entire twelve-month exploration into the Minor Prophets. You could prepare four to five sermons per minor prophet and create a yearly sermon series in such a way. One might also tackle some dominant themes and narratives within the Minor Prophets and coincide them with the Advent season, such as preaching through portions

8. See Elizabeth Achtemeier, *Preaching from the Minor Prophets: Texts and Sermon Suggestions* (Eerdmans, 1998).

of Zechariah. Another possible sermon series would be to incorporate one or two minor prophets into your yearly preaching calendar. A key takeaway from the Minor Prophets is that they are filled with wisdom on how we as unfaithful believers are to relate to and appreciate a faithful, patient, merciful, and loving God.

The Four Gospels

The four Gospels narrate the main stories of the life and ministry of Jesus and his twelve disciples. Matthew, Mark, Luke, and John recount the gospel story represented by Jesus's birth, life, ministry, death, and resurrection. Each gospel account provides a unique human author's perspective on what they witnessed and encountered during the life of Christ. The triune God, the divine author, gave the human authors the words to communicate to a particular group of readers.

Knowing the specific audience to whom it was written provides a contextualized way of understanding and appreciating the Gospel book more fully. For instance, the readership of Matthew's Gospel was Jewish, so you'll find more language and allusions to Jewish culture and history than you would in Mark, Luke, or John. What that means is that there will be some additional exegetical work that we will need to do as preachers to read and preach contextually for our unique church setting. More on contextualized preaching in chapter 7.

The primary literary genre of the Gospels is narrative. Apart from a few instances such as the genealogies in Matthew 1 and Luke 3, the Sermon on the Mount (Matt. 5–7), and the Sermon on the Plain (Luke 6:20–49), numerous parables, and the words of Christ and various dialogical moments with the disciples, the Pharisees and religious leaders, and other biblical people, most of the Gospels contain stories. These stories are told from the perspective of the biblical author. As you prepare to preach on a specific Gospel book, you'll want to become better acquainted with the authorship of the book and his ethnic/cultural background. To maintain the power of the genre, it's worthwhile to consider how the sermon form, when preaching from the Gospels, can remain in story form. Like telling the punchline of a joke at the end, the Gospels pack a powerful principle that we can extrapolate toward the final moments of the sermon. Overloading the Gospel narrative with copious points or principles throughout can shortchange the power of the genre of story. More on this later when we explore sermon forms and outlines.

A quick word about parables: The parables of Jesus are many and varied. Just as the disciples struggled in the moment to decipher their meanings, preachers today may also stumble in preaching them. A parable tells a story that ultimately teaches a major spiritual principle. The specific lesson we are to gain from it isn't readily spelled out for us. That's why parables often stumped the disciples—leading them to ask Jesus what he meant (often in private). Various resources are available for each of these genres. You'll find some resources at the back of the book to guide you.

The Epistles/Letters

Obviously, as a literary genre, the Epistles or Letters of the apostle Paul, Peter, and others make up a significant portion of the New Testament. From the Epistle of Romans through the Epistle of Jude, we find in the New Testament twenty-one different letters written to specific churches and/or individuals. For "logical" or "didactic" (teaching-oriented) thinkers, it's easy to gravitate toward the Epistles/Letters since they are simpler to preach in many ways. The sermon follows the flow of the logic of the letter. You may have also heard, on rare occasions, preachers who decide to narrate a story based on the situational context of a given epistle/letter.

A key element to remember when preaching through an epistle or a letter is that we must distinguish between corporate and individual interpretation and application. Take some extra study time to familiarize yourself with the authorship and readership of a given letter. For instance, Paul writes to the church at Rome and the church at Galatia as communities of faith, while he writes 1–2 Timothy and Titus to his ministry protégés Timothy and Titus (even while the application extends to the churches they pastored). All of Scripture contains application for modern believers—that is us; yet in the sermons we preach, we want to determine what is a corporate application versus what are individual ones. On most occasions, we will want to point out and draw the listeners' attention toward the collective/corporate application of how this epistle/letter shapes discipleship for the congregation *and* the individual person.

Apocalyptic Literature

The final literary genre is apocalyptic literature, found in the books of Revelation and Daniel. Since we've already mentioned Daniel in the Major Prophets section above, we'll focus here on what makes the book of Revelation an apocalyptic text and how that informs our preaching of it.

Revelation is a rather peculiar book. In it, John the apostle describes a vision that he sees, whether literally in front of his face or in his mind's eye, on the Island of Patmos—a picture of the end of days. The word "revelation" means "to uncover" or "reveal."[9] John sees the seven ancient churches of Asia, a glimpse of heaven, the worship and exaltation of the Lord Jesus Christ, heavenly creatures, a cloud of believers who have endured the tribulation (a time of persecution and testing), the devil and his final destiny, and the new heavens and new earth.

The challenge of preaching through Revelation, though it should not be omitted, is helping our listeners understand the meaning of the text without overemphasizing or overpromising what it entails. Frankly, we cannot possibly fathom or comprehend all its imagery, symbolism, and other elements. Yet it is critical to appreciate and understand John's revelation as best we can, since it pertains to our final human days and our entry into our eternal home and future for those who belong to Christ.

CONCLUSION

Recognizing and appreciating the literary genre and preaching sermons that reflect the power of that genre is what we've been exploring in this chapter. Since God is a God of diversity, the Bible is not written with one literary genre alone. Rather, there are several genres that make up the Holy Canon: narrative texts, poetical books/wisdom literature, the prophets, the Gospels, parables, the Epistles/Letters, and apocalyptic literature. Each genre has its own uniqueness and power. In chapter 10, we will go deeper into how these various literary genres play out in the actual sermons we construct as we keep in step with their literary form.

QUESTIONS

1. What did you learn from this chapter regarding literary genres and forms?
2. Is there a preferred literary genre for you? Why?

9. "How to Read the Bible: Apocalyptic Literature," episode 19, Bible Project, https://bibleproject.com/explore/video/apocalyptic-literature.

3. How has this chapter challenged you to consider preaching from a range of literary genres?
4. In which literary genres would you like to develop, both in knowledge and in preaching?

PRACTICES

Summarize in your own words the specific characteristics of each literary genre below.

Narrative Texts

Poetical Books / Wisdom Literature

Prophetical Books

The Gospels

Parables

The Epistles/Letters

Apocalyptic Literature

7

CONTEXT

Do We Understand the Biblical Author and the Ancient World?

> Now there were staying in Jerusalem God-fearing Jews from every nation under heaven. When they heard this sound, a crowd came together in bewilderment, because each one heard their own language. . . . Amazed and perplexed, they asked one another, "What does this mean?"
>
> —Acts 2:5–6, 12

"Context is king!" You've probably heard this phrase mentioned during your theological training or in a Sunday school class. This well-known axiom often used by biblical scholars conveys that all interpretation (whether individual verses or entire pericopes) occurs in an embedded context, including the surrounding verses, chapters, and books (and even the entire biblical canon). Michael J. Gorman notes that "the Bible was written by and for real people, living in specific historical contexts, to address particular individual and community needs."[1] So often, when we think of the world of the Bible, it's a foreign, distant land that makes little sense to us. We rely solely on our own cultural understanding and do little to familiarize ourselves with the world of the Bible.

1. Michael J. Gorman, *Elements of Biblical Exegesis: A Basic Guide for Students and Ministers*, 3rd ed. (Baker Academic, 2020), 76.

The purpose of this chapter is to guide our conversation toward a central aspect of what biblical preaching entails, which is understanding the *biblical* world so that we can then proclaim God's truth properly and effectively to the *modern* world. We are, as John Stott put it, bridge builders whenever we preach or teach God's Word to our congregation:

> In building bridges, we are also following in the footsteps of the great preachers in every age. Chrysostom (who died in 407) is described as a "man of the word and a man of the world" whose preaching was both timeless and timely. Jonathan Edwards in the eighteenth century is said to have had an unrivalled knowledge of the Bible and of the human heart. Both Spurgeon in the nineteenth century and Karl Barth in the twentieth advised preachers to prepare with "the Bible in one hand and the daily newspaper in the other." . . . Both ends of our bridges must be firmly rooted if we are to be able to show that Christianity is still relevant today.[2]

To understand the biblical author's world, we will explore both the historical and cultural worlds of a given book of the Bible on which we will preach. What are the elements of historical and cultural context we want to become familiar with to present this biblical world to our modern listeners? Put differently, what details should I include in my sermon from the ancient context?

Step 4: Understand Your Context

The Worlds of the Bible

Step 4 in the preaching process is to understand the context. If you've ever planned a trip to another country, you've probably made the effort to scope out a tour guidebook about that country. In this guide, you'll find all kinds of helpful information about the nation you'll soon be visiting, such as the currency you'll need to exchange for in order to make local purchases, key landmarks and destination points you won't want to miss, the spoken language(s) and their corresponding key phrases like "hello," favorite hot spots to dine at, and some cultural practices you will want to be aware of. It is a land unfamiliar to you, so the tour guidebook provides a snapshot of the important things you'll want to know before you go.

Similarly, the various books of the Bible, according to their literary genres as we explored in the previous chapter, are situated in a historical land and

2. John Stott, *The Challenge of Preaching*, abridged and updated by Greg Scharf (Eerdmans, 2015), 33, 32.

cultural context often unfamiliar to us. Depending on the specific sermon passage, we'll want to ask: What was it like to be an exile living in Babylon or a Jewish worker living under the rule of ancient Rome? As an initial response, we might honestly say, "I have no idea." This requires exploring a guidebook of the biblical world.

In Scott M. Gibson's collection of essays, *The Worlds of the Preacher*, Haddon W. Robinson wrote an opening piece titled "The Worlds of the Expositor." In this article, Robinson mentions three different worlds of the Bible that preachers want to comprehend: history, language, and culture. Since language will be the subject of our next two chapters, let's proceed with history and culture for the time being. Robinson shares, "As preachers, we want to understand the history of the ancient world. One really cannot understand the Bible unless one understands its history. . . . We might want to ignore history, but history does not ignore us."[3] Why is history so critical to preaching, and how is it that "history does not ignore us"?

As established earlier, the subject in our sermons is the Lord. The triune God is the Lord *of* history and *over* history. The Bible is a historical book. It recounts the history of creation, of Israel, of the Jews, of gentiles, and the new creation, which includes us. Since we cannot escape history when studying the Bible, we are faced with the fact that we cannot ignore or skip over it. We must wrestle with it if we want to preach the Bible properly and effectively.

The World of History

I once preached a sermon on the book of Jonah at a well-known divinity school. After the sermon, one of the professors, who taught ministry courses, spoke with me and said in disbelief, "This is the first time I've ever heard a preacher say that they believed Jonah was literally swallowed up by a fish." Never in my mind had it ever occurred to me that the events that took place in the book of Jonah were not factual and historically accurate.

To preach Scripture means believing what it contains. If we don't believe the Bible is historically factual and accurate, we will have a difficult time saying what God says. Jeffrey D. Arthurs notes in *How to Preach Narrative*, "Christianity is rare, if not unique, among the religions of the world in emphasizing history. . . . I believe that the events narrated happened, even the miracles. Of course, in reducing the events to writing, the authors of the Bible necessarily selected and shaped their material . . . but what is recorded

3. Haddon W. Robinson, "The Worlds of the Expositor," in *The Worlds of the Preacher*, ed. Scott M. Gibson (Baker Academic, 2018), 2, 6.

is historically accurate."[4] What parts of history do we need to understand to communicate the Bible to our listeners?

Authorship

Who wrote this book or letter? Perhaps more than any other question, this is the one we need to start with. Assuming divine authorship and that the Holy Spirit guided human authors in what to write down, who is the human author in each book of the Bible?

Just as authorship is important when reading a book of fiction or nonfiction today, we want to familiarize ourselves with who it is that wrote what we are about to read. I trust in the traditional views on biblical/human authorship. That is, I believe that Moses wrote the Pentateuch or the first five books of the Old Testament (Genesis, Exodus, Leviticus, Numbers, and Deuteronomy). I don't question that the prophet Isaiah wrote the entire book of Isaiah. I believe Paul wrote most of the epistles/letters in the New Testament that bear his signature. I believe the author of Hebrews (whoever that may be) wrote the letter (anonymously) for a reason. And so on.

What's of primary significance to the reader regarding the human author is understanding their ethnicity, culture, position, and purpose. Each of these elements gives us a clue into the historical background of the author. In his book, *Now I Become Myself: How Deep Grace Heals Our Shame and Restores Our True Self*, Ken Shigematsu writes as a person of Japanese descent and heritage (ethnicity), who is Canadian by citizenship and upbringing (culture), as a senior pastor (position), to encourage and offer hope to those who are experiencing personal and collective shame (purpose).

Biblically speaking, the Pentateuch is written by Moses, a Hebrew boy (ethnicity) who later grew up in the land of Egypt (culture), a shepherd turned spiritual leader (position), who led the people of God up to the point of entering the promised land, and who shared the history of creation and the journey of God's people through the time of Joshua (purpose). We'll see another example immediately below regarding the prophetical book Isaiah. Each time we sit down to preach a new book of the Bible, we want to explore in similar fashion who the author is. This provides a perspectival window into the heart of the person who wrote the book. Get to know the author through reading commentaries and other historical and cultural background books.

4. Jeffrey D. Arthurs, *How to Preach Narrative* (Fontes, 2022), 8.

The World of Time

When was this book written? While it's unnecessary to commit to memory the exact year, month, and date of when a Bible book was written, it is beneficial to know the general period. Are we talking about several thousand years BC or in the first century AD? What was going on in history at that time? Was it a time of famine, war, peace, unity, disunity, or conflict? Who was ruling in government at the time? What was that person like? How did he treat those under his control?

Scripture gives various details that preface the historical context of the book you're about to enter. For instance, the book of Isaiah begins, "The vision of Isaiah the son of Amoz, which he saw concerning Judah and Jerusalem in the days of Uzziah, Jotham, Ahaz, and Hezekiah, kings of Judah" (1:1 ESV). This simple verse gives us historical clues on authorship and time involved in this prophetical book.

The author is named clearly in verse 1. This is a vision of Isaiah the son of Amoz (author), who was a prophet (position) from Judah (commentaries tell us his ethnic background) who wrote about his vision regarding Judah and Jerusalem (purpose) in a time of spiritual rebellion. While the specific time frame is not given up front, the descriptive marker "in the days of Uzziah, Jothan, Ahaz, and Hezekiah, kings of Judah," hints through the specific names of kings that he wrote the book around the years 740–700 BC.

The World of Culture

Bible scholars note that "even though the Bible was written *for* us (and for all humanity), it was not written *to* us."[5] Stated differently, we are not the recipients of Scripture, but we are the beneficiaries of Scripture. That means the biblical authors did not write with our specific cultural context in view. Rather, the onus of cultural translation and application is placed on the preacher and listener to apply God's Word to our cultural contexts.[6] Knowing and appreciating the cultures of the ancient world requires work and, dare I say, takes motivation. As J. Kent Edwards notes, "Think of all you have to know in order to preach well. . . . You have to be an expert of ancient culture. Understanding biblical texts is wonderful, but you also have to know the people for whom they were written."[7]

5. E. Randolph Richards and Joseph R. Dodson, *A Little Book for New Bible Scholars: Why and How to Study the Bible* (IVP Academic, 2017), 24, citing John Walton, *The Lost World of Genesis One: Ancient Cosmology and the Origins Debate* (InterVarsity, 2009), 9.

6. For help in this area, consult Elizabeth Backfish and Cynthia Shafer-Elliott, *Grounded Theology in the Hebrew Bible: Exploring the Cultural Context That Formed Ancient Israel* (Baker Academic, 2025).

7. J. Kent Edwards, *Deep Preaching: Creating Sermons That Go Beyond the Superficial* (B&H, 2009), 3, 4.

Sometimes the people group/nation/culture of the biblical author and his readers will be identified immediately. In this case of Isaiah, he is writing to Judah and specifically to the residents of Jerusalem about the visions he received from the Lord about their past and future. In the case of the book of Ruth, the story is a bit complex regarding the people groups/nations/cultures involved in the narrative itself. The main characters are Ruth, a Moabite woman, and her mother-in-law, Naomi, a Jewish woman and native of Bethlehem in Judah (v. 1), who are living in a time of great famine and need to return to Judah for food (v. 7). Get familiar with the people group of the author, the readers, nations, and cultures that are addressed and identified in the book. More about culture soon when we delve into what I call the authorial-cultural model.

The World of Characters

Rather than speaking of large swaths of groups like entire nations, the Bible relates the interactions of specific persons or biblical characters. In the book of Acts, for instance, the author Luke introduces us to many different persons or characters. At times we are given information about their ethnic/cultural/language backgrounds and/or vocation. These are historical/cultural details the biblical author wants the reader to know. For instance, in Acts 2:9–11, those present at Pentecost included "Parthians and Medes and Elamites and residents of Mesopotamia, Judea and Cappadocia, Pontus and Asia, Phrygia and Pamphylia, Egypt and the parts of Libya belonging to Cyrene, and visitors from Rome, both Jews and proselytes, Cretans and Arabians" (ESV). Luke could have said succinctly, "And there were present many from various nations and cultures." Instead, he went to great lengths to provide specific details about their ethnic backgrounds.

While it's easier to gloss over in our sermons the ethnicities/nations represented here (with it being such a large list), sometimes the biblical author adds a specific detail that should be highlighted in our sermon as well. In the very next passage, Luke says, "But Peter, standing with the eleven, lifted up his voice and addressed them: 'Men of Judea and all who dwell in Jerusalem, let this be known to you, and give ear to my words'" (Acts 2:14 ESV). Why do we need to know that the listeners to Peter's sermon are "men of Judea and all who dwell in Jerusalem"? It constitutes the basis for the content of his sermon, which is that he's addressing the Jewish people who have just crucified Jesus on the cross (v. 36). The sermon is contextualized for these Jewish people.

Later, in Acts 4:36, Luke provides additional context regarding the person of Joseph (also called Barnabas), who, in contrast to Ananias and Sapphira in the very next pericope, was "a Levite, a native of Cyprus, sold a field that belonged to him and brought the money and laid it at the apostle's feet" (4:36–37 ESV). Now we know that Joseph was both a Levite and a resident of Cyprus. We can study to learn more about what these designations meant in Luke's day. Much of the time these particulars go unannounced by the biblical authors. Spend some time learning about the ethnic/cultural/national/language markers that the biblical author includes, obviously provided for a purpose.

The World of Archaeology

Archaeology is not necessarily on the top of the list when it comes to contextual investigation for sermons. Many of us are not archaeology enthusiasts. We might marvel at a modern full-size replica of Noah's Ark as re-created in Kentucky and even visit the site, but few of us have the time or resources to travel to the Middle East or Africa to explore landmarks named in our sermon passages. So, how might a modicum of archaeological exploration augment our sermons?

A useful tool here is *The Archaeological Study Bible* (available in ESV[8] and NIV[9]), which provides images of certain maps, locations, and artifacts from ancient periods mentioned in Scripture. There are also entire books dedicated to archaeological findings. You might look at *Behind the Scenes of the Old Testament: Cultural, Social, and Historical Contexts* or *Behind the Scenes of the New Testament: Cultural, Social, and Historical Contexts*, and others.[10] When appropriate, it could be helpful for the congregation to see an image or representation on the screen of Mount Sinai, a Jewish temple, or what a denarius (a Roman coin) looked like. A basic demonstration of archaeology could also provide support for visual learners and establish credibility for skeptics and doubters who distrust the validity of the Bible.[11]

The World of Surprise

The Bible is filled with historical and cultural surprises. As Jennifer Powell McNutt explains in her book *The Mary We Forgot*, "Sometimes something can be so out of place that it draws our attention. By this principle, every time

8. See *ESV Archaeological Study Bible*, ed. David Chapman (Crossway, 2018).

9. See *NIV Archaeological Study Bible*, ed. Walter C. Kaiser and Duane Garrett (Zondervan, 2005).

10. See Jonathan S. Greer, John W. Hilber, and John H. Walton, eds., *Behind the Scenes of the Old Testament: Cultural, Social, and Historical Contexts* (Baker Academic, 2018); and Bruce W. Longenecker, Elizabeth E. Shively, and T. J. Lang, eds., *Behind the Scenes of the New Testament: Cultural, Social, and Historical Contexts* (Baker Academic, 2024).

11. See David deSilva, *Archaeology and the World of Jesus: A Visual Guide* (Baker Academic, 2025).

Scripture names a woman or includes a woman as an exemplar, we should pay attention. Scripture surprises us by going against the grain of its context."[12] Pointing out the surprises in the Bible would be worth noting.

Jesus does something similar on more than two occasions. In Matthew 19:14, Jesus says, "Let the little children come to me, and do not hinder them, for the kingdom of heaven belongs to such as these." Notice how the disciples reacted to Jesus's invitation? In the verse prior, Matthew records, "But the disciples rebuked" those who attempted to bring children to Jesus. With children considered as being "less than" in this society, Jesus reverses cultural norms (surprise) by elevating them to the seat of adults. He does this again in the parable of the good Samaritan in Luke 10:25–37 (Matt. 22:34–40 and Mark 12:28–31), where the protagonist or hero of the story is not a fellow Jew or a religious leader, but a despised Samaritan (half-breed) who does the will of God by showing mercy, care, and hospitality toward a stranger (surprise). Jesus concludes here with the exhortation, "Go and do likewise" (Luke 10:37). Indeed, there are many other examples of surprise recorded in Scripture for our benefit and encouragement.

An Authorial-Cultural Model[13]

As we bring this chapter to a close, I would like to introduce (as I have done elsewhere) a model for grappling with the historical and cultural context of the Bible as it relates (and sometimes fails to relate) to modern times. Depending on our culture of origin or that into which we've been naturalized, the cultural norms and expectations we are accustomed to may vary from what is presented in Scripture. For this reason, I would strongly endorse what I call an "authorial-cultural" model of interpretation. We intentionally learn about the biblical author's culture so that we can compare and contrast it to our contemporary culture (thus an authorial-cultural model).

Why is understanding the biblical author's culture significant? Every time we open the Bible, we are introducing ourselves and our listeners to the world of the author. The Bible is never read out of context. It always has a context. The task for the preacher is to identify and understand this context as best we can.

For instance, the story of Jonah is not just about a cultureless prophet who dismissed and disobeyed the call of God to preach to the cultureless people

12. Jennifer Powell McNutt, *The Mary We Forgot: What the Apostle to the Apostles Teaches the Church Today* (Brazos, 2024), 23.

13. See, e.g., Matthew D. Kim, *Preaching with Cultural Intelligence: Understanding the People Who Hear Our Sermons* (Baker Academic, 2017), 36–44.

of Nineveh.[14] There are different cultures named, represented, and to be understood in this short prophetical book. To omit study of the various cultures mentioned in any biblical book shortchanges us and the listeners. Jonah is a Hebrew, a Jew, who is angry with God because God is calling him to preach a message of repentance (and forgiveness) to people in Nineveh, which was a major metropolis in Assyria. While we could stop there, the astute preacher would want to know, Why is it that Jonah is so upset with God about his mercy and compassion toward the Ninevites?

To understand the author's world and the cultures represented in it, we would benefit from doing some sermonic homework on who the Ninevites and Assyrians were. They were feared and even hated enemies of the Jews, who were violently tortured by them. When we read about the torture of the Jews at the hands of the Assyrians, we quickly come to realize that Jonah's anger is humanly justified. They were people, in the gospel according to Jonah, unworthy of God's mercy, compassion, and forgiveness.

Skipping the study of the biblical author's culture and worlds reduces the sermon to convey: "Jonah was a grumpy prophet who was selfish and didn't understand the heart of God for people." However, when we appreciate the various cultures in a biblical book, it provides opportunities for connection with our listeners today. We can ask: "How are we like the Jews, the sailors, the Ninevites, the Assyrians, and others mentioned in the book of Jonah?" "How are we different from them?" While Harry Emerson Fosdick once famously observed, "Only the preacher . . . proceeds still upon the idea that folk come to church desperately anxious to discover what happened to the Jebusites,"[15] I would contend that it is critical that preachers do not omit the authorial-cultural exploration in our sermon preparation. It takes a few additional moments to read up on these cultures, but they infuse into the sermon an unspeakable richness because the Bible is dealing with people from long ago.

CONCLUSION

For beginning students of preaching, it can be daunting to think about the biblical world and its complexity. In this chapter, my goal has been to attempt to streamline the process of contextualization regarding inclusion of historical

14. I refer to Jonah's example in my book *A Little Book for New Preachers: Why and How to Study Homiletics* (IVP Academic, 2020), 67–68.

15. Harry Emerson Fosdick, quoted in Robert Moats Miller, *Harry Emerson Fosdick: Preacher, Pastor, Prophet* (Oxford University Press, 1985), 342.

and cultural understanding. Becoming familiar with the world of the Bible is a critical step in the preaching task. To omit study of the historical and cultural worlds shortchanges the sermonic process and aim, which is to understand and apply God's Word to God's people. In our next chapter, we will engage in another important step, which is to learn and apply the biblical languages in the writing of our sermons.

QUESTIONS

1. What has been your process of studying the historical contexts found in Scripture?
2. What has been your process to study the cultural contexts found in Scripture?
3. What challenges or reservations do you have about learning the historical/cultural contexts in the Bible?
4. Which historical/cultural contexts do you want to learn about first (this might be for an upcoming sermon or series)?

PRACTICES

1. Summarize the ethnicity, culture, position, and purpose for the books of the Bible you will be preaching on this year.
2. Beyond the surface, go deeper and learn more about the book's author, history, nation, culture, time, people, archaeology, and surprises. For help in locating resources, see the "Further Reading" section.

8

STUDY

What Does It Look Like to Study Our Passage?

> Do your best to present yourself to God as one approved, a worker who does not need to be ashamed and who correctly handles the word of truth.
>
> —2 Timothy 2:15

A professor of biblical languages once shared this illustration with the class. When asked how much biblical exegesis (original Hebrew and Greek *and for the specially learned among us, Aramaic*) should be included in one's sermon, he replied, "Biblical exegesis is like wearing underwear. You want others to know you have it on, but you don't need to flaunt it." Who says seminary professors aren't funny? To be best prepared as biblical preachers, we will want to have taken courses in seminary in the biblical languages (Hebrew and Greek) and learn exegetical and interpretive methods to understand and communicate the Bible using these languages. In an ideal world, every pastor will have received a master's-level seminary education. However, we recognize that not all pastors, for various reasons, will be able to do so.

In most seminary curriculum, students will take at least four semesters of language courses—two in the original Hebrew to study the Old Testament and two in the original Greek to study the New Testament. Advanced students will even take Aramaic. From there, students will take at least one hermeneutics or biblical interpretation course and additional exegesis courses from various books of the Bible using Hebrew and Greek translations.

Getting a comprehensive theological education including biblical languages is not without its potential pitfalls, namely pride. As E. Randolph Richards and Joseph R. Dodson observe in *A Little Book for New Bible Scholars*, "Although all people are prone to pride, training in biblical scholarship can aggravate our hubris all the more."[1] So, why should preachers study the original languages and how can we utilize them in our preaching ministry? This chapter highlights the key components of study in our sermon preparation, particularly the study of the original languages and their benefits.

Step 5: Study Your Passage

Why Invest in Biblical Languages?

Step 5 in the sermonic process is to study our passage. First, it looks like translating the text from the original languages. Awareness and facility of the biblical languages is so important that I will begin this chapter by making a somewhat protracted case for the intentional study of them. We are living in a time of grave corner cutting. If something is inconvenient, we choose not to do it. If something requires sacrifice, we give ourselves a free pass. If something is not mandatory, we will justify moving ourselves to the front of the line.

There are, of course, excellent preachers who were not able to or did not get a seminary education. I completely understand if getting a seminary degree is financially impossible in this season of life. However, choosing the path of least resistance (that is, choosing not to take the biblical languages) seems to be an increasing phenomenon among seminarians. I often hear, "I don't have time for that" or "Nobody I know still uses their languages" (more on this later).

Being trained in the original languages is admittedly a significant investment of time and finances, and it is a sacrifice. Instead of doing a two-year seminary master's degree, you would be investing in a three-to-four-year master of divinity program to learn, experience, and develop skills in the biblical languages. If our reasoning against language acquisition is lethargy, a lack of interest, or even laziness, here are some clear tangible benefits of studying the biblical languages.

Know What You're Talking About

Pastors are sometimes compared to medical doctors. The comparison may seem far-fetched, but it's somewhat appropriate. In both principle and

1. E. Randolph Richards and Joseph R. Dodson, *A Little Book for New Bible Scholars: Why and How to Study the Bible* (IVP Academic, 2017), 71.

practice, pastors are doctors of the soul just as physicians are doctors of the body. The oft-used comparison is rightfully made when we ask, "Would you ever consult a medical doctor who didn't start, let alone finish, medical school?" Of course not! I might even add, "Wouldn't you want a doctor who finished at the top of her class and not the bottom or middle of the pack?" In the same way, "Would we ever want to sit under the preaching and teaching of a pastor who didn't finish, let alone start, seminary?" Of course not! Perhaps I'm assuming too much, but I would hope that one would have the same reaction for both professions.

What's at stake here? Confidence and competence! Study is essential to the preaching task. H. B. Charles says it this way: "I desire to be the kind of preacher that you must listen to. But that requires more than desire. It requires hard work. And the hard work never ends, if you take your preaching assignment seriously."[2] In other words, study elicits confidence by effecting competence. We need to be confident in our pastors' competent interpretations, just as we expect confidence and competence in our medical professionals' diagnoses and remedies and other fill-in-the-blank professions. We want to be confident that they are competent and know what they are talking about. In the case of church ministry, when a pastor/preacher says, "I don't need a seminary education," what they are communicating is, "I can be a pastor/preacher on my own. I don't need another person to teach me how to study and understand the Bible, theology, and integrative practice and praxis."

Put more strongly, not seeking a proper education in the Bible can be a marker of hubris. Why wouldn't any person seeking to be a faithful pastor/preacher want to engage in robust, comprehensive study of the Scriptures, theology, church history, counseling, preaching, apologetics, spiritual formation, and more? I wouldn't want to visit a doctor's office where the physician didn't take basic and advanced courses on human anatomy. Likewise, I want to sit under the preaching and teaching ministries of those who have taken sufficient courses in biblical languages, interpretation, and proclamation, which a rigorous seminary education provides.

Gain Precision in Comprehension

English translations may be adequate, but they vary in precision and ability to match the precise meaning of the Hebrew and Greek biblical writers. As the saying goes, "Something is always lost in translation." Taking the extra

2. H. B. Charles, *On Preaching: Personal and Pastoral Insights for the Preparation and Practice of Preaching* (Moody, 2014), 10.

steps to learn Hebrew and Greek not only develops our minds but increases our appreciation for God's Word. I knew a pastor who carried around his Greek New Testament instead of an English Bible. Though some might call this hubris or showing off, there was something inspiring to see him read and translate on the spot from the Greek. No translation can explain the meaning of a text as effectively as understanding the original language. I'm sure you can attest to the same for those who read and speak another modern language such as Spanish or French.

Go Beyond the Surface

Going deeper into the biblical languages is often described as stepping into and excavating from a golden minefield of knowledge and wisdom that we simply cannot attain by reading an English (or preferred language) translation alone. Studying a biblical language's vocabulary, grammar, syntax, and sentence structure provides a depth and fertility to our interpretive process that cannot be replicated in translations into our preferred language.[3] Similarly, Enoch Okode shares, "It is hard to maintain the centrality of the Word if we view biblical languages as a nonessential and optional extra. Similarly, if preachers don't invest in Hebrew and Greek, their hearers will be deprived of some of the treasures of the Word as well as the informed and informative exposition that they deserve."[4] There is nothing that can replace studying the Bible in the original languages and original contexts.

Develop Dependence and Discipline

A third major benefit of studying the languages is that it causes us to depend on the Lord, to slow down, and even to persevere in discipline. Any time we endeavor to learn a new language, it will be a grind. Language acquisition takes much time, repetition, patience, and frustration. Learning vocabulary words alone requires sacrifice and hard work. Yet, something transpires in us that's challenging to put into words. We become tethered to God and to his Word in new ways. Language study gives us a deeper appreciation for who God is and how valuable his Word is for us and for God's people.

3. See Catherine L. McDowell and Philip H. Towner, *The Rewards of Learning Greek and Hebrew: Discovering the Richness of the Bible in Its Original Languages* (Hendrickson, 2021).

4. Enoch Okode, "A Case for Biblical Languages: Are Hebrew and Greek Optional or Indispensable?," *African Journal of Theology* 29, no. 2 (2010): 92, quoted in Benjamin L. Merkle and Robert L. Plummer, *Greek for Life: Strategies for Learning, Retaining, and Reviving New Testament Greek* (Baker Academic, 2017), 8.

Bible scholars are not shy about gushing over the value of learning the biblical languages. Old Testament professor Carmen Joy Imes writes, "In an age of instant-everything, is it really worth investing hundreds of hours to learn an ancient language? . . . What a difference it makes when we can read the Bible in its original languages for ourselves."[5] Likewise, New Testament professor Nijay K. Gupta says, "Learning Greek and Hebrew in seminary changed my life. It continues to be the most formative experience I had in seminary, and my students have come to expect a 'learn Greek and Hebrew' pitch from me in every class."[6]

What Is Hermeneutics?

"Hermeneutics" is a fancy term for biblical interpretation: the proper understanding and interpreting of Scripture. Let's start with a few definitions. Anthony Thiselton defines "hermeneutics" as "how we read, understand, and handle texts, especially those written in another time or in a context of life different from our own. Biblical hermeneutics investigates more specifically how we read, understand, apply, and respond to biblical texts."[7] Abner Chou explains simply, "Hermeneutics deals with the essential principles by which we accurately understand the Scriptures."[8] Nicholas Piotrowski describes hermeneutics as "the theoretical study of the science and art of how to legitimately and ethically interpret texts."[9] Amy Peeler defines hermeneutics as "the tools we use to discover the deep truths of God's word."[10] Peeler expounds on this definition with two foundational truths when it comes to interpreting the text correctly:

> There are *wrong answers*. There are some things a particular passage cannot mean, but there are many right answers. Beginning there, I think, encourages students to attempt to interpret Scripture without the chilling fear of getting it wrong. Secondarily, then, hermeneutics teaches us that we can never interpret on

5. Carmen Joy Imes, book endorsement of McDowell and Towner, *Rewards of Learning Greek and Hebrew*.

6. Nijay K. Gupta, book endorsement of McDowell and Towner, *Rewards of Learning Greek and Hebrew*.

7. Anthony C. Thiselton, *Hermeneutics: An Introduction* (Eerdmans, 2009), 1.

8. Abner Chou, *The Hermeneutics of Biblical Writers: Learning to Interpret Scripture from the Prophets and Apostles* (Kregel Academic, 2018), 13.

9. Nicholas G. Piotrowski, *In All the Scriptures: The Three Contexts of Biblical Hermeneutics* (IVP Academic, 2021), 4.

10. Email correspondence with Amy L. Peeler on March 4, 2025.

> our own, but must have a community with whom we can test our assumptions about meaning and receive from others confirmation or critique.[11]

We'll start with Peeler's first point and come back to the second in a moment.

Right and Wrong Interpretations

First, most would agree that there are right and wrong interpretations of the Bible. Peeler is correct in giving her students an interpretive leash and yet with clear boundaries. Scripture cannot mean whatever we want it to mean. This is how some students of the Bible go awry. For instance, we cannot tell modern readers of Scripture that the Ten Commandments found in Exodus 20 and Deuteronomy 5 are optional moral principles that no longer apply to us because they are from a different time and place and for a different group of people. The Ten Commandments, though given to the Israelites of old, are still commandments that we, as New Testament believers, need to follow and obey. There isn't wiggle room to say, I'll just follow the odd numbered commandments only. That would be a wrong interpretation. The entirety of the commandments remains applicable to us today as moral, ethical laws for right living.

At the same time, I have struggled throughout my preaching ministry with the second point. Is there only one right, correct interpretation of any biblical text? The short answer is yes. However, I am not God, so I don't have the absolute, final word, nor does anyone else. Yet, as Peeler notes, presuming that the onus is on us to determine "the one and only" interpretive meaning of certain texts can be discouraging if not paralyzing, especially for beginning students of the Bible.

I often tell my preaching students that we could have an arm-wrestling match on who has the correct interpretation of Scripture, but it's only when we get to heaven and ask the Lord that we will realize whether our interpretation was proper or not. Our task is simply to do the best interpretive effort that we can with the language tools in our tool bag. Throughout this process of interpreting Scripture, we are mindful to pray and ask the Holy Spirit to help us in our attempt toward a correct, faithful interpretation. As Henning Wrogemann reminds us,

> There is both an external and internal clarity in Holy Scripture. The interpretation of Scripture—according to Luther—constantly demonstrates the existence of these two kinds of clarity. The *claritas externa*, on the one hand, is the external clarity relating to the wording and the grammar. The *claritas interna*, on the other hand,

11. Email correspondence with Amy L. Peeler on March 4, 2025.

> is the ever-present internal clarity relating to the gospel that may be understood with the help of the Holy Spirit, the true hermeneut (interpreter) of Scripture.[12]

How does this clarity come about? In his preaching courses, Jeffrey Arthurs introduced me, a visual learner, to a helpful interpretive image that uses a baseball diamond (see fig. 8.1). He explains that biblical interpretation can be viewed as the lines on the side of a baseball field, which determine what's a fair ball (fair interpretation) and what's a foul ball (misreading or misinterpretation). I've adapted his image below to fit our purposes. In the same way, there is a fair and proper interpretation of Scripture, and there are foul ones that are improper and incorrect.

What we are seeking to do in our biblical interpretation is to make contact and hit the ball in fair territory. For instance, let's say I were to ask most pastors/preachers, "Can this text mean this?" When the ball is hit in fair territory (proper interpretation), most everyone should agree with me on my interpretation. If it's a foul interpretation, most everyone would say, "I don't think that's a fair or correct interpretation of the passage."

Here's the rub: Our interpretation of the text may not be the same as our application of it. This is where trouble begins to brew, when we try to apply a text before we do our due diligence in interpreting it. The general interpretation of a text should be similar to that of others (who also hold to the authority of Scripture). While our interpretations should be similar or at least agreeable, we might apply the same text in different ways depending on who's listening to our sermon. However, the interpretation can be established with a big picture question: What's the broad subject of this text? Is it about faith? Is it about stewardship? Is it about God's character? Is it about God's work accomplished? Is it about obedience?

Once we get in the ballpark, we will want to narrow down the broad subject by asking, "What's the author's point about this subject?"[13] One way to avoid a misreading is by listing some of the wrong interpretations or foul balls that our listeners might presume as they read and interpret the passage alongside us. So, here are two basic questions we can ask ourselves: What is the author's point about this subject? What point is the author not making about this subject? Make solid contact and get in the ballpark! In the second question, we are anticipating some of the responses that our listeners might have about the Scripture text.

12. Henning Wrogemann, *Intercultural Hermeneutics*, vol. 1 (IVP Academic, 2016), 47.

13. Haddon W. Robinson calls this process getting to the big idea with the following homiletical equation: Subject (What is the author talking about?) + Complement (What is the author saying about what they're talking about?) = Idea. While this is an effective approach in determining the author's main idea, this book will emphasize some other factors in identifying the main, transformational point of the text.

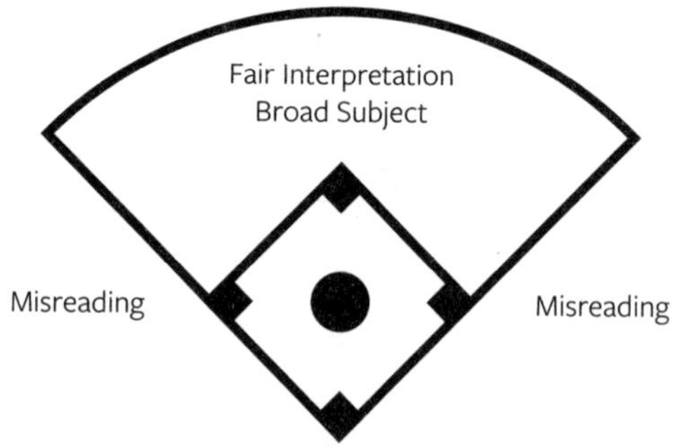

Figure 8.1. Fair and foul interpretations

Let's create an exaggerated and rather obvious case study from Jesus's first miracle, performed at the wedding at Cana in John 2. In this first of many earthly miracles, it may be surprising to readers that Jesus's first miracle would be turning water into wine. You remember the story? Here is the text as a reminder:

> On the third day a wedding took place at Cana in Galilee. Jesus' mother was there, and Jesus and his disciples had also been invited to the wedding. When the wine was gone, Jesus' mother said to him, "They have no more wine."
>
> "Woman, why do you involve me?" Jesus replied. "My hour has not yet come."
>
> His mother said to the servants, "Do whatever he tells you."
>
> Nearby stood six stone water jars, the kind used by the Jews for ceremonial washing, each holding from twenty to thirty gallons.
>
> Jesus said to the servants, "Fill the jars with water"; so they filled them to the brim.
>
> Then he told them, "Now draw some out and take it to the master of the banquet."
>
> They did so, and the master of the banquet tasted the water that had been turned into wine. He did not realize where it had come from, though the servants who had drawn the water knew. Then he called the bridegroom aside and said, "Everyone brings out the choice wine first and then the cheaper wine after the guests have had too much to drink; but you have saved the best till now."
>
> What Jesus did here in Cana of Galilee was the first of the signs through which he revealed his glory; and his disciples believed in him.
>
> After this he went down to Capernaum with his mother and brothers and his disciples. There they stayed for a few days. (John 2:1–12)

At first glance, the point of John's story seems to be that Jesus not only permits drinking, since he transformed an abundance of water into wine, but that he values choice wine of the best variety. With this interpretation, we then communicate the following message to the congregation, "Drinking is permissible, because Jesus obviously condones it. He made water turn into wine." I would hope that all listeners would push back against such a message based on this text. I would similarly hope that all would argue that it is a misreading and misapplication of the point John is making about Jesus's ministry.

Then, what is the purpose behind this story? In chapter 6, we discussed the importance of history and biblical context. How was alcohol viewed in the first century? What was the function of alcohol at an ancient Jewish wedding? Why does the master of the banquet say in verse 10, "Everyone brings out the choice wine first and then the cheaper wine after the guests have had too much to drink; but you have saved the best till now"?

Another misinterpretation (foul ball) of the text would be focusing the sermon on how Jesus speaks to his mother. Without any cultural context, we might gravitate toward Jesus's use of "woman" in verse 4 and think it was a derogatory manner of speaking to his mother. It's essential that we study the text in its proper historical and cultural context. Grab a commentary or background book to gain insight into the customs and cultures of which we are probably unaware.

Then, what is the purpose of this story? What is the point John is making about Jesus? This narrative about the first miracle of Jesus has little to do with wine but with what is stated in verse 11. By transforming water into wine, Jesus showcased his deity. It says, "What Jesus did here in Cana of Galilee was the first of the signs through which he revealed his glory; and his disciples believed in him." This became the moment where Jesus's deity and lordship were manifested and confirmed in the minds of the disciples who placed their faith and belief in him. That is John's point, not Jesus's attitude toward wine or women!

Take God at His Word

Since the Bible is trustworthy, we can take God at his word. Sometimes, due to our finite understanding, we tend to "outthink" God. We might imagine a conversation with God, saying, "God, you couldn't possibly mean what you said here!" There are many verses and passages in Scripture that can and should be taken quite literally, such as in the example of the Ten Commandments above. When God says, "You shall have no other gods before me" (Exod. 20:20), he literally means, "You should have no other gods before me." Case closed.

As someone once quipped, "It's not that the Bible is difficult to understand; it's that the Bible is difficult to obey." No doubt, there are some Scripture passages that are difficult and challenging to comprehend. The apostle Peter in 2 Peter 3:16

says as much: "He [Paul] writes the same way in all his letters, speaking in them of these matters. His letters contain some things that are hard to understand, which ignorant and unstable people distort, as they do the other Scriptures, to their own destruction." Oftentimes the issue is not that we have improperly understood or interpreted a given passage. Rather, the problem is that either we have distorted its meaning (as in the reference above) or we have misapplied the text to the congregation in ways that fail to match the application of the text. In some cases, God forbid, we have outright mishandled the text altogether.

Interpret in Community

In Western cultures like the United States, we often think of reading the Bible as an individual exercise. Reclining on my La-Z-Boy or hunched over my desk under a lamp, I read the Bible in isolation, left to my own thoughts. While reading the Scriptures in solitude can and should happen at times for our own personal devotion, worship, and relationship with the Lord, the importance of interpreting the Bible in community cannot be overstated. Since the Bible was written for entire communities of faith and congregations, we might similarly benefit from the idea and practice of reading the Bible in community or collectively rather than only individually.

In their book *Misreading Scripture with Individualist Eyes*, for example, E. Randolph Richards and Richard James explain, "Shame was a powerful tool in the biblical world. Sometimes it was used well and restored. Other times it was abused and hurt. We can overlook the positive uses of shame, or misunderstand them completely, when we read the Bible as members of individualist cultures. . . . The biblical cultures were just *very* different from ours."[14]

I was taught in seminary how to read and interpret the Scriptures from the original languages by white professors. Not once did they mention that the interpretation of Scripture occurs within their normative white European context of hermeneutics. It was assumed, in their teaching, that proper interpretation occurred within a white European framework, or what Michael J. Gorman calls "majority-culture biblical interpretation," and somehow every non-white person needed to assimilate to the same interpretive framework for it to be correct.[15] This is why, for members of the majority culture, theology does not include a descriptor like "white theology." It is simply referred to

14. E. Randolph Richards and Richard James, *Misreading Scripture with Individualist Eyes: Patronage, Honor, and Shame in the Biblical World* (IVP Academic, 2020), 1.

15. Michael J. Gorman, "Majority-Culture Biblical Interpretation: Reading While White," in *The New Testament in Color: A Multiethnic Bible Commentary*, ed. Esau McCaulley, Janette H. Ok, Osvaldo Padilla, and Amy Peeler (IVP Academic, 2024), 35.

as theology, while others must be labeled with a nonnormative, descriptive prefix like "Asian American theology" or "Black theology."

Thus, one elephant-in-the-room conversation we must have, when it comes to biblical interpretation, is that interpretation is never done apart from one's own cultural context. That includes white-majority interpreters. This statement is not erroneous or a matter of opinion spoken by an ethnic minority person in the United States or the West. It's a fact. Everyone reads and interprets through their own cultural lens (which includes gender, race, ethnicity, education, political views, denomination, etc.).

I was told in seminary that any racial or ethnic minority reading and interpretation of Scripture should be automatically viewed with suspicion as being heretical and unorthodox. Only a white Continental-European (often Reformed/Calvinist) model of hermeneutics was a legitimate reading of Scripture. All others were labeled liberal and therefore heretical. These nonmajority interpretations could not be trusted. If that's the case, then only white people sitting on their own or sitting around a table could properly interpret the Bible.

Our common task as interpreters is to attempt to get into the mind of the biblical author and his cultural context for the purpose of contextualized interpretation. However, we cannot escape the fact that our reading and interpreting of Scripture occurs as an embodied person who has been shaped by a particular cultural context or contexts that are often dissimilar from the biblical world (as discussed earlier).

What might be a solution? Interpreting in community! There's beauty in interpreting the Scriptures with others in community who do not look or think like we do. By this, I'm not advocating for a free-for-all session where the Bible can mean different things for different cultural groups. We can collectively determine the meaning of a given sermon passage with each unique lens offering an additional perspective on the text.

For instance, from an Asian American perspective, Janette H. Ok says, "Asian American biblical interpretation explicitly and intentionally approaches biblical texts not only by means of exegesis but also through diverse and overlapping Asian American experiences and histories."[16] Similarly, Esau D. McCaulley writes of African American biblical interpretation, "To refer to African *American* biblical interpretation, then, refers to the ways in which living in America as a Black woman or man influences the kinds of questions, hopes, and traumas we bring to the Bible."[17] McCaulley continues,

16. Janette H. Ok, "Asian American Biblical Interpretation," in McCaulley et al., *New Testament in Color*, 11.

17. Esau D. McCaulley, "African American Biblical Interpretation," in McCaulley et al., *New Testament in Color*, 1.

"It matters that we have diverse representation in the process of biblical interpretation because it is always ourselves as persons with our experiences, biases, gifts, and liabilities that we bring to the text. We are not disembodied spirits with no histories or cultures. We are not exegetical machines; we are interpreting persons."[18] To interpret the Bible through a particular racial/ethnic lens means to take into consideration the lived experiences and cultural differences that are unique to each cultural context.

Let's take a moment to determine what must stay and what must go when it comes to biblical exegesis and biblical languages. Though it's a painstaking process to leave out exegetical nuggets that we have gathered from our study, preachers will benefit from taking their cues from filmmakers and asking the oft-painful question, "So, what needs to stay on the cutting room floor?"

From Study to Pulpit: Use It or Lose It

An increasingly normative obstacle for many seminarians and pastors is language retention and rehearsal. Language can be lost if not used, even in a short span like a summer break. If I took a straw poll of pastors in America, I would be rather confident to say that many pastors have lost their facility with the biblical languages, especially with Hebrew. Here's what I suggest in terms of using the biblical languages for sermons. You may have your own process for doing things, to each her own, but what I present here may be a reasonable pathway to stay engaged with Hebrew and Greek by minimizing language atrophy or even complete forfeiture, chiefly for use in sermon preparation.

There are resources available for those who have lost the biblical languages completely due to lack of usage. We can regain language function and reintroduce ourselves to the biblical languages and use them. For those with some retention and facility, we can also use the languages in our sermon preparation. Before we get there, a quick word about double-digit-step exegetical processes.

If you've attended seminary, you probably learned some variation of a multistep exegetical method. Aída Besançon Spencer, in her book *The Exegetical Process*, provides a comprehensive pathway, for example, for interpreting the New Testament; she invites her students to a multistep process for writing exegetical papers.[19] Here are some of the major and minor headings offered in her book from the table of contents:

18. McCaulley, introduction to *New Testament in Color*, xii.

19. Aída Besançon Spencer, *The Exegetical Process: How to Write a New Testament Exegesis Paper Step-by-Step* (Kregel Academic, 2025).

Study the literary and historical context of the book
Discern the wider context
Read the book
Study the historical context of the book
Thematic summary of the book
Outline the book or letter

Preparation for the study of the text
Choose the text and its immediate context
Discover the true text
Procedure for choosing the true text

In-depth study of the text
Seek a translation and understand the grammar of the text
Basic grammatical categories
Greek parts of speech
Steps in doing a sentence flow
Comparing different translations with the Greek

Understand the meaning of the words and phrases
Word study references
Example of how to do a word study

Understand the meaning of the text by a stylistic analysis
Identify unusual word order
Identify other figures of speech

Study further contextual resources: Jewish and Greco-Roman background
Elements of background
Three types of literary parallels
References for the study of ancient literatures

Application and completion of study
Make the application to life
Types of direct application

A similar method can be employed for Old Testament texts.[20]

In many ways, preachers work through many of these stages in their interpretive processes. As preachers who also pastor people and shepherd the

20. See also Jason S. DeRouchie, *How to Understand and Apply the Old Testament: Twelve Steps from Exegesis to Theology* (P&R, 2017); and Andrew David Naselli, *How to Understand and Apply the New Testament: Twelve Steps from Exegesis to Theology* (P&R, 2017).

flock, however, going through all ten steps in detail and writing an entire exegesis paper on our sermon text prior to writing our sermon manuscript is an unfeasible task week by week.

What, then, are some of the core steps of the exegetical process that may be both tenable and beneficial in sermon preparation for the purpose of proclamation? While most of us would begin by reading our English translation (more on that later), I would encourage us to start the exegetical process with translating the original Hebrew or Greek.

Translate the Text

First, there is no more significant step than attempting to translate the sermon text on our own. You may not be able to whiz through translating a given text in either Hebrew or Greek, but engaging in weekly, steady translation work of your given sermon passage is a profitable way to retain and expand your facility with the languages. Even though we may skip over some or even many words, we can write down the Hebrew or Greek words we do remember. At the end of this translation process, you can always consult software such as Logos Bible or Accordance to help you parse the nouns, verbs, and other parts of speech. There are free language websites such as BibleGateway.com and others that are valuable translation tools as well.

I confess that I am not an original-language guru. Though it's true that I once aspired to be a New Testament scholar, I don't remember every verb paradigm perfectly. However, during my time as a senior pastor, I tried to keep up the languages by translating the text on which I was preaching each week. Even if you cannot translate the entire passage (particularly lengthy ones), the rhythm of translation work keeps it fresher in the mind. Refer to books like Lee M. Fields's *Hebrew for the Rest of Us* or William D. Mounce's *Greek for the Rest of Us* as texts with concrete pointers on how to maintain your languages.[21] As Douglas Stuart encourages, "Indeed, the pastor who faithfully works from the biblical languages in sermon preparation, no matter how rusty one's knowledge of them may be at the start, cannot help gaining more and more language mastery as time goes by. I hope this primer will encourage many to try."[22] You can start by getting an interlinear Bible workbook such as Jay P. Green's *The Interlinear Bible* or William D. Mounce's *Interlinear for*

21. Lee M. Fields, *Hebrew for the Rest of Us: Mastering the Hebrew Tools to Study the Old Testament*, 2nd ed. (Zondervan Academic, 2023); and William D. Mounce, *Greek for the Rest of Us: Learn Greek to Study the New Testament with Interlinears and Bible Software*, 3rd ed. (Zondervan Academic, 2022).

22. Douglas Stuart, *Old Testament Exegesis*, 5th ed. (Westminster John Knox, 2022).

the Rest of Us and start translating today.[23] There is no shortage of biblical scholars who promote the value of the original languages and who want you to keep using your biblical languages and not forsake them.

Relearn Vocabulary and Paradigms

There is absolutely no shame in admitting that we have forgotten some, much, or all our biblical language knowledge. If you've lost them over time or due to lack of use, you can regain function. Go back to your Greek and Hebrew textbooks and "enjoy" the process of relearning your vocabulary and even verb paradigms and grammar. You would be surprised at how God has given you the ability to recall what was once imprinted on your brain. Like any discipline, the cobwebs will fall off over time.

Robert L. Plummer, in *Greek for Life*, encourages: "How long has your Greek (or Hebrew) been inactive? Ten days? Ten years? . . . I assure you that there is more Greek (and Hebrew) in the deep recesses of your brain than you realize. You can get it back. You absolutely can. Not only can you get it back, but you can also progress in the language and become a skilled reader and exegete of the Greek New Testament (and Hebrew Old Testament)."[24] Keep trying. Don't give up. For many preachers, their Hebrew is rustier than their Greek. Regardless of your situation, you may want to pick up *Greek for Life* and *Hebrew for Life*[25] for tools on how to retrieve your languages.

Do Strategic Word Studies and Look Up Cross-References

As we read and meditate on the sermon passage, pray for the Spirit's guidance to discern what might be the key words or phrases and cross-references as we seek to explain them for our listeners. Some considerations might be the repetition of words, phrases, or themes in a text or in a book. Where else in the Bible does this word or phrase appear? Track them down.

The fact that the human author repeated a word is significant. For example, in 2 Corinthians 1:3–7, the apostle Paul uses the word *paraklēsis* or "comfort" nine times in such a short span of verses. As one reads through the epistles, Paul doesn't always have a reputation for being warm, empathetic, or even mushy. Yet, Paul exhibits profound pastoral care here in this text. What does

23. Jay P. Green, trans., *The Interlinear Bible: Hebrew-Greek-English* (Hendrickson Academic, 2005); and William D. Mounce, *Interlinear for the Rest of Us: The Reverse Interlinear for New Testament Word Studies* (Zondervan, 2012).

24. Merkle and Plummer, *Greek for Life*, 123.

25. Adam J. Howell, Benjamin L. Merkle, and Robert L. Plummer, *Hebrew for Life: Strategies for Learning, Retaining, and Reviving Biblical Hebrew* (Baker Academic, 2020).

Paul mean when he uses the word "comfort" both as a noun and as a verb? How might the original meaning of the word clarify and illuminate the text because we have expounded its original context? Where else does the word *paraklēsis* show up in Paul's letters and in other portions of the canon? When is it used and in what context? While a sermon doesn't require a word study to be shared from the pulpit, sometimes doing a deep dive on certain words might unpack the text in fresh ways for us and our hearers.

Improve Your Facility with Grammar

Remember the days of elementary school and learning English grammar? I'm seeing a flood of drowsy eyelids. To understand a language is to understand its grammar and not just a pocketful of choice vocabulary words. Appreciating and understanding grammar in the original languages is paramount to interpreting a text. It's not enough to go to a foreign country and know a few simple vocabulary words. To become familiar with a language is to understand its grammar.

How does grammar help preachers? Bible scholars at Nelson University observe, "Certain passages of Scripture have multiple possibilities for meaning. Some translations footnote (usually one of) the grammatical options, but many do not. When, say, the King James Version differs from the New International Version, how will you determine which of them gives the best sense? 'Gut feeling?' 'Holy Spirit Woosh?' Urim and Thummim? For this, readers need a knowledge of the Biblical languages and access to grammars, lexica, and scholarly commentaries that deal directly with the original text, little of which will make any sense to those unschooled in Biblical languages."[26]

I once took an art history class during college, thinking it would be an easy A. The first assignment was to write a paper in class about one of the Baroque period pieces that was shown on the screen in front of us. We were asked to describe the piece and make observations about what stood out to us. I straightforwardly wrote the paper the best I could. When the professor returned the paper, she had written to my surprise and shock: "C- You didn't properly discuss what was asked for this assignment." Turns out, after meeting with the professor, I didn't know the *grammar* of art history. I didn't know the verbiage, language, terminology, and so on for how to write a proper art history critique. While I improved over the semester, this course would become the lowest blemish on my college transcript.

26. See "7 Reasons to Study Biblical Hebrew and Biblical Greek," Nelson University, September 24, 2015, https://www.nelson.edu/thoughthub/bible-and-theology/study-biblical-hebrew-and-greek.

More consequential than a low grade in an art history course in college, the gravity of not knowing the grammar of the Scriptures may be quite detrimental to our listeners. We want to do our best to understand the grammar of the original languages so that we can effectively interpret it for our hearers. Investing in learning the grammar of Hebrew and Greek provides the interpreter/preacher with concrete tools to explore the Scriptures in deeper ways with proper methods to determine the original meaning of the biblical authors. As a quick example, William D. Mounce divides his *Basics of Biblical Greek Grammar* into several parts or systems, including: Noun System, Indicative Verb System, Participles, and Nonindicative Moods and Mi Verbs.[27] It is possible to learn these systems of grammar and become competent in applying them to our preaching process. As we move toward the conclusion of this chapter, what might we do if we haven't been able to study the original biblical languages?

Preaching with Your English Translation or in Your First-Language Translation

As you can imagine, translations of the Bible are not as effective at rendering the meaning of the text as the original languages can be. However, that does not mean that they lack value. There are numerous English translations of the Bible, or perhaps your first language is other than English and so you'll be preaching based on that language. There are upward of nine hundred different English translations of the Bible since William Tyndale's English translation published in 1526.[28] What's your favorite translation? Some of the more common translations used across denominations are New International Version and English Standard Version. Your church might also use the New Living Translation or the New American Standard Bible (perhaps one of the most literal translations). There are even multiple translations of the Bible in Spanish. In this chapter, we will do a quick exploration into how we can preach effectively even though we haven't studied the original languages.

Read Several Different Translations

There is no substitute for reading several translations of the Bible in your first language, English or otherwise. Here is an example of what interpreters of

27. William D. Mounce, *Basics of Biblical Greek Grammar*, 4th ed. (Zondervan, 2019).

28. According to Cheree Hayes and Bible Project Team, "Does a 'Most-Accurate' Bible Translation Exist? Understanding Different Translations and Learning to Read Multiple Versions," Bible Project, www.bibleproject.com, January 13, 2023, https://bibleproject.com/articles/does-a-most-accurate-bible-translation-exist.

English translations can do in their sermon preparation. From the influential and well-known resource called the Bible Project, one of their authors, Cheree Hayes, writes, "Seeing and respecting variations helps us humbly continue the work it takes to understand the words of others. We can see how multiple English renderings of the same idea give a deeper understanding of *rakhum*, not to mention all the other words." Let's say you're preaching on Psalm 79 and you get to verse 8. Take a moment to read some different variations of verse 8. Hayes offers these translations.

Different Translations of Psalm 79:8

For one Hebrew example, notice how a selection of translations render the Hebrew word *rakhum* ("mercy" or "compassion") in Psalm 79:8.

King James Version
O remember not against us former iniquities: let thy *tender mercies* [Heb. *rakhum*] speedily prevent us: for we are brought very low.

New American Standard Bible
Do not hold us responsible for the guilty deeds of our forefathers; let your *compassion* [Heb. *rakhum*] come quickly to meet us, for we have become very low.

New International Version
Do not hold against us the sins of past generations; may your *mercy* [Heb. *rakhum*] come quickly to meet us, for we are in desperate need.

Contemporary English Version
Don't make us pay for the sins of our ancestors. Have *pity* [Heb. *rakhum*] and come quickly! We are completely helpless.

The Message
Don't blame us for the sins of our parents. Hurry up and *help* [Heb. *rakhum*] us; we're at the end of our rope.

The Living Bible
Oh, do not hold us guilty for our former sins! Let your *tenderhearted mercies* [Heb. *rakhum*] meet our needs, for we are brought low to the dust.[29]

How does reading various translations aid the interpretive process? Just as in English, a simple word like "chair" can have more than one meaning, such

29. Hayes and Bible Project Team, "Does a 'Most-Accurate' Bible Translation Exist?"

as an object for sitting on or an endowed faculty position at a university. We will benefit from gaining a range of meanings for a Hebrew word such as *rakhum*. Meanings vary from "mercy" to "compassion" and even "help" or "pity." You have descriptive terms like "tenderhearted" as in The Living Bible. To provide a range of meaning in your sermon, you might offer a few of these as examples of how this word has been understood. One meaning of this Hebrew word might resonate more with your listeners than another. While we won't do this for every word, selectively determine, as with a word study, which English words you'd like to "add color" to for your listeners as you walk through the sermon passage. Another straightforward interpretive process would be what we might call "the vowels of hermeneutics."

The Vowels of Hermeneutics[30]

Mark Allan Powell once did a study with US seminary students on the prodigal son story in Luke 15.[31] The first group of twelve students, when asked to recount the story in their own words, failed to mention Jesus's detail of the famine in verse 14: "After he had spent everything, there was a severe famine in that whole country, and he began to be in need." This led Powell to do some further research. He then conducted a study with one hundred American students and found that only six mentioned the famine. His third study was done with fifty Russian students in St. Petersburg. In that Eastern European context, forty-two out of fifty people mentioned the famine.[32]

Powell later brought the same prodigal son story survey to Tanzania in East Africa. With approximately fifty Tanzanian seminarians, Powell asked, "Why does the young man end up starving in the pigpen?" He expected to see replies concerning the famine or squandering money. But to his surprise, about 80 percent responded, "Because no one gave him anything to eat." This small detail is found in Luke 15:16: "He longed to fill his stomach with the pods that the pigs were eating, but no one gave him anything." Powell concludes that the social location of the reader does seem to matter significantly in how one reads, remembers, and interprets a text.[33]

30. Portions of this section have been excerpted and modified slightly with permission from Matthew D. Kim and Daniel L. Wong, *Finding Our Voice: A Vision for Asian North American Preaching* (Lexham, 2020), 64–65.

31. Thanks to Jeffrey D. Arthurs at Gordon-Conwell Theological Seminary for originally sharing this reference with me.

32. See Mark Allan Powell, *What Do They Hear? Bridging the Gap Between Pulpit and Pew* (Abingdon, 2007), 14–18.

33. Powell, *What Do They Hear?*, 26–27.

Like Powell's students, readers of Scripture and preachers of the Word read the text with our own ethnic/cultural perspectives, in my case as a second-generation Korean American preacher, born and raised in the United States. The interpretations that arise from this perspective will land somewhere on a spectrum from Asian to North American values, beliefs, and assumptions. To help preachers consider the challenges of interpreting Scripture for our listeners, I suggest using a hermeneutical approach with five steps that begin with the vowels of the English language.

Vowels hold words together in English and in many other languages, and we might also say that vowels can hold together the process of hermeneutics.[34] In their *Introduction to Biblical Interpretation Workbook*, Klein, Blomberg, and Hubbard Jr. state, "Accurate Bible study must proceed on the basis that we have read the text carefully. We can't move on to interpretation and application until we master the first step of observation. We must see what is actually in the text and not read into it or assume ideas that are not really there."[35]

They articulate a three-part process of hermeneutics using the vowels O (observation), I (interpretation), and A (application). To this method, I would like to add experience and understanding to round out the O-E-U-I-A process of hermeneutics: observation, experience, understanding, interpretation, and application.[36]

Everyone interprets Scripture from their own preunderstanding or perspective and experience. This perspective and experience can be formed by one's gender, ethnicity, culture, generation, vocation, socioeconomic class, political views, or other attributes. While we commit ourselves to interpreting the text through the biblical author's lens as best we can, to interpret Scripture faithfully and systematically we may try walking through the vowels of hermeneutics.

Prior to writing an outline or manuscript, write down some notes (do some initial brainstorming) about your observations, experience, understanding,

34. I present a pathway for cross-cultural hermeneutics using the acronym HABIT (Historical, grammatical, and literary context; Author's cultural context; Big idea of the text; Interpret in your context; and Theological presuppositions) in *Preaching with Cultural Intelligence: Understanding the People Who Hear Our Sermons* (Baker Academic, 2017), 31–44.

35. William W. Klein, Craig L. Blomberg, and Robert L. Hubbard Jr., *Introduction to Biblical Interpretation Workbook* (Zondervan, 2017), 13.

36. Application is a critical element in biblical exegesis. As Douglas Stuart encourages, "My approach to exegesis has certain conscious biases for which I make no apologies. Perhaps the most debatable is my insistence that exegesis should include guidelines for application of the passage being studied. Exegesis is patently a theological enterprise, and a theology that is not applied to the lives of God's people is sterile." See Douglas Stuart, *Old Testament Exegesis: A Handbook for Students and Pastors*, 5th ed. (Westminster John Knox, 2022), xi–xii.

interpretation, and possible applications. Part of this initial legwork will make its way into the sermon later.

Consult Commentaries

Last, but not least, the interpretive process involves reading and gleaning from commentaries. *Nota bene* or reader beware: Not all commentaries are created equal when it comes to tangible and practical benefits for preachers and listeners in the preaching moment. Some commentary series and commentaries are quite technical. Of course, they have a necessary place in scholarship and in the academy. Many times, commentary writers use technical jargon and idiosyncratic speech, which is difficult to decode for the uninformed biblical scholar-pastor. Therefore, when it comes to weekly preaching, technical commentaries and commentary series prove less helpful for the average preacher and listener.

Reading preacher-friendly commentary series, such as the NIV Application Commentary series published by Zondervan Academic or the ESV Expository Commentary series published by Crossway, provide useful background information on history and culture and also address authorship, dates, key biblical and theological themes, and practical connections on how to bridge cultural gaps between biblical times and the modern world. If you find yourself spending exorbitant amounts of time reading commentaries to no avail, you're probably reading a technical commentary and not a user-friendly one for preachers.

CONCLUSION

The original languages are, according to many, an essential part of the preaching process. To understand the Scriptures with breadth and depth, we seek to study, interpret, and apply the biblical languages to our sermons for clarity, accuracy, and efficacy. This chapter has provided several tools for biblical interpretation that can be used by the average pastor/preacher in their study without being a language guru. It is possible to incorporate weekly language study in our sermon preparation and to do it consistently and profitably for the preacher and those sitting in the pews. We have also considered a couple of ways we can preach based on our English translations (or mother tongue).The next step is to determine the main point of the sermon text.

QUESTIONS

1. What is your background regarding the biblical languages?
2. If you have forgotten much, most, or some of Hebrew and/or Greek, are you motivated to regain facility in them? Why or why not?
3. What will help you to start using/relearning the languages again?
4. What is your current practice in using the biblical languages in your sermon preparation?
5. What have been your practices in using an English translation?

PRACTICES

1. Try to translate your upcoming sermon passage, whether it's Hebrew or Greek. Feel free to use software like Logos or Accordance to assist you.
2. Try a word study or two based on your sermon text. Consider which words would be most impactful to help your listeners.
3. Explore cross-references. Where does your text intersect with other Old or New Testament passages?
4. Take some time to understand the grammar of the sermon passage. What did you learn?

9

POINT

Does Our Sermon Convey What the Text Says?

> Consequently, faith comes from hearing the message, and the message is heard through the word about Christ.
>
> —Romans 10:17

We all encounter "what was the point?" moments in our lives. Everyone has pinched themselves to stay awake during a blurry Sunday morning sermon, deciphering a herky-jerky anecdote from a parent or grandparent, watching a purposeless movie, or reading a puzzling book. We scratch our heads and ask, "What was the point?" Making your point, especially a clear one, is a requisite life skill. Preaching is no exception. However, preaching a clear point and a clear sermon is not a given. It takes hard work, discipline, focus, self-awareness, and objectivity to be a clear preacher.

As someone who has taught preaching courses in seminary for many years, I can attest to the fact that most preachers can do a better job with clarity. Haddon W. Robinson once quipped: "A sermon should be a bullet, not buckshot."[1] When we are unclear, the waves of unclarity reverberate across the entire worship space. Clarity cannot be assumed just because *we* think the sermon is clear. It must be objectively clear to *everyone*.

1. Haddon W. Robinson, *Biblical Preaching: The Development and Delivery of Expository Messages*, 4th ed. (Baker Academic, 2025), 16.

Let's start with what to avoid. Clarity seems to be a moving target. Depending on the preaching tradition or denominational context in which we've grown up, preachers will have a different definition of what makes a sermon clear. We think the sermon is clear because we practice certain methods like preaching three points. The traditional "three-point sermon" refers to when the preacher makes three observations about a given Scripture text. Usually, these three points have very little, if anything, to do with one another. They are not cohesive. They often don't build on one another or intersect with each other in any meaningful way.

Consequently, the listener leaves having heard three general observations with no unifying thought, point, principle, idea, or lesson. Sometimes preachers will think they are doing their listeners a favor by presenting five, seven, and (one time I even heard) twelve points or observations about the text expecting that the listener will retain some or all of them. Good luck! That's challenging even for the preacher to recall!

Another common preaching practice is to preach a sermon from two or more passages. The preacher may read one Scripture text and begin the sermon from that opening passage, but then they ask the congregation to flip over to a different text or even two. By the time the preacher launches into that second or third text, the first sermon text has gone into oblivion in the listeners' minds. It proves challenging to bring them back from the second or third text. Both scenarios are more common than we might think. They cause the sermon to lack clarity because nothing concretely unites these points or passages together. So, what makes for a clear sermon?

One of the most important preaching (and I might even add teaching) lessons I hope you will gain from this textbook is that a sermon needs *one* clear main point—and not just any point. In the introduction, I defined preaching as *communicating the triune God's Word to God's people for the purpose of life transformation and Christlikeness through explaining, envisioning, equipping, encouraging, and empowering preachers and listeners to become obedient to Scripture and to live more like Christ Jesus in every part of life.* Since the purpose of preaching is life transformation and Christlikeness, the point of your sermon needs to be what I will call a *transformational point* that God is making in the Scripture text. We will define and determine this *transformational point* using our exegetical and interpretive tools to the best of our abilities. That's what we will learn to do together in this chapter.

You probably know the running joke in children's ministry circles that the correct Sunday school answer to every Bible question is Jesus. While we can probably agree that the main emphasis of the Scriptures, even as Jesus reminds the disciples walking on the road to Emmaus in Luke 24, is the person and salvific work of Jesus himself, every Bible text offers a unique perspective on God's plans and purposes for the world and for us, as Jesus's disciples. Each passage of Scripture has a point, sometimes several points. Our job is to figure out through our study what the major point is that we want to emphasize in each sermon.

Some writers on homiletics call this process determining the *truth* of the passage. For example, in his book *Small Preaching*, Jonathan T. Pennington explains: "We can define preaching as *the invitational and exhortational proclamation of biblical and theological truth*."[2] With this definition, Pennington offers two primary descriptors of proclamation: to be "invitational" and to be "exhortational." In his book *Invitation to Biblical Preaching*, Donald R. Sunukjian has called the sermon's point a "take-home truth."[3] Haddon W. Robinson, in his book *Biblical Preaching*, has called this main point the "Big Idea."[4] Regardless of which terminology you prefer, the key concern for the preacher is to have a clear point or truth that listeners should walk away with so that it can be applied and lived out in our pursuit of discipleship and Christlikeness. Before we nail down a process of determining the point of the Scripture text, let me ask the elephant-in-the-room type question that's probably on your minds.

Aren't There Many Points in a Scripture Text?

This question has been asked in various ways: Isn't it presumptuous for us to think that we can somehow determine *the one and only* main point of a text? Can't there be multiple points in a single Scripture passage? Why do we need to settle on just one? How do we figure out exactly which point God was making? Put differently, isn't the point of a passage subjective, based on one's background or preunderstanding (mentioned in chapter 2)?

Reader-response criticism is a common practice for many aspiring interpreters of Scripture. In this approach, the response of the reader in meaning creation weighs more heavily than seeking to understand and identify the meaning of the original author. We find this practice readily employed in small group Bible studies and devotional readings. The search for meaning is a free-for-all where the Bible passage can mean anything because the reader

2. Jonathan T. Pennington, *Small Preaching: 25 Little Things You Can Do Now to Make You a Better Preacher* (Lexham, 2021), 30.

3. Donald R. Sunukjian, *Invitation to Biblical Preaching: Proclaiming Truth with Clarity and Relevance* (Kregel Ministry, 2007), 65.

4. Robinson, *Biblical Preaching*, 15.

determines meaning from their response or subjective experience. For some preachers, the author's originally intended meaning is a nonissue due to the emphasis on the reader's response. Think of any sermon you've heard where you wondered after hearing the message whether the preacher studied the text on which they preached. The point they made had little or nothing to do with the text that was read.

Put simply, yes, there could be numerous different points or emphases of the divine and human authors in a passage of Scripture. "Polyvalence" is the fancy term for a text that can mean many ("poly") things. To say that, as a modern interpreter, I can generate on my own a single definitive interpretation would signal hubris. I share, to a measured degree, Mark Allan Powell's concern with interpreters' obsession over determining the original author's meaning, where "texts come to mean things that their authors did not consciously intend."[5]

However, I don't believe that modern readers/preachers should disregard pursuing the divine and human author's intended meaning, even if we can and do make errors along the way. I often tell my students that there is a superintended meaning of every biblical text. This meaning is known by the divine author, who supernaturally led the human author to write down what became our Holy Scriptures. One day, when we get to heaven, we can ask God what every passage means. Our earthly task in the moment, however, is simply to do our very best to determine a meaning that most closely aligns with God's original intentions. One way we can mitigate fears of sharing the wrong point is asking: What is *a* main point of this text rather than *the* main point?

Let's explore this process of discerning *a* main point together. Turn with me in your Bible to Proverbs 3:5–6, which reads: "Trust in the Lord with all your heart and lean not on your own understanding. In all your ways submit to him, and he will make your paths straight." This well-known Scripture text is a fan favorite when encountering a crossroad in life as one waits patiently and dependently on God.

What It Can Mean and What It Can't Mean

Let's play a game I'll make up now called, "What it can mean *and* what it can't mean." The first question is what it can mean. The meaning of the text seems straightforward. The author gives three imperative commands that are synonyms with (or resemble) each other. (1) "Trust in the Lord with

5. Mark Allan Powell, *Chasing the Eastern Star: Adventures in Biblical Reader-Response Criticism* (Westminster John Knox, 2001), 3.

all your heart." (2) "Lean not on your own understanding." (3) "In all your ways submit to him."

Some readers of this text might contend that the second and third imperatives provide direct pathways to live out "Trust[ing] in the Lord with all your heart" by "leaning not on your own understanding" and "in all your ways submit[ting] to him." The result of putting our trust and faith in these three imperatives will be that "God will make your paths straight."

What *can* this text mean?

Start with a bird's-eye view. If you were to distill the meaning of this text into one phrase, theme, topic, or word, what would summarize this passage? For many, I believe we would land on the word "trust" or "faith" as the main topic. Next, what does the author say about trust or faith? When one trusts in the Lord with all their heart, not leaning on their own wisdom or knowledge but submitting to him in all things, God will lead them on a straight path. The sermon's point is not whatever I want to say about the text based on "my own finite understanding."

What can this text *not* mean?

Here's the second part of the game: This is where the tension begins to mount as we put our hermeneutical boxing gloves on when determining a text's meaning because of our varied experiences, backgrounds, values, cultures, denominations, genders, and upbringing. Let's offer a few misguided or misdirected understandings of this text.

While it's possible that some reading this passage would diverge in meaning for one or more of the imperative commands, error can strike more easily in the result when one does trust or put their faith wholeheartedly in God, as the author underscores: "and he [God] will make your paths straight." Does that mean that God will give you everything you desire or want? Does that mean that God will provide you with acceptance into your dream college/university, offer you a spouse who's out of your league, give you exceptional children, a highly prized job, or popularity and a platform? Does that mean that God will enable you to do the miraculous? What does it mean to be put on God's straight path? We'll come back to this in a moment.

To provide a template for common interpretive points one might deduce from any given text, I would like to offer the TEACH acronym as a guide since I've found acronyms to be helpful and easy to remember. When we attempt to figure out the point of the passage, we often will explore one of these five interpretive avenues. You might choose to build your sermon on one of these five points. We'll keep Proverbs 3:5–6 as our main example as we go through a range of possible points.

Step 6: Establish Your Point

Considering Theological, Exegetical, Applicational, Cultural, and Homiletical (TEACH-ing) Points

The sixth step in creating a sermon is to establish your point. A helpful way to discern the point is to ask a series of five questions or emphases. Oftentimes, these points will become possible emphases in our sermon along the way. We'll first describe each type and then conclude this chapter by establishing the transformational point we will communicate clearly in the sermon. The most significant question one can ask prior to preaching is: Does my sermon's point convey the point of the Scripture passage? Let's try to create a textual point now for each possibility: theological, exegetical, applicational, cultural, homiletical, and finally transformational. It's impractical to do this exercise for every sermon going forward. So, of course, you don't have to create all of these points for every single sermon you preach.

Theological Point

Here are a series of questions we can ask as we consider potential theological points that the text raises for its readers: What point(s) is God making about the triune God: Father, Son, and Spirit? What does God the Father want us to know about himself in this passage of the Bible? What truth about God are we supposed to appreciate and give praise for? What work has the triune God accomplished in the world and for us based on this text? What is God's will here? What are God's commands that we are to obey?

More generally, what is God saying here or communicating here?[6] What did God want his people to know long ago and far away? What does he want us to know here and now? When people say that the Bible is irrelevant, they are failing to appreciate the multifaceted nature of God's love letter to his people. In the previous chapters, we walked through the various literary genres that can be found in the entirety of the Bible. In every genre, God communicates his truth to us about himself. As Haddon W. Robinson summarizes, "The Bible is a book about God and his redemptive work in human history."[7]

What is God saying about himself in Proverbs 3:5–6, "Trust in the Lord with all your heart and lean not on your own understanding. In all your ways submit to him, and he will make your paths straight"? In many ways, we're asking the

6. Eric J. Bargerhuff and I have written a book with the same title, *What's God Saying Here? How to Navigate Awkward, Troubling, and Bizarre Passages We Would Rather Skip* (Zondervan Reflective, 2025).

7. Robinson, *Biblical Preaching*, 61.

basic theological question: Who is God and what is his character? It seems so simple, but the rationale for this three-part imperative to trust in the Lord with all our heart, to lean on God's understanding and not our own, and to submit to him in all our ways is because ultimately God is trustworthy. Our theological point might be: We can trust God because he is trustworthy and directs our paths.

Exegetical Point

The exegetical point will be your exegetical conclusion based on the results of your study. Placing Proverbs 3:5–6 in its wider context, what else does the author say in Proverbs 3? The exegetical point is the interpretive, objective summary statement of any biblical passage. The exegetical point doesn't necessarily highlight the Trinity as does the theological point. Rather, when seeking to determine the exegetical point, there are two overarching processes by which we typically read and interpret the text: literal versus figurative *and* prescriptive versus descriptive.

LITERAL VERSUS FIGURATIVE

What's the difference between a literal reading and a figurative one?

Not every passage should be taken literally, such as in the cases of Jesus's hyperbole or exaggeration, "If your right eye causes you to stumble, gouge it out and throw it away. . . . And if your right hand causes you to stumble, cut it off and throw it away" (Matt. 5:29–30). Obviously, Jesus is using exaggeration to make a strong point. We must cut off and cut out the sins in our lives. However, in many and most cases, we can assume that we should take God at his word literally. Here, a literal reading of the text allows us to conclude that we can trust God entirely, which involves submitting to him and obeying all that he commands (because we trust that his plans are good).

A more figurative reading of the text might focus on the section "with all your heart" and thereby ponder more creative ways we can trust the Lord with our hearts, desires, or affections. The image or metaphor of the heart represents the totality of our being. When the author writes, "with all your heart," he means there is no wavering of commitment to the Lord. This figurative interpretation provides a concrete image for the listeners to hold on to while hearing the message.

PRESCRIPTIVE VERSUS DESCRIPTIVE

Like the literal versus figurative example is whether a text is prescriptive versus descriptive. Every single passage of Scripture applies to all people: past, present, and future. On certain occasions, the point of the Scripture text is prescriptive (the text gives instructions or commands we are to emulate and do), and other times it is descriptive (the text merely describes the ancient world of the passage).

So, here's a question we can ask ourselves as we read and interpret any passage: Is God prescribing how we are to conduct ourselves, or is God merely describing what took place in the past? Sometimes the answer to this question is yes, no, or both/and. The prescriptive versus descriptive debate is also quite dangerous because we become adjudicators of what we will choose to obey and what we won't. In cases other than obvious hyperbole or exaggeration, it may be safer to say that most passages in the Bible are prescriptive rather than descriptive.

Departing briefly from our example here of Proverbs 3:5–6, here's a question for you: Are the Ten Commandments found in Exodus 20 and Deuteronomy 5 prescriptive or descriptive? The whole process of doing exegesis or biblical interpretation is to ask the Holy Spirit for help to discern not what we want the text to mean but what the text meant in biblical times. Next, we want to discover what that same truth means for us in modern times. Is this passage prescriptive or descriptive? Will we communicate to our listeners that this text only applied to the people back then, or does it still apply to us today?

I would contend that the Ten Commandments are prescriptive in that New Testament believers like us must still obey them. They were not written only for the Israelites living in Moses's time. How do we know the difference? When is a Scripture text merely descriptive versus prescriptive? While this may be viewed as a subjective process, here are two questions we might ask to tell the difference. This might involve some homework and consultation of trusted biblical scholars and commentaries.

Is this text merely providing a historical or cultural description of the biblical world or situational context or does it give an actual command for us to obey? For example, do all laws in the book of Leviticus apply to us today, or are they applicable to the ancient Israelites only? To answer the question: Most laws found in Leviticus would not be enforced upon New Testament believers. However, any laws related to morality/ethical living would be applicable, such as justice issues and caring for strangers/aliens living among us. We can apply marital laws (between one man and one woman, for life) as a moral ethic. Any laws, such as ceremonial laws, civil laws, and dietary laws would not be binding on New Testament believers.

Is this text a universal biblical command (prescription) for Christian living that applies to all times and situations, including today, or is it applicable only for biblical times and people? For instance, Genesis 1:26–28 is God's original design, covenant, and ethic for marriage and is not merely descriptive of the ancient world. It is still prescriptive for today. It applies to all times and places. If we are unsure about any instruction or command in Scripture, we can consult biblical commentaries and speak to trusted pastors who hold to the authority of Scripture, sometimes called biblical authority. Holding to biblical authority means we trust that God's instructions and commandments are best for us in every part of life. If God commanded it, we are wise to obey, even when we don't fully understand or agree. An exegetical point tethered to the text might be: "Trusting in the Lord wholeheartedly leads to a life that is consistent with where the Lord leads."

Applicational Point

If we were to summarize or streamline the Bible, we could say that God's mission is to call people to himself in worship and to call his people toward daily application and living out specific pathways toward discipleship and Christlikeness. Some common applications in Scripture include worship, holiness, obedience, righteousness, confession, repentance, justice, service, giving, and love (love for the triune God and love for neighbor). What does this text invite us to apply to our lives? How do we answer the "so what" factor? How does the point of this passage alter how I live each day? In Proverbs 3:5–6, our applicational point might be a three-part invitation to "Trust in the Lord, lean on God's understanding, and submit to him daily."

Cultural Point

What do we mean by cultural point? This could be interpreted in different ways. As mentioned in chapter 7, there are two primary cultures: the culture in the biblical world and modern culture. The cultural point, for our purposes, takes a bit of crossing "between two worlds."[8] What is God saying to the culture of the ancient world? What is he saying to our culture today? Take a few moments to consider the point God is making to his people long ago as well as what he is saying now. More poignantly, the cultural point will directly respond to our modern times. Here's an example of a modern cultural point: "Trust God in a culture that only trusts in the self."

8. John Stott coined the term "between two worlds" in his classic preaching book, *Between Two Worlds: The Challenge of Preaching Today* (Eerdmans, 2017).

Homiletical Point

A homiletical point is one that resembles the theological point and exegetical point but with a modern twist. Oftentimes a homiletical point would be a "translation" of the theological and/or exegetical point using language that relates directly to one's listeners. The listeners become participants in the wording of your homiletical point. Here's a sample homiletical point: "Following God's path for your life means trusting him with your whole life."

As long as each of your points—theological, exegetical, applicational, cultural, and homiletical—is anchored in God's meaning of the text, it could be an appropriate preaching point to deliver in your weekly sermon. However, we might also consider preaching a transformational point in each sermon.

Transformational Point

How does the transformational differ from what we've already considered? As we pray and consult the Holy Spirit (more on this topic in chap. 16), what message do your listeners need to hear and take home with them this week? Another way to ask the question is: Which point packs the greatest punch or inspires the greatest life transformation? The point of transformation may be one of your TEACH-ing points or it could be something entirely different. What is the transformational point that we will preach to be most impactful in transforming us and our listeners?

The transformational point is one in which God provides his exclamation point on what the individual and collective body need to hear and apply in this sermonic moment and beyond. We might view the transformational point as the point that will help the preacher and the congregation become more Christlike. So, what does a transformational point look like for Proverbs 3:5–6? What's missing in our lives? What is a prominent need? Perhaps it's a sense of fulfillment. So, here's a possible transformational point: "The greatest fulfillment comes from trusting completely in the Lord and not in creating our own sense of fulfillment."

CONCLUSION

We began this chapter by asking, "What was the point"? In *How to Read a Book*, Mortimer Adler and Charles Van Doren suggest various ways to determine an author's message. They write: "From the author's point of view, the important sentences are the ones that express the judgments on which his whole argument rests. . . . But *the heart of his communication lies in the major affirmations and denials he is making, and the reasons he gives for so doing.*"[9] In many ways, the sermonic point seeks the same result. We are trying to relate to our listeners "the major affirmations and denials . . . and the reasons [we give] for so doing." Since listeners are asking, "What is the point?" the entire sermon delivers the answer to that question. The sermon will be constructed based on this transformational point. Once we've discerned what that transformational point will be, we can move from text to sermon. Join me in our next chapter where we will learn how to construct a sermon from the ground up.

QUESTIONS

1. What has been your approach in establishing the main point in a sermon?
2. Do you believe a sermon should have one main point? Why or why not?
3. How do you determine what the primary point of a sermon should be?
4. In what ways could your sermons employ a clearer structure when it comes to making a point(s)?

PRACTICES

1. Work through each of these TEACH-ing points for your next sermon. How are they different in terms of emphases?
   Theological Point
   Exegetical Point
   Applicational Point
   Cultural Point
   Homiletical Point
2. For your upcoming sermon, discern and articulate your Transformational Point.
3. Get some feed-forward on your transformational point. Would others agree with you concerning your point of transformation? Why or why not?
4. Get some feedback on your transformational point after you have preached the sermon. Was the transformational point you preached effective for your listeners? What would you have said differently?

9. Mortimer Adler and Charles Van Doren, *How to Read a Book: The Classic Bestselling Guide to Reading Books and Accessing Information* (MJF Books, 1972), 121.

10

OUTLINE

How Do We Construct Our Sermon Outline?

> But everything should be done in a fitting and orderly way.
>
> —1 Corinthians 14:40

I recently observed for several weeks the process of pouring concrete for two new constructions going up near my neighborhood. Some of you might be thinking, What an exciting life you lead! Well, here's why my attention was drawn to that: As a transplant to Texas, I had never lived in places without basements. If you have ever lived in a home with a basement, you know how invaluable one is.

To my chagrin, homes in Texas, as a standard procedure, don't have basements (unscientifically, it has to do with water being underground). For this reason, concrete foundations are laid directly on top of a grassy field. As I watched the crew work tirelessly over a long stretch of time, whenever I drove by, I came to realize that pouring concrete isn't as simple as I once thought.

The first part of the process is clearing away all the debris where the concrete slab is placed. This took quite some time. Later, they squared off the exact measurements of the foundation to be poured. Once everything was in order (I'm sure there are many other steps I didn't get to see), the cement trucks poured the concrete into the boxes they created to form the perimeter of the foundation. The workers labored tirelessly to make sure the foundation was filled in properly without any cracks and later smoothed it out. Then the concrete needed requisite time to cure.

Why spend such great lengths of time to lay a proper foundation? A sound foundation of any building project is critical to the strength, security, and longevity of the eventual building that will rest on top of it. Remember Jesus's illustrative words in Matthew 7:24–25, "Everyone then who hears these words of mine and does them will be like a wise man who built his house on the rock. And the rain fell, and floods came, but it did not fall, because it had been founded on the rock [in our case, concrete]" (ESV). Laying a faulty or insecure foundation presents a precarious situation for the construction project both short term and long term. A shaky foundation puts the occupants in peril.

This chapter communicates the crucial process of laying a proper foundation for sermonic development, which includes the steps of construction that will ultimately form the sermon. It's not easy to teach someone how to outline a text. In fact, it can be really complex, with a few surprises along the way. Just as constructing a house is not an easy process but worth it in the end, constructing a sermon is similarly a challenging yet rewarding process.[1] Moreover, just as taking shortcuts when erecting a building will lead to collapse and catastrophe, so can taking shortcuts in sermon preparation shortchange our listeners and put them in spiritual harm's way.

As we now enter a critical point of sermon construction, let's remind ourselves of the original definition of preaching put forth in the introduction. Preaching is *communicating the triune God's Word to God's people for the purpose of life transformation and Christlikeness through explaining, envisioning, equipping, encouraging, and empowering preachers and listeners to become obedient to Scripture and to live more like Christ Jesus in every part of life.*

Step 7: Outline Your Passage

The seventh step in the sermonic process is to outline your passage. Let's start with the basics of outlining, which will take us briefly back to your days in elementary school. Your English teacher probably explained the traditional way of outlining a formal paper. In teaching you how to write this traditional outline, the teacher began with an introduction, which includes your thesis statement (stating your main argument or point), followed by three body paragraphs that develop or support this thesis statement, and ending with a

1. John Woods conceives of the sermonic process as entering rooms in a house in his book *God Is in the House: A Fresh Model for Shaping a Sermon* (Langham, 2022).

conclusion (a summary of the paper or argument). See an elementary paper outline below:

Introduction
Point 1
Point 2
Point 3
Conclusion

While this is a standard process of teaching formal paper writing, there is no single, definitive, right way to outline a sermon. Over the years, we've heard of numerous outline forms experimented with by preachers on their listeners. You may have even received a paper fill-in-the-blank style outline included in your weekly worship bulletin.. There are probably as many sermon outline possibilities as there are grandma's favorite chocolate chip cookie recipes circulating around the planet. The most critical lesson about sermon construction we need to remember is that our message must be clearly communicated to our hearers. Now, every preacher automatically thinks they are clear in their own minds. Clear thinking cannot be assumed. Some may even jest, "Why do I need to labor and write out an outline? What's the big deal?"

What makes a sermon clear is that it's clear to everyone, objectively speaking. The outline is serious business and serious work. As Hershael W. York contends, "The outline is the living contract between preacher and listener that assures their mutual time will be well spent, that they will arrive at the destination the text dictates and the Holy Spirit intends."[2] A clear outline is *that* significant! Before we get to the nuts and bolts of outlining, we first need to determine where to place the transformational point.

Place Your Transformational Point

Remember, the transformational point is the foundation of your sermon. You will eventually place all the sermonic building materials on top of that transformational point. Homileticians like Kenton C. Anderson have described this initial process as determining the "sermonic structure."[3] The two major

2. Hershael W. York, "Outlining the Sermon," in *Handbook of Contemporary Preaching: A Wealth of Counsel for Creative and Effective Proclamation*, 2nd ed., ed. Michael Duduit (B&H Academic, 2024), 165.

3. See, for instance, Kenton C. Anderson, *Choosing to Preach: A Comprehensive Introduction to Sermon Options and Structures* (Zondervan, 2006).

ways of structuring your sermon are to begin with the transformational point (what homileticians call the deductive method) or to end with it (the inductive method). Jeffrey Arthurs distinguishes the two forms: "Induction starts with particulars and moves toward a conclusion or principle. . . . Deduction starts with the conclusion or axiom and then explains, proves, or applies that idea."[4]

For this reason, I would like to give a range of possible models for constructing your message. We'll begin with a more "universal" method or approach to outlining that any preacher can "master" in their first year or two of a regular preaching ministry. Later, we'll explore alternate ways of outlining based on the type of passage/genre we are preaching on. Before we can discern what type of approach works best, we'll need to strategically place the transformational point. In principle, any sermon can be preached deductively or inductively. Here are some considerations for how to choose your sermonic shape or structure wisely and effectively. We begin with the transformational point.

Should I Begin with the Transformational Point?

The more logical or left-brained approach to preaching a sermon is to state the transformational point early on and allow the rest of the sermon to unpack and elucidate that transformational point. The whole rationale behind constructing an outline is to know how the sermon begins, to know where it's going, and to know how it will end. Oftentimes, a preacher who favors this method will say at the start, "Here's where this sermon is going. First, second, and third." The advantage of the deductive form is clarity of one's thought and progress. The preacher and the listeners know directionally where the message is going. A sermon without a clear blueprint is a sermonic project that will quickly fall apart.

There are some normative passages/genres of Scripture that preach well as deductive sermons. Naturally, any section, paragraph, pericope, or chapter from an epistle can be preached deductively with the transformational point mentioned toward the beginning of your sermon. The rest of the sermon, as Arthurs points out, explains, illustrates/proves, and applies this transformational point. However, sometimes the preaching passage or genre lends itself toward an inductive approach.

4. Jeffrey Arthurs, "Five Hammer Strokes for Creating Expository Sermon Outlines," in *Sermon Preparation: The Preacher's Toolbox*, ed. Craig Brian Larson (Hendrickson, 2012), chap. 1.

Should I End with the Transformational Point?

In contrast to the deductive model, certain biblical genres like narrative texts, stories, parables, psalms, or proverbs may be better suited by having an organic sermonic shape, placing the transformational point at the end rather than at the start of your sermon. Why does it matter? Well, consider the essential elements of storytelling. As Wayne Baxter notes, stories include "the introduction, the rising action/conflict between characters, the climax, the falling action (invariably following the climax), and the conclusion or resolution of the conflict."[5] To preach a narrative or story-type passage deductively makes less homiletical sense. Stories are not told by leading with the point or principle or lessons learned. For this reason, some passages invite an inductive model that states the transformational point toward the end of the message.

Trace the Flow of the Passage

Once you have determined the transformational point of the passage, take some time to understand the flow of it. One of the most effective ways to outline your sermon is to trace the flow of the passage. Write your notes on paper or in a Word document. If it's an argument, trace the flow of thought. If it's a narrative/story, provide the basic plotline and identify the central characters. Try to determine the point of the argument or story.

Here's the challenge for all preachers. The sermon cannot explain, illustrate, or apply every single verse and cranny of the passage. We have limited time and space, so some things will remain undisclosed. I know what you're thinking: "That's hard to do!" Think of it this way: Even if your sermon was two hours long, I highly doubt you could say everything you wanted to say about a given passage. So, we cut our losses and do the best we can with the time we have.

What does it look like to trace the flow of a text? One way is to summarize themes, going verse by verse or a few verses at a time. Donald R. Sunukjian, in *Invitation to Biblical Preaching*, provides this example from the first chapter of the Epistle of James:

- You should face trials with joy and persevere through them, knowing they're producing maturity and Christlike completeness in you (vv. 2–4).

5. Wayne Baxter, *Preparing Sermons from the Page to the Pulpit: Exegesis to Exposition in Seven Steps* (Lexham, 2023), 70.

- If you lack wisdom regarding the purpose of the trial or how to persevere through it, ask God, and he'll give it to you. But you must firmly believe in his sovereignty and love in order to receive it (vv. 5–8).
- Both poor and rich ought to be able to discern the purposes and benefits that come through their trials (vv. 9–11).
- If you successfully persevere through the trial, you'll receive the crown of life (v. 12).
- But if you respond sinfully to the trial, don't blame God for punishing you too far. Your sinful failure was due to some evil in you, not because God was tempting you (vv. 13–15).
- God never pushes us toward sin. On the contrary, his every action is only and always for our good—from his initial choice to give us birth to his final welcoming of us in heaven as the highest of all his creation (vv. 16–18).
- Therefore, don't become angry with God or blame him if you respond sinfully to a trial. Instead, "be quick to listen" to the wisdom you asked for and to the "word of truth" within you. Be "slow to speak"—do not accuse God or others of causing you to sin. And finally, be "slow to become angry, for man's anger does not bring about the righteous life that God desires." An angry, accusatory response will never bring the maturity or completeness or crown of life that God intends through the trial (vv. 19–20).
- Instead of being angry and blaming God, get rid of whatever filth or evil caused you to react sinfully in the first place, and then return to the Word of God, which is able to guide you safely through the trial (v. 21).
- When you return to the Word, however, you must obey it, and not simply listen to it. You must be a "doer" and not merely a "hearer" (vv. 22–25).[6]

Similarly, as we work our way through the sermon text, we will notice one of several different patterns emerging. As Jeffrey Arthurs notes, there are various flows of thought in any given text, such as:

- Problem-solution
- Cause-effect
- Contrast (not this but that)
- Chronology (first this happened, then this, then this)
- Promise-fulfillment
- Lesser to greater

6. Donald R. Sunukjian, *Invitation to Biblical Preaching: Proclaiming Truth with Clarity and Relevance* (Kregel Ministry, 2007), 20–21.

- Argument-proof
- Explanation-application[7]

After writing down the flow of thought, you now have a choice to make. How much of this chapter do you want to preach this week? If you are planning to preach the entire first chapter, you will need to whittle down all the various principles into one concise transformational point. What is the primary lesson, truth, principle, or point the author is communicating?

You could also divide the chapter into a few pericopes and preach those paragraphs over the course of several weeks. The same process would apply in terms of identifying the transformational point and getting the flow of thought for the selected verses. Tracing the flow of thought in a passage is a helpful exercise because we will gain a better understanding of the letter, story, chapter, or paragraph, and its development. This will also guide and inform our sermonic outline because, in most cases, we will preach the flow of the text.

The Preacher's Roles and Choosing a Home Model

There are two primary roles of the preacher when it comes to the creation of the outline: real estate agent and architect. As a real estate agent, the preacher helps the client or listener figure out which model of home best suits their family and lifestyle. Once they ascertain the home model, preachers will put on the hat of architect.

The Preacher as Real Estate Agent

First, put on your real estate hat, preacher, and think of yourself as a real estate agent. Imagine yourself helping your client purchase a new home. Let's take a stroll through the new home development and consider different model homes. Which one will best suit this family and their needs? To determine the form/structure/shape/model of the sermon, we need to first decide how many levels (or subpoints/moves, more on this shortly) we'll allocate.

CHOOSE YOUR HOME MODEL

We have two major models of homes to choose from: the ranch and the colonial. In my married life of twenty-four years (at the time of publication), I will have purchased two homes without my wife seeing either of

7. See Jeffrey Arthurs, "Five Hammer Strokes for Creating Expository Sermon Outlines," Preaching Today, accessed December 2, 2025, https://www.preachingtoday.com/exegesis/foundations-of-exegesis/five-hammer-strokes-for-creating-expository-sermon-outlines.html.

them in person. Both times, it has been an exercise in complete trust (for her). Yet, thankfully, we have enjoyed living in both homes and have made them our own over time. As a preacher, you will need to choose a home model for your congregation each week based on the Scripture text, genre, and passage length. Thankfully, this process won't be nearly as stressful as literally purchasing a new home each week. You have one major criterion for making this decision. Clarity! What type of home will be most clear for your listeners?

The Preacher as Architect

Second, once we have discerned the best home model to accommodate our listeners, we will next put on the hat of an architect and design the homiletical home. The role of the homiletical architect includes the creation of a clear sermonic blueprint by figuring out where to place the transformational point, provide subpoints, make transitions, and use creativity and pastoral awareness and sensitivities concerning what to include for your listeners' illustrations and applications.

The Ranch: One Transformational Point

The first option is a ranch-style home (single level). In this type of home or sermon, there is one major transformational point. Particularly for shorter sermons or shorter texts, the ranch style is neat and simple without a lot of square footage to navigate and clean up later.

Figure 10.1. The ranch

Each transformational point will have four vertical beams placed in the corners to bear the weight of the home. For a short sermon or sermon text, I would like to propose four corners as Letters A, B, C, and D to mentally aid with the sermon outline:

Corner A: *Explain* your verses.
Corner B: *Illustrate* your verses.
Corner C: *Apply* your verses.
Corner D: *Repeat* your transformational point.

Using the traditional Roman numeral system, your outline would look like this. Provide a complete sentence for each point and subpoint.[8]

Introduction

An effective introduction accomplishes three goals: (1) hooks your listeners, (2) explains why they need to listen, and (3) introduces them to your first move.[9] There are many different ways to launch your sermon. Get creative. You probably know a preacher or two who begins every sermon the same formulaic way: "Please open your Bibles to passage X." Those opening thirty to sixty seconds are so vital in creating a desire for listeners to either tune in or tune out.

Introduction possibilities are bountiful: start with a story, ask a meaningful question, show and tell with an object lesson, read an intriguing quotation, show a brief clip from a movie/show, play part of a song, share news about what's happening in your town, country, or world, recount a memory from the past, praise and thank your listeners, connect something in life to your sermon text, talk about something controversial, draw out a principle from a book or magazine you've been reading, explore current events in culture, and so much more. Give one of them a try this week. Keep your listeners guessing so that you and they won't fall into a sermonic rut.

I. State your transformational point (foundation).

   A. *Explain* the main verses from which you've created your transformational point (corner A). You may need to offer more than one subpoint to explain your verses.

      1. Explanation 1
      2. Explanation 2

      (Transitional statement and/or question)

8. I'm not alone in making the case that your outline should be written in complete sentences. We need to know, as preachers, exactly what we will be saying at each stage. Fragments and incomplete lines do not provide full clarity of thought. See Sunukjian, *Invitation to Biblical Preaching*, 308.

9. Essentially I'm borrowing here from Haddon Robinson, "Start with a Bang and Quit All Over," in *Biblical Preaching: The Development and Delivery of Expository Messages*, 4th ed. (Baker Academic, 2025), 116–20, where he says that effective introductions command attention, uncover a need, and introduce the body of the sermon.

B. *Illustrate* the verses you've just explained (corner B).[10] You may need one longer or two or more (shorter) illustrations to explain your verses.

1. Illustration 1
2. Illustration 2

(Transitional statement and/or question)

C. *Apply* the transformational point for the congregation (corner C). You may have one or more applications for your listeners.

1. Application 1
2. Application 2

(Transitional statement and/or question)

D. *Repeat* the transformational point with the congregation (corner D). It can be easy for everyone to forget what the point is, so repeating it here will help both the preacher and listeners stay on track.

(Transitional statement and/or question)

Conclusion

Now that your people have listened to the sermon for 30–45 minutes, what's next? Conclusions have similar qualities to introductions but achieve a different end. The conclusion is not just a point of finality when we stop talking and take our seats. Rather, an effective conclusion summarizes your sermon's moves, reminds the listeners of your transformational point, illustrates and/or applies your transformational point, invites listeners to respond to the sermon through participation, facilitates visions/dreams of how to live the message this week, challenges the listeners to be and make disciples, and encourages the congregation to embody the sermon individually and collectively. As Robinson and others have asked, "So what? What difference does this make?"[11] Failing to answer these questions is a disservice to our congregants. In terms of storytelling dynamics, the sermon's conclusion is not just a denouement (a point of deceleration and finality). Rather, an effective conclusion will motivate, inspire, encourage, challenge, remind, galvanize,

10. J. Kent Edwards and Scott M. Gibson suggest a similar approach (which I have appropriated using an A, B, C, D structure) and provide the option of giving listeners a counterargument instead of an illustration. Where would some congregants object to the point of the sermon? This counterargument would be addressed here. Gibson gives credit to Edwards for this structure (conversation with Gibson, April 28, 2026).

11. Robinson, *Biblical Preaching*, 123.

excite, support, promote, and empower your listeners to live victoriously for Jesus this week.

What to Do When We Need More Than One Explanation

Depending on the content of the preaching text, you may want to oscillate between two different subpoints for A, B, and C so that the outline structure might resemble the following format:

I. State your transformational point.
  A1. Explain your verses (e.g., verses 1–3).
    1. Explanation 1
  B1. Illustrate your verses.
    1. Illustration 1
  C1. Apply your verses.
    1. Application 1
    (Transitional statement and/or question)
  A2. Explain your verses (e.g., verses 4–8).
    1. Explanation 2
  B2. Illustrate your verses.
    1. Illustration 2
  C2. Apply your verses.
    1. Application 2
  D. Repeat your transformational point.

Now that we have a basic outline structure, we will explore what each lettered subpoint and transitional statement or question looks like.

State Your Transformational Point

First, in terms of the transformational point, a key guideline is to focus on main clauses or main ideas in a given sermon passage. This transformational point comes directly from the biblical text. It's not something that you simply conjure up on your own. In his preaching textbook, *Preparing Sermons from the Page to the Pulpit*, Wayne Baxter shares this nugget:

> There is a fundamental principle in language: main or independent clauses convey primary thoughts, and subordinate or dependent clauses convey secondary thoughts. A main clause is a complete thought that can stand on its own and

> makes perfect sense by itself. A subordinate clause, however, is an incomplete thought, grammatically speaking, and needs to be attached to a main clause for it to make sense.[12]

Similarly, as we construct our outline, we are focusing on main or independent clauses or verses that the transformational point can stand on. Now, I've received some pushback over the years from beginning preaching students who articulate some version of this: "Why can't we preach on a subpoint of the text rather than on a main point?" Usually, I'll chime back, "Why would you want to preach on minor points rather than major points?" There may be rare occasions where we do end up preaching on minor or secondary characters such as Hagar, Jonathan, Naomi, or Eutychus. However, in general, as someone once put it, let's "keep the main thing the main thing" or let's "major on the majors, not on the minors."

Some homileticians believe that outlining should be constructed in two or even three stages of development by first creating a passage outline, an exegetical outline, and finally a sermon outline.[13] While that's certainly not verboten by any means, a two-step or three-step process may not be entirely necessary. You will always provide the biblical, historical, and cultural details in your explanation of the text anyway, so writing an initial exegetical outline may slow down the sermonic outlining process. Word the transformational point in today's language, and write the point in such a way that your listeners feel included. This can be accomplished by using second-person pronouns or with application-oriented language that includes the listeners.

Explain Your Verses (Corner A)

After naming your transformational point, start by explaining your verses and sharing your most critical exegetical insights. It's been helpful for me to put the appropriate verse numbers in brackets for easy reference next to corner A. This will enable you to reread those verses to guide your listeners and refresh them on where this transformational point derived from.

What is happening in your passage? If it's a narrative/story text, describe the characters, context, situation, or conflict. If it's a letter, what is the author

12. Wayne Baxter, *Preparing Sermons from the Page to the Pulpit: Exegesis to Exposition in Seven Steps* (Lexham, 2023), 54.

13. For instance, Jeffrey Arthurs suggests writing an exegetical outline prior to writing the homiletical outline. See Arthurs, "Five Hammer Strokes for Creating Expository Sermon Outlines." Donald Sunukjian encourages writing a passage outline, a truth outline, and a sermon outline. See chapter 2 of Sunukjian, *Invitation to Biblical Preaching*, 27–41.

communicating to the recipients? If it's a psalm or proverb, what's the main principle God wants us to know, experience, or apply? What do these verses mean, historically, culturally, situationally, morally, linguistically, or grammatically, and so on? Subpoint A is your opportunity to explain the passage as thoroughly as you can.

No matter how few or how many verses you are preaching on, you won't be able to cover every detail in your sermon text. So, be selective and explain the main verses from which you've created your transformational point (corner A). Being selective in what to include and what to leave out in your exegetical information is a painful process. We cannot discuss everything we learn in our time of study. That's perfectly fine. Your sermon is not strictly an intellectual exercise, though it will include relevant exegetical details.

EXAMPLES OF EXPLANATION (CORNER A)

What do I need my listeners to understand? What needs explanation? In any given sermon text, there will be two primary explanations that will be helpful for our listeners. First, we explain the situation/context. Second, we explain the historical/cultural significance.

EXPLAIN THE SITUATION/CONTEXT

One of the challenges of preaching to modern listeners is that they may not be familiar with the customs and practices of ancient Israel or people in biblical times. It will be important, depending on which passage you are preaching, to provide context or situational background on what's happening in your text. For instance, if you are preaching on Genesis 15, you'll want to spend some time educating the congregation on the nature of biblical covenants, in particular the Abrahamic covenant. Or, if you are preaching on the letter of 1 Corinthians, the Greco-Roman ceremonial food laws that Paul refers to may not be familiar to your congregation.

EXPLAIN THE HISTORICAL/CULTURAL SIGNIFICANCE

While it may be well and good that stories and examples are in the Scripture passage, what do they have to do with us today? Why is this historical/cultural detail worth mentioning and explaining in your sermon? Sometimes the best thing we can do in our sermon is to explain the historical and cultural significance of our passage. For example, let's say we are preaching through the book of Ruth. What do we need to teach the congregation about Jewish marriage customs and the concept of the kinsman-redeemer? For most people listening today, these cultural practices mean little to nothing. Take some time to explain their significance to connect the dots for them.

TRANSITIONAL STATEMENT AND/OR QUESTION

Transitions are quite significant in maintaining the order and continuing the progress of your sermon. The point of having a transitional statement or question is to connect the dots for your listeners. How does your explanation of the passage relate to your illustration? What wording will help you get there? Sometimes it's best to provide a statement only. Sometimes it might be more effective to ask a question. And sometimes the best approach is to give both a statement and a question. Write out your transition in full.

Illustrate Your Verses (Corner B)

EXAMPLES OF ILLUSTRATION (CORNER B)

Sprinkling your sermon with illustrations accomplishes three goals: It brings clarity, provides connection, and helps with recollection. If you are familiar with *Aesop's Fables*, it contains memorable stories that teach children a lesson or moral principle, with animals acting as the primary characters. These fables are creative and useful illustrations for life and how to live wisely.[14]

Similarly, effective illustrations are powerful for our preaching ministries. First, illustrations bring clarity to our speech. That's why someone once said, "A picture is worth a thousand words." Jesus, the master preacher, used illustrations in his teaching and preaching regularly. For instance, while each of the parables is an illustration in its own right, think of the everyday examples Jesus used to bring clarity to his sermons or teachings for his disciples and the crowd. In his Sermon on the Mount, Jesus teaches on the subject of worry, saying, "Look at the birds of the air; they do not sow or reap or store away in barns, and yet your heavenly Father feeds them" (Matt. 6:26). In verse 28, he provides another illustration on worry: "And why do you worry about clothes? See how the flowers of the field grow. They do not labor or spin." Both of these illustrations regarding birds and flowers help us better understand the concept of worry because they clarify. Jesus uses birds and flowers as clarifying examples to show the opposite of worry with an if/then model of communication. If birds and flowers don't worry, then

14. I was reminded of the significance of *Aesop's Fables* in Mikeal Parsons, "Jesus the Fabulist? Jesus's Parables in Light of Aesop's Fables," W. C. Dobbs Endowed Lecture, Baylor University, George W. Truett Theological Seminary, April 22, 2025, available at https://youtu.be/S2eovtKJt6A.

you shouldn't either. If your illustration requires additional explanation, it's not an effective illustration. Illustrations should immediately make sense to the listeners.

Second, illustrations can connect the teaching of your subpoint with the real lives of your listeners. Without illustrations, our sermons become dry lectures imparting dry information. Illustrations also provide a purposeful mental reprieve from all the information we are communicating in the sermon. Some like to call lecture-style preaching an information dump or information overload. Illustrative material is highly beneficial in keeping your listeners engaged in the message. Illustrations need not be long or voluminous.

Third, illustrations help the sermon with recollection or recall. It's easier to remember a sermon that incorporates a few choice illustrations. The reality is our brains can only handle so much information at a time. Yes, our sermons should contain plenty of necessary exegetical information including history and culture, dates and figures, archaeology and artifacts; however, that same information will be easier to retain if we offer a memorable illustration. Our brains react well to stories or other forms of illustration.

Some words of caution when using illustrations: It's tempting, when you need a quick illustration, to explore books of illustrations or to do a quick search online. These books promise a plethora of a thousand or more illustrations. You might think: I've hit the sermon illustration jackpot! But not all sermon illustrations are created equal. Some examples and stories may be helpful, but others may not prove beneficial for use. The illustrations may be inaccurate, and the sources may be improperly cited, among other inconsistencies. While personal illustrations are often used because they are convenient, we can find illustrations in various places and sources, such as nature, a walk, an insightful quotation, history, music, art, language, science, sociology, literature, magazine articles, biblical references, and more.

Here are a few criteria for selecting illustrations. Illustrations do not have to be lengthy. They should, in fact, be brief. The temptation for any preacher is to elongate a story or example because it takes up pulpit time. Illustrations should be crisp and impactful.

Illustrations should also be factual and truthful. If you are looking up a statistic or something that can be verified, go the extra step and make sure what you are communicating is indeed a fact. Similarly, some preachers have been caught stealing and using the illustrations of others and employing them in first person as if that story had happened to them. Refrain from lying in the pulpit or even exaggerating.

Illustrations should be culturally appropriate. Not every illustration works for every ethnicity and culture. Check ahead of time if you are using an illustration that may be inappropriate or distasteful for someone of another cultural context. I've made some mistakes in this regard over the years by not inquiring beforehand if what I was going to use as an illustration would be misunderstood or hurtful to someone from a cultural background unfamiliar to me.

Finally, as a quick testimony, it's always helpful to pack a backup illustration (especially when preaching two or more services). I have had sermon illustrations that flopped in the first service and have needed to come up with another one before the next service(s). If you aren't sure how a sermon illustration will go, be prepared with a plan B or C.

Apply Your Verses (Corner C)

EXAMPLES OF APPLICATION (CORNER C)

What's the purpose of preaching a sermon if nothing and nobody changes? The purpose of a sermon application is to apply or practice in some way the eternal truths of God's Word and to look more like Christ. As Haddon W. Robinson explains, "Application gives expository preaching purpose."[15] More concretely, it is the point of transformation where we, as hearers of the Word, mature as disciples through obedience and Christlikeness. An application helps the listeners to know, to embody, to experience, to practice, to share, and to obey the transformational point and truth of God's Word as part of their discipleship journey.

A pet peeve of mine is when the sermon's application does not come directly from your sermon text. We don't cherry-pick applications from other parts of Scripture. The application derives from the biblical text on which you're preaching. The preacher, for example, preaches an entire message on Exodus 3, but then says, "How do we apply this? Turn with me to Philippians 3." No, the application comes directly from Exodus 3 and not another text. The secondary text might serve as an example or illustration of your main sermon text's application. However, the application should not derive from a secondary passage.

Another temptation or homiletical malpractice for any preacher is to preach the wrong application from the sermon text. Robinson memorably observed, "More heresy is preached in application than in Bible exegesis."[16]

15. See Robinson, *Biblical Preaching*, 10.

16. Haddon W. Robinson, "The Heresy of Application: It's When We're Applying Scripture That Error Most Likely Creeps In," in *The Art and Craft of Biblical Preaching: A Comprehensive*

Similarly, Robinson shares, "Inappropriate application can be as destructive as inept exegesis."[17] Sometimes, we insert faulty application in biblical narratives when we apply a biblical principle or moral to the story of what to do and what not to do, such as, "Dance like King David when you worship," or in the account of David and Bathsheba, "Don't go on the roof like King David did or bad things will happen." Both types of applications are not the proper applicational principle.

Then, what should an application aspire to be? Applications are often direct and tied directly to the text, such as in Proverbs 3:5–6. The applications are clear: "Trust in the Lord." "Lean not on your own understanding." "In all your ways submit to him." Sometimes the application is implied and not directly stated.

Here are a range of questions to help discern the sermon passage's application, moving from the individual believer to the corporate body of Christ. Often the text will provide more than one applicational response. Strike a balance between the two: individual and corporate.

Individual applications

- What does God want me to know?
- How is God asking me to respond?
- What is God asking me to be?
- What is God asking me to do?
- What is God asking me to give up?

Corporate applications

- What does God want the congregation to know?
- How is God asking the congregation to respond?
- What is God asking the congregation to be?
- What is God asking the congregation to do?
- What is God asking the congregation to give up?

To know how to specifically apply a passage involves knowing the people in the congregation. We'll talk in depth in chapter 18 about pastoring the people to whom we preach.

Resource for Today's Communicators, ed. Haddon W. Robinson and Craig Brian Larson (Zondervan, 2005), 306.

17. Robinson, *Biblical Preaching*, 11.

Repeat Your Transformational Point (Corner D)

By the time you've explained, illustrated, and applied your transformational point, it's a helpful reminder to you and your listeners to repeat the transformational point before you go to your conclusion or before you move on to your second main subpoint or move.

Telling the Story (The One-Point Narrative Sermon)

Another approach to the one-point transformational sermon is to tell the biblical story as your sermon. People love stories. People love to tell stories. People love to hear stories. Sometimes, as preachers, we forget to tell the story. In *Nourishing Narratives*, Jennifer L. Holberg observes, "But no matter what one's childhood—even if one was not or is not really much of a reader—we are *all* profoundly story-shaped people. We live in a world that, for better or worse, most often seems to process through narrative, not facts."[18]

A narrative sermon still has one transformational point. Your entire sermon will tell a story through the inductive approach that eventually makes the transformational point of the Scripture text. As you make your way through the story, you can explain, illustrate, and apply. Ultimately, you will state your transformational point toward the end of the message.

The Colonial (Two-Story Home): One Transformational Point with Two Main Subpoints or Sermonic Moves

The two-story home offers listeners one transformational point and two subpoints, or what homiletician David Buttrick refers to as sermonic "moves." Buttrick explains, "For years, preachers have talked about making *points* in sermons. The word 'point' is peculiar; it implies a rational, at-a-distance pointing at things, some kind of objectification. Of course, for many decades preachers did seem to suppose that there were fixed truths 'out there' to be talked about or pointed. Instead, we are going to speak of moves, of making moves in a *movement* of language."[19] The sermon only has one transformational point but the additional subpoints or moves help the sermon with its movement as it journeys toward a final destination. Sometimes these moves or subpoints will be building on another, expanding on the other, or contrasting the other (rarely) in nature.

18. Jennifer L. Holberg, *Nourishing Narratives: The Power of Story to Shape Our Faith* (InterVarsity, 2023), 3.

19. David Buttrick, *Homiletic: Moves and Structures* (Fortress, 1987), 23.

Figure 10.2. The colonial

Here's an example of a two-story sermon with two subpoints and ending with a transformational point. Some might consider this a three-point sermon but it's really two subpoints that lead to a transformational point.

Sermon Title: "What's Your Eau de Toilette?"[20]
Sermon Text: John 12:1–11 (see also Matt. 26:6–13;
Mark 14:3–9; Luke 7:36–50)

Introduction

1. **Move 1: When we worship Jesus, we don't calculate the cost** (vv. 1–5).
    A. Jesus received honor from his friends (vv. 1–2). [*Explain*]
    B. Mary's gift of worship was expensive (v. 3). [*Illustrate*]
        1. Nard or perfume was extraordinarily expensive in Jesus's day.
            a. Imperial Majesty is one of the most expensive perfumes today.
        2. The nard Mary offers was worth an entire year's salary.
    C. Judas calculated the cost of Mary's gift and sometimes we do too (vv. 4–5). [*Apply*]
        1. Here are examples where we tend to calculate the cost when giving to Jesus.
            a. We calculate the cost of our career.
            b. We calculate the cost of our home.
            c. We calculate the cost of our retirement.

20. Adapted from Matthew D. Kim, "What's Your Eau de Toilette? An Extravagant Example for an Extraordinary God," Preaching Today, https://www.preachingtoday.com/sermons/sermons/2023/march/whats-your-eau-de-toilette-extravagant-example-for-extraord.html. Used by permission.

d. We calculate the cost of our tithe.

e. We calculate the cost of our children.

D. When we worship Jesus, we don't calculate the cost. [*Repeat*]

(Transition: Judas seems to be charitable in his question, "Why wasn't this perfume sold and the money given to the poor?" But really, Judas was counting the cost because he wanted something. What was it that he wanted?)

2. **Move 2: When we worship Jesus, we don't expect something in return (v. 6).**

A. Judas wasn't interested in helping the poor. [*Explain*]

B. Judas wanted to use the money for his own gain. [*Illustrate*]

1. Illustration: A little girl gives her father $2.00.

2. Illustration: The Christian life is a paradox.

C. We give generously and freely because we want to give to others. [*Apply*]

D. When we worship Jesus, we don't expect something in return. [*Repeat*]

(Transition: When we worship Jesus, we don't count the cost or expect something in return. How else does Mary show the proper attitude toward worship?)

3. **Move 3: Transformational Point: When we worship Jesus, we don't count the cost or expect something in return, because Jesus is worth it (vv. 7–11).**[21]

A. Mary's gift shows us that we don't wait to worship Jesus (v. 7). [*Explain with subpoints A, B, and C*]

1. Mary is urgent in her act of worship.

2. Mary isn't concerned about her reputation.

B. Mary's gift shows us that Jesus is the most valuable person in this life (v. 8).

1. Caring for the poor will never end.

2. The poor are important but Jesus is most important.

C. Not everyone will recognize Jesus's worth (vv. 9–11).

21. Scott M. Gibson emphasizes using sermonic moves instead of sermonic points because there is only one point or "big idea" in the sermon. Gibson also refers to this sermonic movement as moving toward a "running homiletical idea" or preaching idea where each subpoint builds and combines into one major homiletical idea or point at the end of the sermon. This structure can be used to provide a framework for inductive sermons. Scott M. Gibson, Preaching: Principles and Practice Course, Gordon-Conwell Theological Seminary.

1. The chief priests wanted to kill Jesus and Lazarus.

D. Sometimes, we have a preoccupation with our reputations. [*Illustrate*]

E. What if we only had one month to live? [*Apply*]

F. When we worship Jesus, no gift is too precious, because Jesus is worth it. [*Repeat*]

(Transition: When we worship Jesus, we don't count the cost. We don't expect something in return. We don't hold anything back. So, what's your eau de toilette? What is your gift and act of worship to the Lord? What will you fully surrender to Christ?)

Conclusion

The Three-Level Home: One Transformational Point with Three Subpoints

A three-level or three-story home has one transformational point with three subpoints. The process will look very similar to the two-story colonial, except you will add an additional subpoint/move to the overall movement of the sermon. Here's an example from a sermon I preached on Matthew 6:19–24. The transformational point comes at the end.

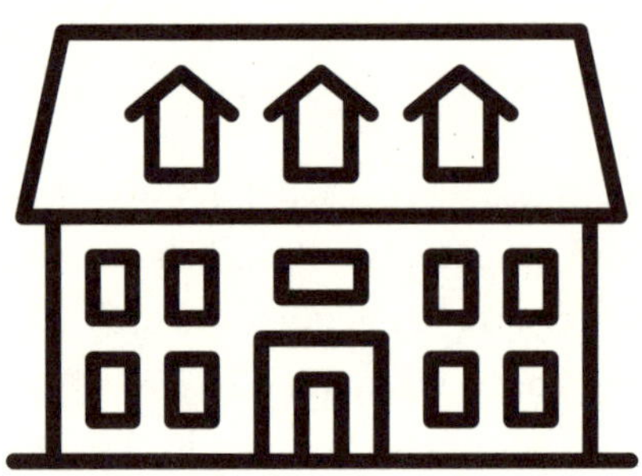

Figure 10.3. The three-story home

Introduction

1. Move 1: Earthly treasures are temporal so don't hoard them (v. 19).

A. Earthly treasures are temporal. [*Explain*]

1. They can be destroyed (moths).
2. They can be damaged (rust).
3. They can be stolen (thieves).

B. The earthly treasure is what we store up that we leave behind. [*Illustrate*]

1. We like to store up earthly treasures: home, cars, salary, vacation, position, financial investments, children, toys, gadgets, clothing, purses . . .
2. *Toy Story* the movie is a prime example of what happens when we hoard.

C. There is no end to our materialism. [*Apply*]

1. Hoarding leads to losing and not winning.

D. Earthly treasures are temporal so don't hoard them. [*Repeat*]

(Transition: We focus so much in this life on earthly treasures. If we don't hoard earthly treasures, what should we do instead?)

2. **Move 2: Heavenly treasures are eternal so build your heavenly bank account** (v. 20).

A. A heavenly treasure is anything we use to build up God's kingdom. [*Explain*]

1. Treasures in heaven are things that cannot be destroyed, damaged, or stolen.
2. We store up treasures in heaven because they have eternal value, like giving of time, resources, and talents.

B. The Bible speaks frequently of the consequences of hoarding versus giving. [*Illustrate*]

1. Proverbs 1:19 says, "Such are the paths of all who go after ill-gotten gain; it takes away the life of those who get it."
2. Acts 20:35 says, "In everything I did, I showed you that by this kind of hard work we must help the weak, remembering the words the Lord Jesus himself said: 'It is more blessed to give than to receive.'"

C. Name some ways to build your heavenly bank account. [*Apply*]

D. Heavenly treasures are eternal, so build your heavenly bank account. [*Repeat*]

(Transition: Why do we focus so much on earthly treasures?)

3. **Move 3: We treasure what's in our hearts** (vv. 21–23).

A. There is a direct connection between our treasure and our heart. [*Explain*]

1. "For where your treasure is, there your heart will be also."

2. Jesus speaks of this principle as "the eyes of the heart," which the religious leaders didn't understand.

B. What we treasure reflects our spiritual condition. [*Illustrate*]

1. "Our approach to money and possessions is central to our spiritual lives." From Randy Alcorn in *The Treasure Principle*.

C. List the things that you love and the things you like to look at. [*Apply*]

D. We treasure what's in our hearts. [*Repeat*]

(Transition: Since we treasure what's in our hearts, what is the pathway to be free from earthly treasures?)

4. Move 4: Transformational Point: Give freely because we cannot serve both God and money (v. 24).

A. Jesus says we cannot serve both God and money. [*Explain*]

1. The word for "serve" is also translated as "slave."

2. We can become a slave to God or a slave to money.

B. We place our hope in money or in God. [*Illustrate*]

C. When we're tempted to buy another treasure, consider buyer's remorse. [*Apply*]

1. Will I regret purchasing this item tomorrow?

2. However, will I regret giving to someone in real need?

D. Give freely because we cannot serve both God and money. [*Repeat*]

Conclusion

CONCLUSION

The sermon outline is a crucial step after determining a clear transformational point. Your sermon needs a purpose and a destination. If you are a beginning preacher, it may be helpful to get another pair of eyes on the outline. Get some feed-forward or feedback from an experienced preacher and ask them if the sermon outline is clear to them. Once you have written out a clear outline, the next step of biblical readiness is to point to the Trinity as you write the manuscript.

QUESTIONS

1. What does your process look like for outlining the sermon?
2. Are there any areas of the outlining process that have been particularly challenging for you? Why?
3. How can you develop in your sermon outlining?
4. When was the last time you received assistance from a more experienced preacher?

PRACTICES

1. This week, work on getting familiar with the outlining process. Take some notes on what you appreciated and didn't appreciate about the outlining process prescribed here.
2. Show your working outline or finished outline to a trusted preaching colleague. Ask them to be honest about its flow and clarity.

11

WRITE

Why Write Our Sermon Manuscript?

Whatever you do, do it from the heart for the Lord and not for people.

—Colossians 3:23 (CEB)

When I served as a youth pastor, preaching every Sunday, I thought it was good enough to write a skeletal outline of the sermon and not write out a full-length manuscript. As a busy seminarian, I didn't have time to bother with writing a full manuscript. That would take too long or be unnecessary, or so I thought. In short, I was being lazy. The problem is that when you're introverted and not always quick on your feet, the right words don't seem to fall gracefully from your lips.

I remember toward the end of my master of divinity program, I was encouraged by the preaching faculty to study for doctoral work in homiletics. My wife, who was then my fiancée, and I had an exhausting conversation one night that went something like this: "Sarah, I've been encouraged to do doctoral work in preaching. I was hoping that after we get married, we could move to Scotland so I could pursue a PhD in homiletics." To this, she bluntly replied: "Why would you want to do that? You're a terrible preacher."

After two years of listening to my sermons as a youth pastor, no less than one hundred sermons, my wife had heard her share of not-so-stellar messages. She kindly went on to explain that the ineffectiveness of my preaching stemmed from the fact that I didn't write out my sermons word for word. She was right. My weekly sermon preparation had consisted of conjuring up a few bullet points for an outline and then filling in the sermon content on the spot as I went along. What some have called shooting from the hip.

From day one at my church in Colorado, however, when I began my ministry as a senior pastor, I wrote a manuscript for every single sermon. Every single word. In fact, I wrote a manuscript any time and every time I did any form of preaching (even giving short devotionals). Sarah later commented on how writing a manuscript revolutionized my preaching for the better. Through the technical process of writing a manuscript and writing for the ear, I became a more effective preacher because I knew what I would say and I had taken the time to craft words for a specific group of listeners. I have carried this habit of writing a manuscript into academic work as well in preparing my lectures.

Step 8: Write the Manuscript

Writing the full manuscript, word for word, is step 8 of the sermonic process. In this chapter, we will consider what makes for an effective sermon manuscript and then I'll share a manuscript written from the outline shared in the previous chapter on John 12:1–11.

Clear Thinking

Alistair Begg, in his book *Preaching for God's Glory*, discloses his process for sermon preparation: "Think yourself empty, read yourself full, write yourself clear, pray yourself hot, and be yourself, but don't preach yourself."[1] Let's concentrate on the third element here, write yourself clear. I have found that the most significant reward of writing down every single word in my sermon manuscript is facilitating clarity of thought. A question every preacher must ask is, Am I being clear to my listeners?

By writing a sermon manuscript, we can trace the flow of the message by reading sequentially through each sentence and each paragraph. If we stumble over words or find ourselves pausing, that means something is unclear. We can read it and reread it aloud and determine if it is clear or fuzzy. Begg explains, "When we take the time to commit not only our thoughts but our sentences and paragraphs and linking phrases to paper, we will quickly detect the *non*

1. Alistair Begg, *Preaching for God's Glory* (Crossway, 2011), 50–64.

sequiturs and be able to make corrections long before we are presenting the material in a public forum."[2]

James S. Stewart, the well-known Scottish preacher, tells of an exchange that took place between a young preacher and Dr. Joseph Parker of City Temple regarding sermon feedback. When the young minister shared his concern that his own preaching was "producing only apathy," Dr. Parker replied, "I think I can tell you what is the matter. For the last half hour you have been trying to get something out of your head instead of something into mine!"[3] Clarity of thought in a sermon comes intentionally from the rigorous process of writing and rewriting as well as placing and re-placing. Clarity happens before we enter the pulpit and not after.

Clear Structure

After reading through the manuscript, we can assess whether the entire structure of the message is smooth, rough, or hazy. There have been several times over my preaching ministry when I've found that either the structure could be reorganized or I needed to remove a paragraph and add another. It is only through having an entire manuscript in front of us, a true give-and-take process, that we can make that determination. Even a polished outline can only give us so much information on the clarity of our organization. When words fill the paragraph and the page, we can visually locate areas that are lacking.

Pastoral Tone

Writing the manuscript aids us in evaluating our tone, specifically our pastoral tone. One of the major cautions against communicating via email or text is that we cannot hear the tone of the messenger. By pastoral tone, I am referring to speaking in a way that is loving, encouraging, warm, and uplifting, rather than yelling or diminishing. As Paul writes to Timothy, "Preach the word; be prepared in season and out of season; correct, rebuke and encourage—with great patience and careful instruction" (2 Tim. 4:2). The Greek words that stand out to me here are great patience or *pasē makrothymia*. *Pase* can be translated as "complete" or "all." Depending on our spiritual condition, it's easy to preach with exasperation. We can become accusatory or hostile in our tone rather than pastoral and loving. Reading through the manuscript aloud gives us an opportunity to hear the words spoken and the tone in which they are conveyed.

2. Begg, *Preaching for God's Glory*, 54.
3. Story shared by Begg in *Preaching for God's Glory*, 54.

Write to Be Heard, Not Read

A key difference between writing a sermon manuscript and writing a paper is that we are, as preachers, writing for aural (hearing/audible) communication and not for visual or optical communication. What's the difference? Sermons are meant to be heard, even if they are sometimes read. So, this requires a mental paradigm shift because we are writing for listeners and not for readers.

Think of it as writing in a conversational style. In a formal paper, you wouldn't begin with, "Hey church, how's everyone doing today? It's so good to see you at worship!" In a sermon manuscript, however, I might say something quite informally in that exact manner. In oral communication, we often use contractions like "isn't" and "wouldn't" rather than in a formal paper that elongates the words as "is not" and "would not." Oral communication is also repetitive, which means if I want to emphasize a statement or question I will write it twice or thrice. That doesn't happen in formal research papers. So, in many ways, we are retraining our minds to write in a way that's easier on the ears.

Every preacher has a different experience level and gifts when it comes to writing. Some of us are more natural writers who have the facility to "turn a phrase" or compose sentences in a pleasing manner. For others, it's a chore and challenging. No matter our starting place, I want to encourage you to keep honing your weekly craft. After you have written a first draft of the manuscript, read it over and take just twenty to thirty minutes and ask yourself if there are any places where you could say something more creatively or illustratively. Work on using active, strong verbs and creating word pictures or images. Do the best you can. It's a process for all of us to develop as writers. Ask the Holy Spirit to help you say something more compellingly and interestingly.

Think of Manuscripting as Filling in Your Outline

Rather than thinking of writing the manuscript as an altogether different part of the sermonic process, it might be useful to think of it as filling in the outline. Take your existing outline, as you've written it, and fill it in underneath the corresponding transformational point and moves. Each move or subpoint might include one or more paragraphs to fully explain, illustrate, and apply. Indent each subpoint and sub-subpoint to know where you are in the manuscript. I'll show you an example from my previous outline on John 12:1–11.

Sermon Title: "What's Your Eau de Toilette?"[4]
Sermon Text: John 12:1–11 (see also Matt. 26:6–13; Mark 14:3–9; Luke 7:36–50)

Introduction

If you had one opportunity to show Jesus how much you loved him, what would you do? What might you say? What offering might you bring? One of my favorite songs of all time is Mercy Me's "I Can Only Imagine." The songwriter invites the listener to envision what it will be like when we first encounter Jesus face-to-face in eternity. We don't have to wait for glory to free our imagination. Perhaps you can do a little exercise now: Fill in the blank. I can only imagine that when I see Jesus I will _______.

Let's read John 12:1–11 together.

As we just read, what might you have done if you were Mary Magdalene? Like Mary, what would you do if you had one chance, one shot at showing Jesus how much you loved him? Here, in this passage, Jesus is approaching the last week of his earthly ministry. As we've seen throughout the Gospel of John, John is giving us a wide-angle, panoramic view of who Jesus is. Most importantly, John drills down to show us that Jesus is God. Jesus is the Messiah and the Savior of the world.

We come to a familiar story where Jesus is honored in the form of a dinner celebration. He's at the home of Martha and Mary. We have come to appreciate from previous passages that they were Jesus's close friends. How does Mary demonstrate her love and devotion to Jesus?

1. **Move 1. When we worship Jesus, we don't count the cost (vv. 1–5).**

   A. Jesus received honor from his friends (vv. 1–2). [*Explain*]

   The story we are reading is so important to the Gospel writers that it is also described by Matthew and Mark. In this event, referred to by some as "The Anointing at Bethany,"[5] we see that Jesus's public ministry has concluded. He's spent three years pouring his heart out to his disciples and teaching the crowds about the kingdom of God. And we come to this momentous occasion where Jesus receives respect and honor from some of his closest disciples, Lazarus, Martha, and Mary.

4. Adapted from Matthew D. Kim, "What's Your Eau de Toilette? An Extravagant Example for an Extraordinary God," Preaching Today, https://www.preachingtoday.com/sermons/sermons/2023/march/whats-your-eau-de-toilette-extravagant-example-for-extraord.html. Used by permission.

5. Andreas J. Köstenberger, *John*, Baker Exegetical Commentary on the New Testament (Baker Academic, 2004), 357.

At that time, there was no dinner table as we know it. People didn't sit on chairs. They didn't sit on the floor. So, what did they do? They reclined at the table. Essentially, what that looks like is that they lay down on something like a sofa, leaning on one arm while eating with the free hand.

In verse two, Lazarus was conversing at the table with Jesus as Martha is serving the food. If you remember from Luke 10:38–42, Jesus was also hanging out at Martha and Mary's home. On that occasion, Martha was frantically preparing food for Jesus. Rather than keeping the meal simple,[6] she came to the point of exhaustion preparing this meal. What was her sister Mary doing though? She was learning at Jesus's feet. Jesus taught her the Word of God. At the end of Jesus's public ministry, Martha is busy serving again. And her seemingly slacker sister Mary enters the room.

B. Mary's gift of worship was expensive (v. 3). [*Illustrate*]

1. Nard or perfume was extraordinarily expensive in Jesus's day.

Verse 3 says, "Then Mary took about a pint of pure nard, an expensive perfume; she poured it on Jesus's feet and wiped his feet with her hair. And the house was filled with the fragrance of the perfume." Back then, people didn't invest their retirement savings in the stock market, a 501K, IRA, TIAA-CREF, or any other interest account. They didn't have Charles Schwab, Fidelity Investments, or E-Trade. What they had was nard. That sounds gross, doesn't it? You just picture this clump of fat. Well, that's the image that comes to my mind, anyway.

For most people in the ancient world, they placed much value in fragrances, perfumes, and oils. Stores like Bath and Body Works or Ulta Beauty would've been very popular back then as well. We can only guess that the reason why perfume was so valuable was because people didn't take showers very often. Also, water supply for baths was hard to come by. They lived in the hot sticky desert and didn't wash themselves frequently. That can be a "lethal" combination.

Nard was an extremely expensive commodity. What is nard? Nard, or spikenard as they called it, was an aromatic plant not grown locally in Israel. If you wanted some nard, you had to get it from Arabia,

6. An allusion to Haddon W. Robinson's sermon, "Don't Just Do Something, Sit There," February 14, 1991, preached at Gordon-Conwell Theological Seminary chapel, available at https://youtu.be/Sz5A2YaAsZw.

Iran, India, or elsewhere. It was imported. You know that imports are expensive.

So, we see that Mary brings a pint of pure nard into the dining room. A pint is 16 fluid ounces. If you go to any department store, you can't buy a pint of perfume. Those who like to put a dab of fragrance on their necks know that most such fragrances come in bottles of 1.6 or 3.4 fluid ounces. Mary had her entire life savings in this bottle.

2. Imperial Majesty is one of the most expensive perfumes today.

Most perfumes and colognes cost about $40–$100. But on Forbes .com I found out that the most expensive perfume in the world is called "Imperial Majesty," which costs $215,000 a bottle.

Here's the description of this supposedly exquisite scent: Imperial Majesty is a limited edition of a Clive Christian signature scent. Sold simply as No. 1, the fragrance is priced at $2,150 an ounce. But the reason Imperial Majesty costs so much is that Christian, a British designer-turned-perfumer, poured 16.9 ounces of No. 1 into a Baccarat crystal bottle, stuck a five-carat diamond into the 18-carat gold collar, and unveiled it at Harrods in London and Bergdorf Goodman in New York City.

3. The nard Mary offers was worth an entire year's salary.

To Mary, her nard is the equivalent of Imperial Majesty. This is her life fortune. She has only one opportunity to show Jesus how much she values him, how much she worships him, how much she loves him. So, what does she do? She pours the entire bottle on his feet and wipes it off with her hair. It seems strange, doesn't it? Why would someone in her right mind do such a thing?

To Mary, when she worshiped Jesus, she didn't calculate the cost. It didn't matter to her. What mattered most was worshiping Jesus Christ, her Lord and Savior, with everything that she had. She gave Jesus every drop of this expensive perfume for no other reason than to prove her love and worship to her "Imperial Majesty," the Lord Jesus Christ.

C. Judas calculated the cost of Mary's gift and sometimes we do too (vv. 4–5). [*Apply*]

This bothered Judas in particular. Judas Iscariot was Jesus's disciple who later betrays him. He knew about nice things because all he cared about was money. And, in verse five, Judas tells us that what Mary has in her hands is worth an average worker's entire yearly salary. The US Department of Labor decided that the minimum wage in the US would be $7.25. If you make minimum wage, your annual income will be approximately $14,000–$15,000. We don't know exactly how much this perfume would cost, but it's probably a lot more than $15,000.

What does this Bible lesson mean for us today? Does not calculating the cost of offering worship to Jesus mean we give our life savings to the church? No. Not necessarily. I don't think there's a direct correlation.

This passage is more descriptive than prescriptive. It describes Mary's act of devotion without prescribing the same example for us. However, Mary's example gives us the biblical principle that when it comes to worshiping Jesus, there must be a willingness in our hearts to abandon every earthly thing to follow him. If we truly love Jesus and desire to worship him with our lives, we won't calculate what we may have to give up to follow him. We'll give of ourselves joyfully and freely just as Mary does here. When we worship Jesus, we don't calculate the cost. Sometimes, if we're honest, we do calculate, don't we?

1. Here are examples where we calculate the cost when giving to Jesus.

   What is the most valuable thing to you that you would have much difficulty giving up to worship Jesus and show how much you love him? Just think about that for a moment. Do we calculate the cost of following Jesus? Would we withhold our careers? Our homes? Our cars? Our retirement savings? Our tithes and offerings? Our TVs? Our children? Our time? Our convenience?

D. When we worship Jesus, we don't count the cost. [*Repeat*]

(Transition: Judas seems to be charitable in his question, "Why wasn't this perfume sold and the money given to the poor?" But really, Judas was counting the cost because he wanted something. What was it that he wanted?)

2. Move 2. When we worship Jesus, we don't expect something in return (v. 6).

A. Judas wasn't interested in helping the poor. [*Explain*]

In any human relationship or friendship, we innately desire a give-and-take experience. That's the only natural human response. If we only give, we feel cheated. Yet, if we only take, I would hope that we would feel guilty before the person who is always giving us something.

Judas was probably one of those guys who only received *from others*. He didn't give *to others*. John calls Judas a thief, meaning he would help himself to the offering. He would secretly withhold money and use it for himself. He was selfish and self-interested. He didn't *really* care about the poor. His private motive was to snatch the funds from selling Mary's perfume and use it for his own devices.

B. Judas wanted to use the money for his own gain. [*Illustrate*]

1. Illustration: A little girl gives her father $2.00.

I once heard a story about a little girl who was given two dollars by her father. He told her that she could do anything she wanted with one and that the other was to be given to God on Sunday at church. The girl nodded in agreement and asked if she could go to the candy store. With visions of all that she could buy with her dollar, she happily skipped toward the store, holding tightly to the two dollars in her hand. As she was skipping along, she tripped and fell and the wind blew one of the dollars into a storm drain at the curb. Picking herself up, the little girl looked at the dollar still in her hand and then at the storm drain and said, "Well, God, there goes your dollar." We often live by the following principle: Me first. God, you second, third, or fourth.

2. Illustration: The Christian life is a paradox.

Many Christians have forgotten that Christianity is paradoxical. To the world, Jesus's teachings don't make sense. Jesus calls us to an other-worldly and profoundly upside-down life. For instance, Jesus says things like: The last shall be first and the first shall be last. Those who have little on earth will be rich in heaven and those who have much on earth will have little in heaven. Jesus uses uneducated fishermen to become disciples who bring the gospel to the world. Much of Christianity doesn't make worldly sense.

C. We give generously and freely because we want to give to others. [*Apply*]

The same principle holds true here. When we worship Jesus, we don't expect something in return. There's a Latin phrase, quid pro quo. It means "this for that." God, I'll give you $5 if you'll give me back $10. God, I'll give you fifteen minutes for my daily devotional, but I want to do as I please for the rest of the day.

This type of mentality permeates the church at large. It's seen in what others have called the prosperity gospel, the health and wealth gospel, or the name it and claim it gospel. We want to be fed, but we don't want to fast.

This is not the attitude of a generous giver that Jesus had in mind for his disciples. We give to Jesus and others because we love him and them.

As it says in 1 John 4:19, "We love because he first loved us." We come to church because we want to worship him. We share our tithes and offerings because we want to be a blessing to expand God's kingdom. We give our time and resources to those in need because Jesus says it's better to give than to receive (Acts 20:35 and other places).

John sets up a clear contrast. Judas got it wrong, but Mary got it right. Mary's heart is a true disciple's heart. She gave to Jesus without expecting anything in return. I wonder what would happen in our church if we possessed more of Mary's heart.

D. When we worship Jesus, we don't expect something in return. [*Repeat*] (Transition: When we worship Jesus, we don't calculate the cost or expect something in return. How else does Mary show the proper attitude toward worship?)

3. **Move 3. Transformational Point: When we worship Jesus, we don't count the cost or expect something in return, because Jesus is worth it (vv. 7–11).**

A. Mary's gift shows us that we don't wait to worship Jesus (v. 7). [*Explain with subpoints A, B, and C*]

1. Mary is urgent in her act of worship.

How did Jesus respond to Mary's extravagant example? Jesus defends her against Judas's insincere question. He is stern: "Leave her alone." And then he says something peculiar: "It was intended that she should save this perfume for the day of my burial."

Mary most likely was saving this perfume for Jesus's burial and not for this dinner party. It was common practice to use perfume in the embalming process to help with the odor of bodily decay. But, here in this story, it was a powerful gesture to honor Jesus while he was still living.

2. Mary isn't concerned about her reputation.

Mary worships Jesus without holding anything back. She is in many ways reckless in her worship. She doesn't care about what others think of her. The only opinion that matters to her is what Jesus thinks of her. And clearly Jesus is pleased with her worship and sacrifice.

B. Mary's gift shows us that Jesus is the most valuable person in this life (v. 8).

Then, in verse eight, Jesus says something even more bizarre. He says, "You will always have the poor among you, but you will not always have me." Does that mean Jesus doesn't care about the poor? Absolutely not.

Jesus cares greatly for the poor. He frequently mentions and ministers to those with physical needs.

1. Caring for the poor will never end.

So, what is he saying then? He's stating that giving to the poor will never end. But, you won't have many opportunities left to worship me. In fact, for Lazarus, Mary, and Martha, Palm Sunday is tomorrow, marking the final week of Jesus's earthly life and ministry.

2. The poor are important, but Jesus is most important.

Since Jesus isn't here physically anymore, what does that mean for us today? Do we have to do extravagant things for Jesus to be pleased with us? I don't think so. We can't make a direct correlation between what Mary did and what we are to do.

C. Not everyone will recognize Jesus's worth (vv. 9–11).

1. The chief priests wanted to kill Jesus and Lazarus.

When we fail to recognize something's or someone's worth, it's easy for us to think they are discardable. Sadly, in our sinful world, even people who make life more difficult for us become dispensable in our minds. For the chief priests, Jesus and Lazarus were a problem they needed to solve, to get rid of.

D. Sometimes, we have a preoccupation with our reputations. [*Illustrate*]

In Europe, one way Christians tried to please God was to build him extravagant buildings. If you travel to many parts of Europe, the cathedrals built for God are magnificent. Think of St. Peter's Basilica in Rome, St. Paul's Cathedral in London, or Notre-Dame de Paris. They are usually ornate and laden with gold and precious stones.

Is that what Jesus wants from us? I don't think so. So, what is our eau de toilette? How are we going to show Jesus how much we love him?

E. What if we only had one month to live? [*Apply*]

Years ago, a book that caught my eye at Barnes and Noble was called *One Month to Live* by Pastor Kerry Shook. He serves as senior pastor of Woodlands Church near Houston, Texas. He asks readers to consider some profound questions such as: What if you only had one month to live? How would you make each day meaningful? How would you relate to others differently? What would you do to make the rest of your life really count?

Truth is, we often avoid thinking about our mortality. Shook emphasizes that if we spent the rest of our lives living as if we only had one month to live, it would dramatically transform every part of our lives. It would help us reprioritize. We would focus on what's most important to God and advancing the Great Commission and the Great Commandments.

I think what Jesus is asking us to do is surrender our lives to him completely. Jesus wants our lives, every part of our lives. He wants to be the Lord of everything. Every part of our life should be worship to God. When we worship Jesus, we shouldn't hold anything back. We should give him our best.

When my brothers and I went to church growing up, my dad would go to the bank and go to the teller to get brand-new one-dollar bills for us to give as offering to the Lord. I used to think that it was silly. Why does the condition of the dollar bill matter? But, as I've grown up, I appreciate my dad's example. Jesus wants us to give him our best in everything. It may or may not matter to Jesus. I'm sure not many of us are going to ask Jesus whether he appreciated the crinkle-free money we put in the offering basket. However, when we worship Jesus, no gift is too precious. Nothing is wasted when we offer our best to him.

F. When we worship Jesus, no gift is too precious, because Jesus is worth it. [*Repeat*]
(Transition: When we worship Jesus, we don't count the cost. We don't expect something in return. We don't hold anything back. So, what's your eau de toilette? What is your gift and act of worship to the Lord? What will you fully surrender to Christ?)

Conclusion

I want to challenge us today concerning our attitudes, especially about worship. Are we giving the triune God our best worship every Sunday? Are we truly living a Christlike life? Can you imagine a church where everyone worshiped God without holding anything back? How can we ask the Holy Spirit to help us worship him with every part of our lives? Wouldn't it change the world around us?

Today, our focus is on worshiping Jesus, worshiping God the Father, through the help of God the Spirit. Mary gives us an extravagant example. But how can we worship Jesus with more reverence, passion, and joy? Let's start with praise. Can you imagine a church where everyone sang their hearts out to God? We can express through song how much we love him. We can sing passionately from the depths of our hearts. That is our offering of praise to him. Can we do that as a church? Can we sing to the Lord with all our heart, soul, mind, and strength?

Can we serve this congregation using the unique gifts that God has given each person, whether it's cleaning, teaching, cooking, welcoming, inviting, gathering, leading, or encouraging?

This is not to induce guilt, but what about coming to church on time? I know that people don't like hearing about this, but it's something that we must discuss as a church family. I want to challenge us to give God our best in all parts of worship even in our timeliness. I want to challenge us as a church to come fifteen minutes early and quiet our hearts to worship God. When we're always late, it can mean subconsciously that we don't value God enough to set this time apart for him. Let's start coming to church earlier and showing Jesus that we truly value him.

Finally, how do we spend our time? Can we make God the highest priority of our lives? Can we spend time with him? Can we read the Word throughout the week? Can we spend time in prayer, asking the Spirit to strengthen our prayer lives? Can we truly worship Jesus daily? Can we serve sacrificially the people God sends our way? Can we ask the Spirit to help us build relationships with people in our neighborhoods, schools, workplaces, and more?

There's a poem by Theodore W. Brennan called "Those Wasted Years" that I'd like to share with you:

> I looked upon a farm one day, that once I used to own;
> The barn had fallen to the ground, the fields were overgrown.
> The house in which my children grew, where we had lived for years . . .
> I turned to see it broken down, and brushed aside the tears.
> I looked upon my soul one day to find it too had grown,
> With thorns and nettles everywhere, the seeds neglect had sown.
> The years had passed while I had cared for things of lesser worth.
> The things of heaven I let go while minding things of earth.
> To Christ I turned with bitter tears and cried, "O Lord, forgive!"
> I have not much time left for Thee, not many years to live.
> The wasted years forever gone, the days I can't recall.
> If I could live those days again, I'd make Him Lord of all.

A slew of questions may be circulating in your brain: Is this necessary? Do I really have to give something to Jesus? Isn't that promoting moralism or simply behavior modification? Aren't grace and forgiveness free? Yes, salvation is a free gift. And those who experience Christ's mercy and forgiveness cannot help but give their entire lives to him.

So, what's your eau de toilette? Is Jesus your Lord of all? How will you demonstrate how much you love him? Would you give everything to have Jesus, or would you trade Jesus to have everything in the world?

John 12:1–11 communicates a profound message. If we truly understood who Jesus is and what he's done for us, we would give everything to worship him. We would have different values and priorities. We would spend our time and money differently. We would love God and people more intentionally. When we worship Jesus, there is no gift too precious. He's worth more than we could ever give in response to him.

Can we start offering Jesus our best worship? Can we spend time with him during the week? Can we allow him to have control over every area of our lives? Can we relinquish every earthly thing and prioritize the kingdom of God?

The truth is: We only get one life to live. Unlike cats, which have nine lives, we only get one. We only have one life to make a difference in this world. Let's make it count for Christ. When we worship Jesus, we don't count the cost or expect something in return, because Jesus is worth it.

Step 9: Point to the Trinity

The ninth step of the sermon developmental process is to point your listeners to the Trinity. As you write your sermon manuscript, go back and find a place where you can point to each person of the Trinity—if you haven't done so already. As we spelled out in chapter 4, we are going to identify how each member of the Trinity fits into your sermon text this week. We won't mention each member of the Godhead in every single line, paragraph, or subpoint, but let's try at least once per message. Even if one or more members of the Trinity is not mentioned by name, we can use our exegetical study to think through how each member of the Godhead plays an active role in this sermon (refer to chapter 4 under "Identifying the Trinity at Work" for a refresher).

In this process, I'm asking you to consider how God the Father, God the Son, and God the Spirit inform and transform listeners. Our role as preachers is to facilitate Christlikeness in our congregation by explaining, envisioning, equipping, encouraging, and empowering them to be obedient to Scripture and live more like Jesus in every way.

Where in your sermon can you point to each member of the Godhead either as a primary character in the text or working behind the scenes to cultivate your discipleship and Christlikeness? The foundation of every biblical sermon is a robust and clear theology communicated to the congregation by highlighting the centrality of the Trinity. What does this text say about the triune God, and how does each member of the Trinity transform and empower God's people in living out the truth of the text?

Earlier, in chapter 1, we discussed the salience of knowing God more concretely and experientially through our Scripture text. We asked the following questions about the text on which we are preaching: (1) What has God done (in my Scripture text)? (2) What are God's names? (3) What will God do (his promises)? How can some of these elements be incorporated into our sermon manuscript? This is how we can regularly introduce our congregation to the triune God in each sermon. Take your observations from studying each member of the Trinity in your sermon text and share those findings with your church.

CONCLUSION

Writing out the full manuscript may seem like an unnecessary exercise in an already crowded week. However, nothing helps our preaching precision and clarity more than working on this vital step. I have yet to regret writing out the manuscript. I have regretted failing to do so.

Here's a quick and hopefully useful tip: If you are a verbal processor, writing a manuscript might be best accomplished by speaking into an app or on your computer, where dictation is possible. You don't have to suffer silently at your desk staring at a blank document. Speak your sermon, and have it transcribed for you as you go along.

Preaching isn't just a hodgepodge of exegetical material that magically becomes a clear message. It's an intentionally organized, well-conceived, well-blueprinted opportunity to speak into the lives of the people God has entrusted to us to love and to serve. Writing a manuscript each week does require time, lots of time, depending on the text. However, don't shortchange your listeners because you don't want to put in the effort. Make the time, keep the time, say no to those wanting to encroach on that time, and be laser focused during that time. It will be worth it for yourself and for those to whom you preach.

QUESTIONS

1. How do you feel about writing a manuscript?
2. What has been your practice in terms of writing a full manuscript?
3. Do you have any reservations about writing a manuscript?
4. What would most help you to be able to write a manuscript each week?

PRACTICES

1. Once you have written out your sermon outline, try to fill in the manuscript for this upcoming Sunday's sermon.
2. Remember, you don't have to write the sermon manuscript in one sitting. Once your outline is complete, write the manuscript over a course of one or two days.
3. In chapter 20, we will rehearse or practice reading and internalizing the sermon manuscript, with additional tips on how that can be accomplished consistently.

PART 3

Culturally Ready

Cultural readiness is a critical step in sermonic development because we need to know the people to whom we preach. Sermons should be tailored for those gathered in the worship space. This third part, on being culturally ready, equips preachers to know our people better, to introduce the gospel regularly in our sermons, and to think more concretely about discipling our listeners through the proclamation of the Word. In terms of writing style, you might envision the rest of the book (parts 3–5) as us sitting together in my backyard roasting s'mores over a warm fire while we talk.

12

LISTENERS

Who Is Hearing Our Sermons?

> To the weak I became weak, to win the weak. I have become all things to all people so that by all possible means I might save some.
>
> —1 Corinthians 9:22

The joy and challenge of any preaching ministry is that we preach to real people, real listeners. Listeners embody various cultures. It is for this reason that we shouldn't preach the exact same sermon in every location, place, and time. For any aspiring and seasoned preacher, "Who are my listeners?" is a question as equally significant as "What am I preaching about?" A sermon is a unique word that is prepared and written for a particular community of believers, whether that's in a local church, at a church camp, or perhaps while preaching to a group outdoors.

The reality of ministry life is that we cannot hand select those who attend our churches. Even if we could choose them, a sermon will still require contextualization or tailoring for the specialized group of listeners God sends our way. That being the case, there are several different types of people we want to become better familiar with as they hear us. In this chapter, we will identify groups of listeners and provide some strategies for understanding the people to whom we preach.

The Myth of the Monocultural Church

Homogeneity gives preachers the optical illusion and false impression that "everyone in my church is the same, so I don't need to contextualize my sermons." Whenever there is a clear majority demographic, it's convenient for the preacher to tell themselves: We look alike, think alike, believe alike, behave alike, and so on, based on racial congruity. While some congregations may be racially homogeneous, there are various kinds of diversity to consider if we look beyond the surface.

The notion of a monocultural church is a myth. Years ago, there was a movement called the Homogeneous Unit Principle (HUP) that suggested that churches grow fastest when they remain one racial culture. The original architect of the HUP, Donald A. McGavran, argued, "People like to become Christians without crossing racial, linguistic, or class barriers."[1] In certain pockets of Christianity, crossing such barriers may very well be impossible, especially regarding racial diversity. However, no congregation is completely monocultural because underneath the surface there are numerous subcultures within every congregation. To better equip ourselves for crossing those barriers, we want to grow in developing cultural intelligence or CQ. If you would like to explore this topic further, refer to my book *Preaching with Cultural Intelligence*, also published by Baker Academic.[2]

CQ Preaching Is Loving Preaching

I have found over the years that preaching with cultural intelligence is not an academic exercise but merely an expression of pastoral love. Rather than thinking that we have to develop cultural intelligence as part of our job description in order to preach more effectively, we want to think of cultural intelligence in preaching as an act of love for our people to get to know them better. Granted, it's not easy to love people, especially with all of their complexities and idiosyncrasies. Yet, enhancing one's cultural intelligence is part of what it means to be an effective pastoral shepherd and leader. Nobody wants to feel like they are just a "project" for their preacher to develop a particular skill. We want to cultivate our cultural intelligence as a way to love people from the pulpit.

The intertwining questions we need to ask ourselves are: Who's hearing our sermons, and do we know them? In this chapter, we'll consider the concept of

1. Donald A. McGavran, *Understanding Church Growth*, 3rd ed., ed. C. Peter Wagner (Eerdmans, 1990), x.

2. See Matthew D. Kim, *Preaching with Cultural Intelligence: Understanding the People Who Hear Our Sermons* (Baker Academic, 2017).

cultural intelligence and how it helps us better contextualize our messages for our listeners. As this process may overwhelm some, we'll limit our discussion to the following forms of diversity: biblical literacy, cultural, economic, educational, ethnic/racial, gender, generational, geographical, marital, political, religious, special needs, spiritual, and theological diversities. While space limitations prevent us from going deeply into each context, I will briefly bring to consciousness how each of these distinct forms of diversity factors into our sermons.

Biblical Literacy

Let's start with biblical literacy since we are Bible preachers. Of course, it seems obvious that a congregation will have varying levels of biblical literacy represented across the worship space. The number of people who read their Bibles continues to plummet year by year. According to one statistic, those who read or listen to their Bible at least four times a year outside of a worship setting is only 66 percent among those who attend church in person.[3] That means among churchgoers, 34 percent are opening or listening to their Bibles less than four times *per year* of their own accord. That's an alarmingly low number.

So, what can be done about it from the pulpit? Instead of scolding our listeners, make the Bible come alive for them from your weekly preaching ministry. Mike Burnette encourages, "Expository preaching can help spark an interest in Bible reading. . . . The goal is to create a hunger for God's Word, so congregants will want to engage with it daily. . . . Preaching through entire books makes it easier for people to see the big picture. . . . Model love for God's Word. As a leader, your passion for Scripture is contagious. In your sermons, on social media, and during conversations, share how God is speaking to you through your personal Bible study."[4] As preachers, we can help change the congregational attitudes toward the Bible. Recognize that there is a plurality of experiential knowledge when it comes to biblical literacy. We cannot assume that everyone knows the basics, even naming a few of the Ten Commandments—let alone knowing what they mean—in our sermons.

Culture

Generally speaking, cultural diversity can represent an infinite number of possibilities. We might think of culture more concretely as two groups: majority

3. Mike Burnette, "Igniting Passion for Scripture: How to Grow Bible Engagement Through Preaching," *Influence Magazine* (Winter 2025), 88.

4. Burnette, "Igniting Passion for Scripture," 89–90.

culture and minority cultures. Every congregation possesses a critical mass of people from one primary, overarching demographic. For instance, if you are pastoring a predominantly white American congregation, the majority culture in your church is that of white American culture and all that that represents. You will also have congregants who are not white Americans and who may retain their national culture of origin, such as that of Spain or Uganda. You will have a third pocket of people who are bicultural or multicultural, who may be American culturally but with a mixture of other cultural traditions and practices. The panorama of cultures emphasizes different foci in what people value and believe, how they see the world, and how they operate.

Economics

The demographic of class in our congregations is probably seldom discussed in open conversations. And yet, economic class is a visible form of diversity in every church. Congregations have worshipers who are living in poverty as well as members of the upper echelons of society, so the way we speak about money in our sermons matters. The location where we worship and where our congregation meets will attract different segments of the population. One way we can demonstrate cultural intelligence is to not assume people come from a specific income bracket and to be able to speak in such a way that everyone can feel included in the sermon. I have found this particularly true in wealthier congregations, where the pastor might speak of everyone taking certain vacations or eating at certain restaurants. Those who have less will feel marginalized rather than have a sense of belonging.

Education

Another area of diversity in our congregational membership concerns educational backgrounds. If we are ministering in a college town or in an urban setting near universities, we might make a comment that presupposes that everyone has experienced college. Words like, "Remember senior year of college when you . . ." though statistically only about half of your congregation has earned a four-year college degree.[5] It used to be commonplace that only people from older generations did not attend university. Today, age plays a smaller role in who goes to college, since many younger people don't

5. Michael T. Nietzel, "Percentage of Adults with College Degree Hits New High, Finds Lumina," *Forbes*, January 30, 2025, https://www.forbes.com/sites/michaeltnietzel/2025/01/30/percentage-of-adults-with-college-degree-hits-new-high-finds-lumina.

find pursuing a college degree compelling or worthwhile. Using illustrations and examples from college or even from the world of literature and the arts may not resonate with our listeners. So, it's best to assume that you have a hodgepodge of listeners who may or may not have a college degree and especially a postgraduate degree.

Ethnicity and Race

The most obvious form of diversity in our congregations is racial diversity (ethnic diversity is a close second). It is not good enough just to sit next to someone of a different race/ethnicity from you in a worship gathering. Diverse friendships and discipleship partnerships with those who look different from us is the goal, not simply attending the same church. Pastors can model intentionally crossing racial barriers to welcome those who are different from them. In her bestseller, *Why Are All the Black Kids Sitting Together in the Cafeteria?*, educator Beverly Daniel Tatum addresses this noticeable attitude of majority persons who fail to cross the room to make a connection with someone of another race/ethnicity.[6] The onus is on the pastor to take the first step and greet a visitor or congregant of a different race/ethnicity.[7] This cross-racial relationship will only deepen our discipleship and our preaching ministries.

Gender

It used to be the case that preachers would see more women at church than men. However, recent studies have shown that there has been an exodus of females leaving the church primarily due to various forms of unequal treatment, church hurt, misogyny, harassment, and disillusionment with the church as a whole.[8] Male preachers especially fall into the trap of preaching primarily to men rather than speaking to both women and men. Female preachers tend to preach across genders more effectively because they are more used to speaking with both genders. While this is a rather complex topic, we want to thoughtfully consider the way we interpret and communicate the Scriptures for both genders.

6. Beverly Daniel Tatum, *Why Are All the Black Kids Sitting Together in the Cafeteria? And Other Conversations About Race*, revised and updated (Basic Books, 2017).

7. See Matthew D. Kim, *Becoming a Friendlier Church: A Pathway to Genuine Community* (Baker Books, 2026).

8. Daniel A. Cox and Kelsey Eyre Hammond, "Young Women Are Leaving Church in Unprecedented Numbers," Survey Center on American Life, April 4, 2024, https://www.americansurveycenter.org/newsletter/young-women-are-leaving-church-in-unprecedented-numbers.

Generations

This type of diversity is tricky, as we are called to preach to either our grandparents' generation or our grandchildren's generation or in between. There are numerous resources available on intergenerational ministry, less so on intergenerational preaching. However, a good starting place is not to get overwhelmed by who's sitting in the pews. If most of your congregation is elderly or middle-aged or youthful (including college and high school), then they should be the priority for whom you are tailoring your message. Of course, you will want to speak to specific generations and across the generations at times.

Thankfully, we don't need to fret too much about appealing to all generations at all times. As Darrell E. Hall observes, "People come to church to hear a specific perspective on life: *people want to hear the Bible and its contents in preaching*."[9] This should put us somewhat at ease lest we become overly anxious about whether we've missed the generational mark each week. If you are hearing regular murmuring, however, that your preaching isn't connecting with your hearers from various generations, then it would be helpful to take stock of that and make some adjustments. When I was a younger pastor, I found it most beneficial to sit with elderly congregants and hear their stories. Even though they might repeat themselves, you will glean a host of wisdom by becoming familiar with what older generations value and devalue. The same principle is true for older preachers communicating to younger listeners.

Marital Status

A natural blind spot in our preaching consideration is speaking to both married couples and singles in our congregations. Most pastors are married themselves, and so they default to addressing marital issues and forget to include singles in their sermons. As noted by Bridget Gee, in *Single, Just Because*, comments are often made without thinking, as if singleness is a plague and marriage is expected:

> "How are you still single, Bridget?"
>
> "How is it that you have not been snatched up yet?"
>
> "It's an injustice that you're not married."
>
> "Your husband is going to be so lucky."[10]

9. Darrell E. Hall, *Speaking Across Generations: Messages That Satisfy Boomers, Xers, Millennials, Gen Z, and Beyond* (IVP Books, 2022), 8.

10. Bridget Gee, *Single, Just Because: A Pilgrimage into Holy Aloneness* (IVP, 2022), 6.

Even though a preacher isn't so blunt or direct, we can still make unintentional and unwanted comments about another person's marital status and cause unnecessary ill feelings or even trauma. Most of us have either heard or preached sermons where we've unintentionally elevated married couples, shamed the divorced and separated, or marginalized single folks. The same can be said about when we communicate with married couples or those who are divorced or widowed, as well as those who have children or not. Cultural intelligence in this regard means we should be more judicious when speaking of marital status. Unless we are preaching to a crowd of married couples or college students on the topic of marriage or to a group of widows and widowers, or divorcées, and so on, marital status and drawing attention to singleness is a topic to avoid.

Politics

Mentioning politics and political divisions in our congregations is often taboo. We are living and will continue to live in polarized political times.[11] To cultivate our cultural intelligence with regard to preaching and politics, we want to be careful to promote unity and mitigate disunity through our proclamation. In general, it's wise to bring up politics from the pulpit only when politics or something political is mentioned in the text. When this happens, we can generally address it in a bipartisan way and ultimately bring the discussion back to Christ Jesus, the only wise King and Ruler. Of course, there are times when, no matter what we communicate in the realm of politics, we will be misunderstood. Therefore, be judicious when it comes to what we proclaim from the pulpit on political topics.

Religions

Preaching with cultural intelligence also invites purposeful reflection on hearers who come from other religious backgrounds and faith traditions. We may have people listening in the pews who are Muslims, Buddhists, Hindus, Jehovah's Witnesses, Mormons, and followers of a host of other religions. Preach with a loving tone and present the gospel clearly. We want them to wonder why we are so convinced that the gospel is truthful and life changing. Why is the person of Jesus so radically different from other "gods"? We are often

11. For more information on preaching on politics, see Matthew D. Kim and Paul A. Hoffman, *Preaching to a Divided Nation: A Seven-Step Model for Promoting Reconciliation and Unity* (Baker Academic, 2022).

the ones telling our congregants to bring to church their family members, neighbors, and coworkers who don't know the Lord, so it's our joyful responsibility to preach sermons with them in mind. Instead of speaking pejoratively and making them feel like their religion is a joke, communicate God's Word in such a welcoming way that it invites dialogue and further conversations.

Social Locations

Think, for a moment, about the importance of social location. Where is your church physically located? It may be situated on the corner of Fourth Street and Main Street in a small, rural village or Fourth Street and Main Street in an urban metropolis. Wouldn't your sermon sound different based on the coordinates of your church building because it includes a variety of listeners? Being culturally ready in our preaching means becoming familiar with the social location of our people. How is preaching in a farming community dissimilar from preaching in a middle-class suburb? Gaining intelligence about who the people are in our neighborhoods and surroundings will be one of the first pastoral assignments I would give you as you begin a new ministry.

Functional Needs

A growing population of people who need more intentional focus in preaching are those with access and functional needs in our congregations. While I will miss some groups of people, we are thinking especially of those with the following: physical disabilities (wheelchair users, the blind, the deaf and hearing impaired, the mute), temporary illnesses or chronic conditions, cognitive/intellectual disabilities (including Down syndrome, dyslexia, ADD and ADHD, autism, neurodivergence, dementia, and Alzheimer's), and those with emotional/behavioral disorders. Some of these people might benefit from individualized attention given to them in a separate facility in the church building. However, is it also possible for churches to think creatively to welcome and include these brothers and sisters into the worship gathering? Providing creative solutions for those with special needs goes beyond the purview of this book, nor is it something that I am, in full transparency, prepared to confidently address. Yet, in our preaching ministry and ecclesiology, we must remember and show hospitality to those with special needs.[12]

12. Here are some helpful resources on some of these topics: Patricia M. Batten, "Evangelical Preaching and the Transformation of Listeners with Intellectual Disability," unpublished PhD Thesis, University of Aberdeen, 2026; Sandra Peoples, *Accessible Church: A*

Spiritual Maturity

A penultimate consideration is knowing the spiritual maturity levels reflected in your congregation. Scott M. Gibson shares, "There are different levels and layers of spiritual maturity in any congregation. At the same time, congregations vary from one to another. Some are mature, while others are less spiritually vibrant. These factors come into play when a preacher considers what to preach."[13] How do you know whether a church member is mature spiritually or not? Here are some diagnostic questions: Do they read Scripture regularly? Do they want to serve? Do they want to give of their time, treasures, and talents? Do they seek to live in obedience to Scripture? Are they walking in pathways leading to Christlikeness? How do they respond to constructive criticism or rebuke? Do they speak well of others, or are they usually criticizing others and gossiping about them? Though spiritual maturity levels will be all across the map, help your congregations take weekly steps toward deepening their discipleship. This will take relationship building and doing life together in the church and in our community.

Theology

Oftentimes preachers get shy when speaking out on theological differences and for good reason. Nobody wants to get an earful or email from a disturbed congregant concerning something theological that we have raised in our sermons. Tim Cooper writes, "It seems almost inevitable that theology is involved when Christians disagree. They may fall out over explicit differences in doctrine, or they may differ over how theology is worked out in practice. Usually, each side in a disagreement bolsters its position by appeals to the

---

Gospel-Centered Vision for Including People with Disabilities and Their Families (Crossway, 2025); Chris H. Hulshof, *Jesus and Disability: A Guide to Creating an Inclusive Church* (B&H Academic, 2022); Amy Kenny, *My Body Is Not a Prayer Request: Disability Justice in the Church* (Brazos, 2022); Lamar Hardwick, *Disability and the Church: A Vision for Diversity and Inclusion* (IVP, 2021); Stephanie O. Hubach, *Same Lake, Different Boat: Coming Alongside People Touched by Disability*, revised and updated (P&R, 2020); Bethany McKinney Fox, *Disability and the Way of Jesus: Holistic Healing in the Gospels and the Church* (IVP Academic, 2019); Jolene Philo and Katie Wetherbee, *Every Child Welcome: A Ministry Handbook for Including Kids with Special Needs* (Kregel, 2015); Amy Fenton Lee, *Leading a Special Needs Ministry: A Practical Guide to Including Children and Loving Families* (Orange, 2014); and Brian Brock and John Swinton, eds., *Disability in the Christian Tradition: A Reader* (Eerdmans, 2012).

13. Scott M. Gibson, *Preaching with a Plan: Sermon Strategies for Growing Mature Believers* (Baker Books, 2012), 19.

Bible."[14] We can expect disagreements when it comes to theology. I'm sure there is no church on the planet where everyone agrees on every theological nuance. Much like the section on different religions, preach theology seriously but loosely (when it comes to nonessential doctrines). Do not ostracize or chastise those who hold different theologies on minor theological disparities.[15] I realize the threshold here will vary greatly from church to church and pastor to pastor. Speak the truth in love.

People Are People

A final reminder in this opening section is that at the end of the day, with all of our human diversity, people remain people. We are God's beloved creation, image bearers, and human beings. What are the bare-bones basics that every person needs to live: food, water, shelter, income, community, relationship, love, and most importantly, the gospel, and a relationship with the Lord Jesus Christ. There may be moments in a sermon to highlight our differences, and yet as a general homiletical principle, focus on what unites us and what we need to do to grow in Christlikeness and advance the kingdom of God where God has placed us.[16] Love your people by helping them love God and love one another as well. Before we move on to our next topic on cultural readiness, this second part of the chapter will conclude with practices for developing our cultural intelligence in preaching.

Practices for Developing Cultural Intelligence

Build the Homiletical BRIDGE

In *Preaching with Cultural Intelligence*, I offered the acronym BRIDGE to explain how we can sermonically consider and engage our listeners right where they are. BRIDGE stands for Beliefs, Rituals, Idols, Dreams, (view of) God, and Experiences.[17] If it's overwhelming to think of all of the different types of

14. Tim Cooper, *When Christians Disagree: Lessons from the Fractured Relationship of John Owen and Richard Baxter* (Crossway, 2024), 57.

15. Three theological differences that cause some of the greatest rifts in ministry are baptism, women in ministry, and human sexuality. However, I would place human sexuality in the major theological camp as I hold to a traditional biblical view of marriage between one man and one woman for life. Of course, sexual sins are not salvific, but they do carry significant consequences in how we view and approach biblical/theological differences, more so than baptism or women in ministry.

16. See Kim and Hoffman, *Preaching to a Divided Nation.*

17. See Kim, *Preaching with Cultural Intelligence*, 18–24.

people listening to your message, narrow your focus to one or two subcultures or types of people in your congregation per week using the BRIDGE.

For instance, depending on the passage at hand, I might select the topic of Beliefs and do a mental survey of some listeners who might disagree with the biblical truth this text is communicating. Ask yourself, What do they believe and why? Another Sunday, it may be more pertinent to challenge various idols that permeate the congregation. There may be occasions where the sermon benefits from investigation of multiple aspects of the BRIDGE. Using the BRIDGE metaphor aids cultural intelligence because it provides six distinct areas of life that shape who we are as individuals and as congregations.

Read and Participate

This next practice for developing cultural intelligence is twofold. In many ways, these two practices go hand in hand. If a cultural group is foreign to you, read about them (history, culture, practices) as you attend and participate in their cultures. For instance, you may be unfamiliar with the Vietnamese congregant who has been attending your church for a few years. You can read about their cultural history and experiences, attend a birthday party when invited, and participate in their cultural expressions. Some may push back and say, "I'm a busy pastor. I don't have time for that." Well, do the best that you can to develop cultural intelligence so that you might be able to effectively communicate God's Word to their culture.

Meet and Listen

Similarly, there is often no substitute for meeting with those who are different from you and listening to their stories and experiences. It should be a no-brainer to know that pastoral ministry and preaching ministry require getting to know and knowing our people. Even if you cannot meet with everyone in a given calendar year, try to meet more and more congregants and their families. Listen to them, both in terms of their spiritual joys and concerns but also culturally speaking. Ask them if your sermons are reaching their heads and hearts. If not, ask them what you might do differently and do better.

Get Feedback and Feed-Forward

How can we respond to this diversity and hear the different perspectives in the room? Even in a smaller congregation, we can invite participation in our preaching ministries through feedback and feed-forward sessions. Perhaps once a month or as frequently as once a week, get together for a time of sermonic feed-forward and feedback with your listeners. Find people of various demographics in your churches (including some of the categories mentioned in this chapter) and talk about the sermon text beforehand and afterward. How is your sermon reaching everyone, and what can you do to improve?

Play Duck-Duck-Goose

Playing duck-duck-goose is my homiletical game of focusing your sermon on one person per week. As you make your way mentally around the church membership list, occasionally stop at strategic points and ask who might be sitting here regularly that I never think about in my sermon preparation. We usually preach to the ducks. But what about the geese? The geese are the people least like me. Ponder and ask the Holy Spirit to consider who the geese might be in your congregation and target your sermon for them this week.

Target Your Sermons on One Person Per Week

It's daunting to think we must consider every single type of person out there when writing and delivering sermons. One way to cope with the vast diversity of listeners is to tailor my weekly sermons for one person in the room. Try writing the entire sermon for that person who may be a white, thirty-something, single parent, who is college educated, works as a schoolteacher, who grew up in Upstate New York, and is raising two young children on his own. The next week, I write the sermon for another person who is very different from him. She's a retired, seventy-year-old, African American woman, married, with three adult children, who had a successful career in the banking industry and lives in a well-established condominium downtown. Trying to write a sermon for both individuals can be discouraging and overwhelming. However, this is where we must rely on the power of the Holy Spirit. I cannot tell you how many times I have written a sermon for one person in the room and someone who's completely different shares how God spoke into their lives that week. It's a mystery I cannot understand but one I do appreciate.

CONCLUSION

It can be maddening and anxiety inducing to think about every different culture represented in my church. There are some seasons where growing cultural intelligence as pastors and preachers is mandatory because people change and congregations experience turnover. There are other seasons where we cannot handle another item on our to-do list. Cultural readiness for preaching is a step-by-step and season-by-season process. Nobody is fully culturally ready to preach. Yet, as best we can, we want to develop intentional ways to increase our cultural intelligence to become more effective pastors and preachers. Culturally prepared sermons enable our diverse listeners to feel seen and loved and to experience a sense of belonging.

QUESTIONS

1. Who are the cultural groups that you regularly think about when preparing your sermons?
2. Which cultural groups might you forget in your sermons?
3. Who are people you could ask to help you name your blind spots?
4. What are regular rhythms you can implement to grow in cultural preparation?

PRACTICES

1. Read an article or book about a cultural group represented in your congregation that you are unfamiliar with.
2. Participate in a cultural event or gathering of a congregant who you know little or nothing about.
3. Try a feedback or feed-forward session with a handful of listeners who come from different cultural backgrounds.
4. Try to write your sermon for one goose this week. Ask yourself what questions they may be asking of the text. What are their struggles and concerns as they read this passage? What illustrations or applications can you tailor for this individual?

13

GOSPEL

Does Our Sermon Proclaim the Gospel?

> For when I preach the gospel, I cannot boast, since I am compelled to preach. Woe to me if I do not preach the gospel!
>
> —1 Corinthians 9:16

The Bible imparts to us the gospel or the good news of salvation, which is an all-consuming, all-important story about God: God the Father, God the Son, and God the Holy Spirit. Christianity is, in a nutshell, the gospel story: the announcement of good news that God sent his Son, Jesus Christ, to the world to save it from sin and condemnation (John 3:16–18). Through the perfectly lived earthly life, to suffering death on the cross, burial in a tomb, and bodily resurrection of Jesus Christ, God reconciled a broken, fallen, sinful world to himself. Jesus was and is the only sufficient atonement for the penalty of sin. And through the work of the Holy Spirit, those who repent of their sins and put their faith in Jesus Christ alone become regenerated and are given a new spiritual life for the remainder of their earthly existence and into eternity in heaven.

There's much gravitas or weight in the gospel story. So much is at stake! What this means is that preachers cannot be wishy-washy when it comes to presenting the essence of the Christian message. As C. S. Lewis once claimed, "Christianity is a statement which, if false, is of *no* importance, and if true, of infinite importance. The only thing it cannot be is moderately important."[1] Every single passage of Scripture conveys something concrete about God and asks in some shape or form: What does this text communicate about God? And yet, there is another consequential question preachers must ask: "How does the gospel intersect with this Scripture passage?"

In 1 Corinthians 9:16, mentioned above, the apostle Paul asserts, "For when I preach the gospel, I cannot boast, since I am compelled to preach. Woe to me if I do not preach the gospel!" At the risk of speaking out of turn, vis-à-vis Paul's admission here, could it be argued that our preaching is woeful if the gospel is missing from it?

I became increasingly convicted by the Holy Spirit of the importance of preaching the gospel in every sermon during the global COVID-19 pandemic that began in March 2020. During the pandemic, people were taking ill and dying every single day. Dozens, hundreds, even thousands were passing away each week. As preachers tried their best to stream their sermons online, the centrality of the gospel became crystal clear. It dawned on me that any sermon a person hears may be their very last.

The apostle Paul is adamant that gospel proclamation is a requisite component to the sermon. So should we view the gospel as homiletically indispensable! In this chapter, we will unpack the core elements of the gospel and encourage all preachers to communicate the gospel clearly in each sermon we construct and communicate, even if it's not explicitly mentioned in our Scripture text.

The Gospel Is Trinitarian

In some Christian circles, the gospel centers solely and at times exclusively on the person and work of Jesus Christ, the Son. To some extent, this argument is true. In its most simple form, as I have argued elsewhere, the gospel concerns the perfect sacrificial life, death, burial, resurrection, ascension, and return of Jesus.[2] The gospel is nothing less than the divine/human person and finished work of Jesus Christ.

Yet, while the gospel emphasizes Jesus, it's not exclusively about Jesus. Since the Bible is trinitarian in nature, the gospel cannot omit the persons and works of God the Father and God the Spirit. In his book *The Trinity*, Donald Fairbairn elucidates, "The gospel begins with the Trinity, and it centres

1. C. S. Lewis, "Christian Apologetics," in *God in the Dock*, ed. Walter Hooper (Eerdmans, 1972), 101.

2. Matthew D. Kim, *Preaching to People in Pain: How Suffering Can Shape Your Sermons and Connect with Your Congregation* (Baker Academic, 2021), 7.

around the Trinity—around the eternal love between the Father and the Son, a love that God shares with us when he sends his Son into the world, and when he sends his Spirit into our hearts."[3] Amy Gannett similarly advocates for a trinitarian gospel: "A non-Trinitarian God not only lacks love, but lacks the warmth of the gospel narrative."[4] Finally, Michael Reeves explains helpfully the trinitarian and trifold efficacy of the gospel: "The Christian gospel is good news concerning the Father, the Son, and the Spirit, and the work of the Father, the Son, and the Spirit, in revelation, redemption, and regeneration. . . . The gospel, after all, is not merely revelation. It is a revelation that *redeems* and *regenerates*."[5] As we consider the work of preaching, let's take each in turn: revelation, redemption, and regeneration.

Gospel Preaching Reveals

First, gospel preaching reveals. Our presentation of the gospel narrative invites reflection on what Scripture has revealed about the triune God. Every text reveals some salient truth about who God is. In addition, every text reveals some salient truth about who we are: our depravity and our need for Christ's work of justification and the Spirit's assistance in our sanctification.

At its core, Scripture manifests a gospel arc or emphasis culminating in the work of Christ's death and resurrection for our justification and illuminates the Spirit's assistance toward our personal and collective regeneration and transformation as God's children. Without the gospel, what hope do we have for our justification and sanctification? Without the gospel, all that's left is doom and gloom. Just refresh yourself by rereading some of the prophetical books. Without Christ, people in the past, present, and future have zero hope.

With the gospel, however, we have access to hope present and hope future. One of the most important implications and applications of the gospel is that it reveals and offers hope to God's people no matter where we are in the Christian journey. Because of what Jesus accomplished on our behalf, through the presence and power of God the Father and God the Spirit, in each sermon we preach, we provide tangible expressions of hope revealed in God's truth. We have hope because we have the gospel expressed through and executed by the triune God on our behalf.

3. Donald Fairbairn, *The Trinity* (Union, 2024), 51.

4. Amy Gannett, *Fix Your Eyes: How Our Study of God Shapes Our Worship of Him* (B&H, 2021), 60.

5. Michael Reeves, "Essentials Series Preface" in Fairbairn, *The Trinity*, 8–9.

Gospel Preaching Redeems

Next, gospel preaching, when done rightly, redeems all participants—both the preacher and the listener. The book of Ruth is a beautiful reminder of our need for redemption. Every person on the planet needs a kinsman-redeemer, not just a Boaz, but the Lord Jesus Christ himself! Gospel preaching is preaching redemptive sermons. Mark S. Young explains how the gospel infuses hope through a redemptive lens: "*Redemption* describes how God is resolving those three problems [sin, death, and evil]. The present brokenness of this world does not remain unchallenged; it will not last forever. Through the life, death, and resurrection of Jesus, God intervenes on humanity's behalf, rescues us from that which holds us in bondage, and restores us to relationship with himself. The good news of redemption brings *hope* to humanity. Hope is the gospel made immanent, incarnate, and certain."[6]

Weekly proclamation of gospel redemption introduces nonbelievers to their theological and practical need for salvation from sin and death. Romans 3:23 is clear: "For all have sinned and fall short of the glory of God." The salvific enterprise that Jesus offers to those who have placed their complete faith and trust in him is worth reiterating time and time again to both nonbelievers and believers alike. Part of the struggle for longtime Christians is that we can so easily forget from whence we came: a life pre-Christ embedded and emboldened in sin. The gospel is a daily and weekly reminder that our Redeemer lives and desires for us to look more like him, through obedience and surrender, in every part of our being.

Gospel Preaching Regenerates

Finally, gospel preaching regenerates. Every Christian is on a pathway toward regeneration or rebirth through the assistance and power of the Spirit. What disrupts our regenerative process and Christian formation is the obvious and blatant obstacle of our sin. In his sermon, preached at the Metropolitan Tabernacle, Charles Spurgeon proclaimed:

> But what is it to be born again? I have already said that I cannot tell you how the Spirit of God operates upon the unregenerate, making them to be new creatures in Christ Jesus. I know that he usually operates through the Word, through the proclamation of the truth of the gospel. So far as we know, he works upon the mind according to the laws of mind by first illuminating the

6. Mark S. Young, *The Hope of the Gospel: Theological Education and the Next Evangelicalism* (Eerdmans, 2022), 7.

> understanding; he then controls the judgment, influences the will, and changes the affections. . . . A new nature is created within him, although the old nature is not entirely eradicated. It will ultimately be destroyed, but it is not destroyed at first; when a new nature is born within the man, a nature which hates what the [old] nature loved, and loves what the old nature hated, a new nature which is akin to the nature of God.[7]

The gospel is part and parcel of every biblical message we preach because apart from it we have no authority and power to initiate and substantiate the process of regeneration. The Lord transforms people mysteriously, as Spurgeon observes, "through the proclamation of the truth of the gospel." As a result, we focus our sermons not on behavior modification per se, but rather on the life transformation that takes place when God reorients our desires and passions toward holiness, godliness, and righteousness because of his great and efficacious gospel.

I would like to leave us with practical applications as they relate to gospel preaching: Preach the gospel to yourself, preach the gospel contextually, preach the gospel passionately, and preach the gospel regularly in every sermon.

Preach the Gospel to Yourself

We've heard it said often: "Preach the gospel to yourself." The question is, Can we ever preach the gospel too often, especially to ourselves? The thing about the gospel is that it's never one and done. We never outgrow the gospel or our need of it. Since the gospel encapsulates our entire existence, there can never be a time where I've somehow arrived and no longer have need of it!

The temptation for many preachers is that we can be myopic and only think about our listeners when preparing the sermon. Sermon preparation can often feel like an external exercise and not an internal one. I'm intentionally writing the sermon for them, my people, out there, externally. The reality, however, is that I'm also writing the sermon for myself. John Koessler's insight is useful here: "In the written record of redemption—the inspiration of Holy Scripture—God's Spirit superintended the process but did not eclipse the personality and vocabulary of the writers. A human process resulted in a divine product. Why should we be surprised, then, to find that our humanity

7. Charles Haddon Spurgeon, "The Necessity of Regeneration," *Metropolitan Tabernacle Pulpit* 54 (December 3, 1908), available at https://www.spurgeon.org/resource-library/sermons/the-necessity-of-regeneration.

is also fundamental to the task of preaching?"[8] At the core of the homiletical process is our need for the gospel. We preachers are not above our listeners or above the gospel itself. Our need for the gospel is a requisite qualification of preaching: a gospel accepted, internalized, embodied, and actualized in the preacher himself or herself. When the gospel story fails to affect and grip me, the preacher, what does that mean for my hearers? What hope can I possibly convey?

As you prepare your message, take an extra few minutes each week to internalize how the gospel intersects with your sermon text. How does the gospel concretize whatever truth God may be imparting to you and your congregation in this text? Hold tightly to the gospel. Never let it waiver in your head and heart. Preach the gospel to yourself daily. Preach the gospel to yourself from your sermon passage.

Preach the Gospel Contextually

The cruciform nature of the gospel is compelling because it introduces us to something so foreign: death to the self in exchange for a crucified life in Christ. In *Cruciformity*, Michael J. Gorman says, "'Cruciformity' is my own term for a concept commonly believed to be central to Paul's theology and ethics: conformity to the crucified Christ."[9] Instead of a cruciform theological lens or worldview, the world we inhabit, including our beloved church members, is receiving a different gospel or false gospel every day. This different gospel champions self-promotion, self-congratulation, self-superiority, self-worth, self-gratification, self-indulgence, self-identification, and more self, self, self. The crux of the gospel communicates daily death to self to experience true life. Later, in Galatians 2:20, Paul says: "I have been crucified with Christ and I no longer live, but Christ lives in me. The life I now live in the body, I live by faith in the Son of God, who loved me and gave himself for me." Why did Christ give his life for me according to this text? So that I might die to self and live for Christ.

One of the central messages of the gospel is to kill our idols in order to follow Christ more closely. For this reason, the gospel must be contextualized for our specific hearers. Acts 17, which highlights Paul's ministry in Athens, is a text where a contextualized gospel is modeled for us. After

8. John Koessler, *Folly, Grace, and Power: The Mysterious Act of Preaching* (Zondervan, 2011), 46–47.

9. Michael J. Gorman, *Cruciformity: Paul's Narrative Spirituality of the Cross* (Eerdmans, 2021), 4.

surveying the city and its rampant idolatry, Paul stood up and said in verses 22–23: "People of Athens! I see that in every way you are very religious. For as I walked around and looked carefully at your objects of worship, I even found an altar with this inscription: TO AN UNKNOWN GOD." Paul meets them contextually where they are: people religiously devoted to idols and not to the Lord. He spoke in such a contextual, knowledgeable, observant way that while some rejected his message, others said, "We want to hear you again on this subject" (v. 32).

Winning souls for the gospel will, in most cases, not be instantaneous. To get a second or third hearing, like the apostle Paul, is a major win! Every country, region, area, culture, individual has any variety of idolatrous commitments. To preach the gospel contextually involves knowing our people well and knowing their idols and speaking to them in their area of gospel need.

Preach the Gospel Passionately

Since the gospel is the greatest story ever told, the most effective thing we can do in the pulpit is to preach the gospel with greater passion. The sheer familiarity of gospel preaching breeds contempt. If we're not careful, we can preach a tepid, lukewarm gospel as if it were a lackluster message. On the contrary, the gospel demands a passionate plea. Eternal life and death are at stake. The eternality of the gospel compels us to preach boldly and passionately every time we share about the person and work of Jesus Christ through the power of God the Father and the assistance of the Holy Spirit.

Since it is true that the only way to eternal life and reconnection with the Father is through Christ and Christ alone, the onus is on preachers to communicate the gospel message both passionately and urgently. It's not a wishy-washy, conviction-less, feel-good story of minor proportions. No! The gospel is everything for life today and life eternal. For those who don't place their faith in Christ, eternal separation from God is final and permanent! I'm reminded of the powerful moment Luke records where Jesus tells the story of a rich man who dies and sees Abraham and Lazarus, the beggar, and he calls to Abraham, "Father Abraham, have pity on me and send Lazarus to dip the tip of his finger in water and cool my tongue, because I am in agony in this fire" (Luke 16:24). I'm haunted by Abraham's words to the rich man: "And besides all this, between us and you a great chasm has been set in place, so that those who want to go from here to you cannot, nor can anyone cross over from there to us" (Luke 16:26). The gospel of Jesus Christ requires passionate proclamation. Preaching has a crucial component of persuasion attached to it (see chapter 20 on communication). Impassive preaching fails to persuade or convince others of the truth. Once this earthly life is over, there is no other opportunity for our listeners to invite Jesus Christ into their hearts and to receive him as Lord and Savior.

Preach the Gospel Regularly

Last, I want to encourage you to preach the gospel regularly, even in every single sermon. In Galatians 1:6–9, the apostle Paul reminds the believers in Galatia of how easy it is to listen to a different or false gospel. He writes, "I am astonished that you are so quickly deserting him who called you in the grace of Christ and are turning to a different gospel—not that there is another one, but there are some who trouble you and want to distort the gospel of Christ. But even if we or an angel from heaven should preach to you a gospel contrary to the one we preached to you, let him be accursed. As we have said before, so now I say again: If anyone is preaching to you a gospel contrary to the one you received, let him be accursed" (ESV). With every sermon possibly being the last one someone will hear, isn't it worth it to tell or remind our hearers of God's love demonstrated through the gospel? It will take thirty sermonic seconds or less.

Over the last couple of decades, there has been, in my estimation, less discussion and emphasis on evangelistic preaching. Perhaps too many of us have been desensitized by hellfire-and-brimstone street evangelists who have erred on the side of judgment rather than grace. Regardless, at the heart of the gospel story is a commitment to lost souls and spreading good news. Andrew Root instructs, "Evangelism comes from the Greek *ev* or 'good,' and *angel* or 'message' or 'messenger.' To be part of the event of evangelism is to find yourself in the angelic act of bringing or receiving the message of good news."[10] Remember the apostle Paul's encouragement for preaching the gospel: "For, 'Everyone who calls on the name of the Lord will be saved.' How, then, can they call on the one they have not believed in? And how can they believe in the one of whom they have not heard? And how can they hear without someone preaching to them? And how can anyone preach unless they are sent? As it is written: 'How beautiful are the feet of those who bring good news!'" (Rom. 10:13–15). What a privilege it is to impart the good news of the gospel

10. Andrew Root, *Evangelism in an Age of Despair: Hope Beyond the Failed Promises of Happiness* (Baker Academic, 2025), xii.

to ourselves, to skeptics, to prodigals, and to the already saved. Preach the gospel every time you stand and deliver God's Word.

CONCLUSION

Do you remember the first time you heard the gospel? For some, it's a life-altering moment and one that leads to immediate transformation. For others, they heard the gospel spoken or proclaimed, but it will take another hearing or many hearings before they recognize their need to embrace the gospel. Heartbreakingly, some may never come to appreciate their need for the gospel. Regardless of how one encounters and experiences the gospel message, the gospel is foundational to the Christian life. In his book *Evangelistic Preaching*, Roger Carswell exhorts preachers with these challenging words: "We are to proclaim [the gospel] in complete dependence upon God to use our words. Before every sermon I preach, I pray, 'Lord, without You I can do nothing, therefore will You please accomplish that which counts for eternity through this message?' Only God can 'give the increase.'"[11]

Never tire of hearing the gospel nor of preaching it. Preaching the gospel in every sermon is a preacher's opportunity to participate in the sufferings of Christ here on earth so that ultimately we will live with Christ eternally. The same is true for our hearers. As we preach the gospel and introduce or reintroduce our listeners to the triune God's revelation, redemption, and regeneration, I press upon you the importance to preach the gospel also to yourself, in context, with passion, and with regularity. I cannot emphasize enough how the gospel is vital to an effective preaching ministry! In the next chapter on cultural readiness, we'll take a deeper look at how our preaching ministry connects with discipleship.

QUESTIONS

1. What is your definition of the gospel?
2. How often do you preach the gospel in your sermons?
3. Has this chapter changed how you will approach preaching the gospel going forward?
4. What concerns or questions do you have after reading this chapter?

11. Roger Carswell, *Evangelistic Preaching: Proclaiming the Gospel to Non-Christians Who Are Listening* (10 Publishing, 2022), 18.

PRACTICES

1. Preach the gospel to yourself this week. What aspect of the gospel story hits home for you? What parts of the gospel feel distant?
2. Preach the gospel in your upcoming sermon or sermon series. Write down your observations. How can you explain the gospel more clearly to your listeners?
3. As you preach the gospel, take some time to consider how you are engaging your listeners contextually, passionately, and regularly. What could use more intentionality? What else have you noticed when preaching the gospel?

14

DISCIPLESHIP

Is Our Preaching Ministry Making Disciples?

> Him we proclaim, warning everyone and teaching everyone with all wisdom, that we may present everyone mature in Christ. For this I toil, struggling with all his energy that he powerfully works within me.
>
> —Colossians 1:28–29 (ESV)

Steve Bezner opens *Your Jesus Is Too American* with commentary on the oft-too-familiar condition of the American Christian heart. Bezner writes: "This is a book about obedience to the way of Jesus. It is also a book about how the way of Jesus often stands in stark contrast with the American way."[1] He continues: "Christians must become recommitted to knowing and obeying Jesus in a way that will set them apart. The church needs to be distinctive again—like it was in its earliest days."[2]

I begin this chapter with Bezner's cultural analysis and suggested recalibration because it resonates deeply with what I would like to communicate in this chapter on discipleship as it relates to our task of preaching. We are facing a shortage, perhaps more aptly a discipleship crisis, in the American Christian church. If I were to ask a direct question about the preaching happening in our time, it would be this: "Does your preaching match the way of Jesus, or is it too American?" Are we preaching for warm fuzzies or preaching for hearts ablaze for Jesus?

1. Steve Bezner, *Your Jesus Is Too American: Calling the Church to Reclaim Kingdom Values Over the American Dream* (Brazos, 2024), 1.

2. Bezner, *Your Jesus Is Too American*, 14.

Christians define discipleship in assorted ways. Sometimes we limit it to a program: "Discipleship is one of the ministries in our church." Sometimes we equate it with a book: "We're reading this great discipleship book." Sometimes it's only a descriptive adjective: "We are a discipleship church" (as if discipleship is not the key agenda of every church). Sometimes, we refer to it as an exercise in spiritual formation: "Do you engage in the practice of discipleship?"

Instead of these types of uses for the word "discipleship," I would like to offer this equation: The gospel + obedience to Christ = discipleship. Put differently, the gospel (the focus of our previous chapter) + discipleship (the focus of our current chapter) leads to obedience to Christ. We cannot have the gospel or discipleship without Christlike obedience. Unfortunately, I question how many preachers are explaining the gospel and discipleship in such terms.

Where do we get that notion? The Great Commission text, of course! Jesus said it himself in Matthew 28:19–20, "Go therefore and make disciples of all nations, baptizing them in the name of the Father and of the Son and of the Holy Spirit, teaching them to observe [obey] all that I have commanded you. And behold, I am with you always, to the end of the age" (ESV). Similarly, I drew our attention to Colossians 1:28–29 at the start of this chapter, where Paul stirs the preacher's affections toward complete maturity in Christ, or to the act of obedience. He writes, "Him [Jesus] we proclaim, warning everyone and teaching everyone with all wisdom, that we may present everyone mature in Christ. For this I toil, struggling with all his energy that he powerfully works within me" (ESV). Preaching devoid of the call to obedience cannot be called preaching that makes disciples; nor can it be called preaching that disciples one's listeners.

Preaching as Discipleship

Part of the conundrum Christianity finds itself in with regard to discipleship is that preachers are afraid to speak boldly concerning full obedience to Jesus out of fear of being thought of as fanatical. For instance, when we preach full submission to what the Bible says, we might be labeled legalistic. Preachers who challenge societal and cultural values with biblical ones are called intolerant or uncharitable. When we preach the exclusivity of Jesus, we are considered hateful, ungracious, judgmental, or narrow-minded. However, preaching as discipleship necessitates absolute, complete, total obedience to the triune God in every part of our lives. Never have I read in Scripture advocacy for a partial, half-hearted obedience to Jesus (remember "all that I have commanded you"). Have you?

In fact, according to Scott M. Gibson, discipleship and maturity are the primary reasons that preachers preach in the first place. In his book *Preaching with a Plan*, Gibson unpacks what it means for preachers to place highest priority on discipleship and Christlikeness. Gibson says, "We engage in what we do for the growth of men and women and boys and girls in the faith. We want to stretch believers to expand their faith and obedience as they grow in grace. Our goal is Christlikeness, and we know that believers in Jesus Christ will mature in their faith through faithful sermon planning and the preaching of God's Word. . . . Preaching is a means of discipleship, a shaping of men and women into the people God wants them to be—growing, deep believers able to face the world in which they live because they have been nurtured to do so by the Word."[3]

The trajectory of discipleship, according to Gibson, is not always up-and-to-the-right but can be visualized as a bell-shaped curve (see fig. 14.1).[4] Our spiritual development can experience highs and lows, peaks and valleys. Nobody's spiritual life is always growing in a positive direction. The bell-shaped curve reveals the up-and-down nature of spiritual maturity for all believers. The spiritual maturity of our congregations might be variously described as infant, toddler, child, adolescent, young adult, middle-aged, and older adult. Congregants move along the spiritual maturity path from one stage to the next. What determines the spiritual age of a person is not their ability to recite correct biblical answers (which is valuable) but putting the Word of God into practice, obeying God's commands, and becoming Christlike in every way. In aggregate, where is your congregation on the path to discipleship presently?

Similarly, Bill Hull and Ben Sobels detect the noticeable void of discipleship in gospel proclamation in *The Discipleship Gospel*:

> The true gospel is Jesus' gospel, which he referred to as the "gospel of the kingdom" (Matt. 24:14), and this gospel was crystal clear to the early church (Acts 2:14–41). Since then though, the church has drifted away from preaching Jesus' gospel—at various times and in different ways—and has believed in different "gospels," which aren't really gospels at all. They have one common characteristic: they remove the necessity of discipleship from Jesus' gospel. The type of preaching that comes from believing these gospels ultimately suffocates disciple-making in the church. Yet making disciples is one of the greatest tasks that Christ has called the church to do until he returns.[5]

The problem is that we cannot preach toward discipleship if we are unwilling to communicate the hard truths about discipleship from the pulpit.

3. Scott M. Gibson, *Preaching with a Plan: Sermon Strategies for Growing Mature Believers* (Baker Books, 2012), 13, 17.

4. See Gibson, *Preaching with a Plan*, 127–28.

5. Bill Hull and Ben Sobels, *The Discipleship Gospel: What Jesus Preached—We Must Follow* (HIM Publications, 2018), 14.

Discipleship and Transformational Preaching

Death to Self and Christlike Obedience

Jesus doesn't mess around with the concept of discipleship. For our Lord Jesus, discipleship means "being found in human form, he humbled himself by becoming obedient to the point of death, even death on a cross" (Phil. 2:8 ESV). Remember, Jesus taught his disciples the same death-to-self principle of discipleship in Matthew 16:24: "Then Jesus said to his disciples, 'Whoever wants to be my disciple must deny themselves and take up their cross and follow me.'" To take up one's cross to follow Jesus means full surrender and nothing less. In many ways, we have succumbed to an à la carte type of discipleship where, like in a buffet line, we can pick and choose what we want to live out and what we want to avoid.

For true and lasting transformation to take place in the life of every believer, it will require discipleship manifested by selflessness and absolute obedience to the Scriptures and all that God has commanded of us in his holy Word. In other words, life transformation doesn't just happen without daily sacrifice and intentionally practicing submission and compliance. It happens through daily obedience—to the easier things (if there are such things) and to the hardest things. Now, some will raise their fists at such a comment. That sounds legalistic! Well, no, not really.

The apostle Paul identifies a clear marker of Christian maturity, which is death to the old self and putting on the new self. In Colossians 3:1–3, he explains, "If then you have been raised with Christ, seek the things that are

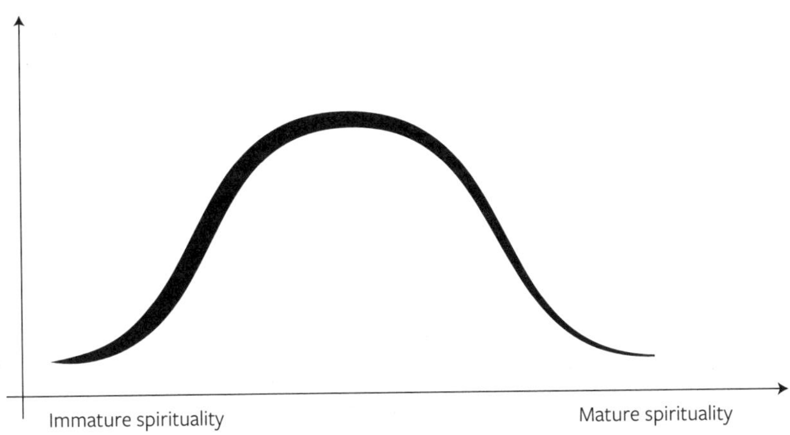

Source: Scott M. Gibson, *Preaching with a Plan: Sermon Strategies for Growing Mature Believers* (Baker Books, 2012), 128. Used by permission.

Figure 14.1. Gibson's bell-shaped discipleship curve

above, where Christ is, seated at the right hand of God. Set your minds on things that are above, not on things that are on earth. For you have died, and your life is hidden with Christ in God" (ESV). Paul continues in Colossians 3:5–10, "Put to death therefore what is earthly in you: sexual immorality, impurity, passion, evil desire, and covetousness, which is idolatry. . . . But now you must put them all away: anger, wrath, malice, slander, and obscene talk from your mouth. Do not lie to one another, seeing that you have put off the old self with its practices and have put on the new self, which is being renewed in knowledge after the image of its creator" (ESV). Mature believers do not actively commit themselves to selfish living and practicing sinful behaviors that lead to death. One of the reasons why I believe there is often little transformation in the lives of believers today is because preachers are timid in renouncing various sins and calling for repentance.

Repentance

There has been no spiritual revival or awakening, as far as I'm aware, without fervent prayer and repentance. From the First and Second Great Awakenings to the revivals on Azusa Street to the recent "outpouring" at Asbury University, repentance is assumed to be a crucial part of the equation when it comes to spiritual transformation, whether it's personal or corporate spiritual maturity.[6] The word "repent" occurs in the NIV translation some seventy-eight times in Scripture.[7] In Matthew 3:8–9, Jesus rebukes the Pharisees and Sadducees: "Produce fruit in keeping with repentance. And do not think you can say to yourselves, 'We have Abraham as our father.' I tell you that out of these stones God can raise up children for Abraham." In other words, Jesus says we cannot rest on our laurels (or rest on our spiritual ancestors, in this case).

We never become "too good" for repentance, and bearing fruit requires continuous repentance from the believer. Repentance is not a one-and-done deal where the first time we repent and receive Christ is the only time we need repentance. Repentance, confessing our sins and turning away from them, is necessary every time we sin, which unfortunately is every single day, numerous times per day. As 1 John 1:9 states, "If we confess our sins, he is faithful and just to forgive us our sins and to cleanse us from all unrighteousness" (ESV). When we fail to repent, our Christian faith will eventually degenerate because we will cease to fight the battle against sin.

6. Instead of the term "revival" or "awakening," Vickers and McCall refer to this spiritual encounter or experience as an "outpouring." See Jason E. Vickers and Thomas H. McCall, *Outpouring: A Theological Witness* (Cascade Books, 2023).

7. BibleGateway, https://www.biblegateway.com/quicksearch/?quicksearch=repent&version=NIV.

Make it a weekly rhythm to create space in the worship gathering to repent individually and corporately. Whether we recite a liturgical confession together or simply incorporate a time of silence, repentance is a core element in developing as Christ's disciples. John Ortberg says, "Repentance is remedial work to mend our minds and hearts, which get bent by sin."[8] Since sin is a nagging, daily problem, we preach against sin and invite regular repentance as its remedy. If we are not preaching against sin and preaching repentance normatively, sin will become normative. Moreover, we will continue to malnourish our congregants with a champagne diet, which tastes extraordinary, but leads to spiritual gluttony and indolence. Preaching devoid of repentance fails to aid our discipleship process.

Discipleship Starts with the Preacher

This daily death to self and call for Christlike obedience is first required of the preacher. One of the most challenging life verses for me has been Galatians 2:20, where the apostle Paul declares, "I have been crucified with Christ and I no longer live, but Christ lives in me. The life I now live in the body, I live by faith in the Son of God, who loved me and gave himself for me." What Paul is teaching here is contrary to the popularized prosperity gospel that teaches we are to live for the self: self-preservation, self-profit, and self-promotion. I tell my students at the beginning of every semester that I pray for them that they would not seek to be famous—to the chagrin of some. For pastors and preachers, our flesh seeks to live self-centeredly and not to be crucified. We want to make a name for ourselves rather than or in addition to making Christ's name known. Self-orientation is constantly at war against self-crucifixion. Every time the flesh rises up, we put it to death. Truth be told, we struggle with this every day (at least I do).

Steve Bezner uses the film *Shawshank Redemption* to illustrate this principle: "In dying to self, we find the secret to living. At first I thought Jesus would rephrase Andy's charge to Red along the following lines: Get busy dying so you can get busy living. But after reflecting on the kingdom, I think it would be something more like this: Get busy dying so you can get busy helping others live. This is the final great paradox of the kingdom—it promises greater life, but it requires a radical death, a death to ourselves."[9] When pastors and preachers exemplify being "crucified with Christ" to their listeners, it is

8. John Ortberg, *The Me I Want to Be: Becoming God's Best Version of You* (Zondervan, 2010), 165.

9. Bezner, *Your Jesus Is Too American*, 191.

contagious. We cannot expect our hearers to change if we are unwilling to change first. As Christian leaders, preachers lead the charge toward discipleship and Christlikeness. In this manner, preachers model obedience to the Word in its entirety (as best we possibly can).

Discipleship Is Both Taught and Caught

We often like to distinguish matters of life as being innate, taught, or caught. Since discipleship is not innate to anyone, whether discipleship is taught or caught is a non sequitur. In fact, discipleship is clearly both caught and taught, not either/or. The word "disciple" (*mathetes*) means "learner" or "practitioner." We learn by knowing, doing, and *practicing*. I can say I am an avid pickleball player, but if I never show up on the court to practice or play, how can I get better? Similarly, discipleship is cerebral *and* practical. We often talk a big game about discipleship, but few work at it intentionally. Intellectual knowledge must lead to practice: experiential knowledge. Preachers and their listeners don't develop discipleship simply by knowing more. We, all Christians, become Jesus's disciples by living and obeying God's truth, as the British like to say, full stop.

When I think about what it was like for Jesus's first disciples, I imagine a daily apprenticeship where Jesus gave the twelve verbal instructions followed by practical exercises. He taught them the Word of God daily and it was their responsibility to implement it in action. One moment stands out to me where the disciples were impotent to cast out demons:

> When they came to the crowd, a man approached Jesus and knelt before him. "Lord, have mercy on my son," he said. "He has seizures and is suffering greatly. He often falls into the fire or into the water. I brought him to your disciples, but they could not heal him."
>
> "You unbelieving and perverse generation," Jesus replied, "how long shall I stay with you? How long shall I put up with you? Bring the boy here to me." Jesus rebuked the demon, and it came out of the boy, and he was healed at that moment.
>
> Then the disciples came to Jesus in private and asked, "Why couldn't we drive it out?"
>
> He replied, "Because you have so little faith. Truly I tell you, if you have faith as small as a mustard seed, you can say to this mountain, 'Move from here to there,' and it will move. Nothing will be impossible for you." (Matt. 17:14–20)

What a mystery for the disciples, who in the past had successfully exorcised demons! The teaching moment comes in verse 19, when the disciples approached him privately and asked Jesus why they were ineffective. Jesus comments on their lack of faith. Some manuscripts insert in verse 21 words that are similar to Mark 9:29: "This kind can come out only by prayer." Earlier in Matthew 6, in the Sermon on the Mount, Jesus had taught the disciples about giving, praying, and fasting in secret to the Father. By chapter 17, the disciples, now put to the test in a real-life ministry moment, cannot exorcise the demon. It takes more than intellectual faith to develop discipleship. It must be coupled with faith in action, often referred to in ministry as praxis.

Listeners Become Disciple Makers

The Christian life has a transitional and transformative quality to it: It moves commonly through four phases of spiritual formation: nonbeliever/skeptic, convert, disciple, disciple maker. Once we become disciples who have put our faith and trust in the Lord Jesus Christ, we immediately move into the disciple and disciple-making stages of faith that continue in perpetuity. Many seem to struggle postconversion. We, pastors and preachers, have at times waffled in our teaching/exampling of how to be a disciple and disciple maker.

Years ago, when I was serving as a senior pastor, I regularly preached or taught a Bible study on Friday evenings. Frankly, my sheep were hungry, so I often taught the Bible in various contexts several times per week (including leading a small group Bible study, preaching one or two different sermons, and teaching Bible study for the entire congregation on Sunday afternoons). I still remember one Friday evening when I asked my leaders to put into practice the things they were learning from our Bible study, one member shouted out: "Pastor Matt, we still need to be fed more!" In my disbelief, I remember responding incredulously, "When are we going to start practicing what we've learned?"

Preaching to form disciples and disciple makers demands regular invitations to participate in the life of Christ. Explore pulpit discipleship with a piece-by-piece perspective, where we might address specific areas of discipleship in a given year. This relates back to planning our preaching (chap. 5). Be concrete and discern how the church might grow in discipleship over the next year, three years, and even five years.

Prayerfully ask the Spirit to reveal the most pressing issues of discipleship for your congregants. Similarly, ask your leadership and pastoral staff what people most need to hear about from the pulpit. Just as physical exercise is never welcome per se, spiritual exercise also presents various challenges and barriers. Nobody likes to be pushed into doing uncomfortable things, and oftentimes spiritual maturity lends itself toward going into uncomfortable areas of life that are not surrendered to the Lord.

Preaching on Discipleship's "Big Three": Money, Sex, and Politics

Anecdotally, if I were to name the "big three" discipleship issues that cause the greatest disruptions, divisions, and vices in the Christian life, they would include the arenas of money, sex, and politics. Pushback at the highest levels comes when the preacher administers sermonically God's truth on these difficult topics. Why?

Money (stewardship, tithing, giving), sex (biblical marriage, sexual ethics, and gender identity), and politics (praying for political leaders, bipartisanism, political divisions) are heavily personal issues and identity issues at their core. We don't have the space to go deeply into these topics. But suffice it to say, preachers would be wise to preach regularly on money, sex, and politics.[10] The big three are a Pandora's box of sorts to open from the pulpit. They are some of the toughest topics for disciples to fully digest so that they can trust and obey God's Word. Temperatures rise in congregations when we broach these sensitive topics, particularly human sexuality and LGBTQ+ issues.[11] To our detriment, rather than engaging in healthy dialogue, oftentimes we, as preachers, have failed to demonstrate understanding and compassion and have approached these issues in a heavy-handed manner that conveys: "God said it, so get with it." We can be more winsome and irenic.

Preach with nuance by addressing the kaleidoscope of perspectives on these divisive concerns. Acknowledging another's views (even if different from your own) goes a long way, but do so in a loving manner. In most cases, we are not going to win over skeptics with one sermon (no matter how impressive or persuasive). Preach in a way that invites further conversation, and welcome those who take you up on the offer. Don't quickly dismiss them or their perspectives.

10. For books that may help us preach on money, sex, and politics, see Nathan Meador and Heath R. Curtis, *Stewardship: For the Care of Souls* (Lexham, 2021); Randy Alcorn, *Giving Is the Good Life: The Unexpected Path to Purpose and Joy* (Tyndale, 2019); Tony Scarcello, *Love All Our Neighbors: How Churches That Hold a Traditional Sexual Ethic Can Care for LGBTQ People* (IVP, 2026); Sam Serio, *Sensitive Preaching to the Sexually Hurting* (Kregel, 2016); Timothy Keller and Kathy Keller, *The Meaning of Marriage: Facing the Complexities of Commitment with the Wisdom of God* (Dutton, 2011); Miranda Zapor Cruz, *Faithful Politics: Ten Approaches to Christian Citizenship and Why It Matters* (IVP Academic, 2024); Matthew D. Kim and Paul A. Hoffman, *Preaching to a Divided Nation: A Seven-Step Model for Promoting Reconciliation and Unity* (Baker Academic, 2022); and David T. Koyzis, *Political Visions and Illusions: A Survey and Christian Critique of Contemporary Ideologies* (InterVarsity, 2019).

11. Transgenderism relates to identity and is not expressed through sexual behavior. However, that does not preclude the fact that we should, when appropriate, preach on gender and gender identity and dysphoria as well.

Discipleship Occurs with Greater Love for Christ

Ultimately, discipleship through obedience happens with greater love and affection for the Savior. Jesus said it plainly and simply: "If you love me, keep my commands" (John 14:15). There is no greater correlation between discipleship and obedience than love for Christ. The more we preach on the love of Christ and love for Christ, the more discipleship through obedience will gain traction. Of course, in our postfall world, there is no foolproof way to guarantee obedience to Christ. I sin and struggle with sin every day even though I do claim to love Jesus and want to love Jesus more and more.

At the end of John's Gospel, we read about Peter's reinstatement to ministry. It's a sobering narrative, as we often in hindsight lambaste Peter for his thrice denial at the end of Jesus's earthly ministry. However, it is interesting, isn't it, that Jesus asks Peter three times if he loves him. Rereading the account, it struck me how I never noticed that when the disciples realized it was Jesus who came to visit them on the shore, Simon takes center stage in the story. John narrates: "As soon as Simon Peter heard him say, 'It is the Lord,' he wrapped his outer garment around him (for he had taken it off) and jumped into the water" (John 21:7). If anyone loved Jesus, it was Simon Peter. I cannot imagine how badly Peter wanted to see Jesus again after his failure-by-denial. He could not wait the extra few minutes on the boat, so he swam to him. Then in verse 11 we read: "So Simon Peter climbed back into the boat and dragged the net ashore. It was full of large fish, 153, but even with so many the net was not torn." Simon takes on supernatural strength to bring Jesus the fish he requested in verse 10. Then comes Jesus's piercing question to Simon Peter: "'Simon son of John, do you love me more than these?' 'Yes, Lord,' he said, 'you know that I love you.' Jesus said, 'Feed my lambs'" (21:15).

We like to give Simon Peter a hard time, but I'm convinced more than ever that Simon Peter followed through on his thrice-repeated profession of love for Christ by obeying Jesus's thrice-repeated commands to feed Jesus's lambs, take care of Jesus's sheep (v. 16), and feed Jesus's sheep (v. 17). Simon Peter would go on to be one of the most evangelistically prolific disciples among the twelve. He wrote the letters of 1–2 Peter. And, according to church tradition, Peter would ultimately give his life for his beloved Savior via upside-down crucifixion on an inverted cross because he was unworthy to die in the same way as Jesus, in Rome.[12]

12. "Martyrdom of the Holy Apostle Peter," in *The Ancient Martyrdom Accounts of Peter and Paul*, trans. David L. Eastman (SBL Press, 2015), 19.

CONCLUSION

Discipleship is an apprenticeship to Jesus and the process of growing in obedience to his ways. Easier said than done, discipleship is a journey that will never become fully actualized. Yet if our preaching is not a regular exercise in discipleship, I don't know what the proper purpose would be. This is why preaching is so vital to the health of a congregation. At the core of what we do, preaching aims at discipleship and disciple making. In part 4, we move into the all-important neighborhood of spiritual preparation for preaching.

QUESTIONS

1. What is your definition of "discipleship"? Would you include obedience in your definition? Why or why not?
2. How is your congregation maturing spiritually? Where is it stagnant?
3. How have you approached preaching as discipleship?
4. In what areas would your congregation benefit from greater intentionality in discipleship?

PRACTICES

1. Pray for discernment as you engage matters of discipleship in your preaching and teaching ministries.
2. Make a list of recent discipleship topics you've covered over the last one or two years.
3. Ask your pastoral staff and church leaders how the church is doing regarding discipleship. What is most urgent in your pursuit of discipleship as a congregation?
4. Prayerfully incorporate some of these discipleship topics in your upcoming sermon series as you develop your preaching calendar.

PART 4

Spiritually Ready

As Ephesians 6:12 reminds us, "For our struggle is not against flesh and blood, but against the rulers, against the authorities, against the powers of this dark world and against the spiritual forces of evil in the heavenly realms." We know too many excellent communicators who have fallen into sin and moral failure. How does the preacher thrive in their own spiritual/prayer life and thereby lead the people from the overflow of that thriving spiritual life? This part is crucial for the preacher's life and ministry. We will answer a salient question: How does the preacher lead out of integrity, with the power of the Holy Spirit, and bring the congregation closer to Christ via discipleship and leadership? In this section, I write with the voice of one who seeks to be an encourager, cheerleader, and mentor, going on the same journey as you. By no means have I arrived nor will I ever arrive—nor will any of us. That's why we need encouragement in our spiritual lives. I trust that part 4 will assist you in this regard.

15

HOLINESS

Why Does Our Integrity Matter in Preaching?

For the Scriptures say, "You must be holy because I am holy."
—1 Peter 1:16 (NLT)

I must confess that I never wanted to be a pastor or preacher. What a strange admission toward the end of a preaching textbook. While there were many reasons for this hesitancy and at times even reluctance toward full-time, vocational ministry, one of the primary reservations regarded the unspoken expectations of holiness and integrity. Pastors are expected, by nature, to be more spiritually mature than those they lead. More emphatically, some expect pastors to be perfect. I didn't want that kind of pressure.

When I was serving as a senior pastor, one of my congregants said in an informal conversation, "Matt, your life must be really hard." When I asked him why, he responded, "Because you have to be perfect, but I don't." This was coming from a person who had gone through his share of scuffles with the legal system. His comment struck me between the eyes. It reiterated my fear of entering pastoral ministry in the first place. Holiness and integrity are indispensable in pastoral life and for anyone aspiring to preach and teach.[1]

1. See Matthew D. Kim, *7 Lessons for New Pastors: Your First Year in Ministry*, 2nd ed. (Cascade Books, 2021), xx–xxi; and Matthew D. Kim, "Being a Person of Character and Integrity" in *A Little Book for New Preachers: Why and How to Study Homiletics* (IVP Academic, 2020), 106–13.

The spiritual target on our backs from the enemy is real and so is the responsibility and weight of living a virtuous, morally exemplary life.

Some have a strange attraction to the pulpit and preaching ministry. When we see the panorama of celebrity pastors who seem to be idolized by their adoring listeners, who host podcasts and write bestselling books, who have church leaders hanging on their every word at pastors' conferences, it makes pastoring a large, well-known congregation rather alluring. Yet, like the clacking of falling dominoes, every day it seems like another minister of the gospel has succumbed to moral failure. Let me put it starkly: We are never immune to falling into temptation. The apostle Paul says it this way: "So, if you think you are standing firm, be careful that you don't fall!" (1 Cor. 10:12).

The call and pursuit of personal holiness for preachers is not unique to our time. As Nathan Finn observes, for example, "In his *Pastoral Rule* (c. 590), Gregory [the Great, the bishop of Rome] argued that preachers need not only be skillful homileticians but to live lives of holiness that confirm their preaching."[2] This is a good and right thing, to be certain. The life and lifestyle we project from the pulpit needs to be the same life we live outside of the pulpit every mundane moment of every day.

Those who advocate for the marriage between character and preachers are many in number. As a sample, Christopher A. Hall explains, "The [church] fathers affirmed a deep connection between the spiritual health of biblical interpreters and their ability to read the Bible well. . . . The character of the exegete would determine in many ways what was seen or heard in the text itself. Character and exegesis were intimately related."[3] In *How to Prepare Sermons*, William Evans notes, "What we are does indeed speak louder than what we say and certainly is more effective in the long run. . . . If the preacher is not living up to his [or her] preaching, the people will soon find it out—then woe be to that man [or woman]. . . . The preacher must be clean in the habits of his [or her] life."[4] Dwight Moody exhorted preachers saying: "The preaching that this world needs most is the sermons in shoes that are walking with Jesus Christ."[5]

In more recent years, Steve Norman states, "Preachers don't need more tricks and tips; we need help cultivating a life that generates great sermons. . . . The preacher's formation shapes the preacher's preaching. How I live influences

2. Nathan Finn, "Preaching in Historical Perspective," in *Handbook of Contemporary Preaching: A Wealth of Counsel for Creative and Effective Proclamation*, 2nd ed., ed. Michael Duduit (B&H Academic, 2024), 21.

3. Christopher A. Hall, *Reading Scripture with the Church Fathers* (IVP Academic, 1998), 41.

4. William Evans, *How to Prepare Sermons* (Moody, 1964), 17.

5. D. L. Moody, *Thoughts for the Quiet Hour* (Moody, 1941), entry for February 6.

how I preach and how I don't. Who I am shapes what I will say and what I won't."[6] Tara Beth Leach admonishes in *Radiant Church*: "Maybe it's time for us to look in the mirror, examine our hearts, and ask the Lord to show us where we've fallen short, confess, lament, and repent."[7] The sobering reality of ministers falling short and being disqualified from ministry service needs to be addressed head-on. The rest of the chapter will name some common battles preachers fight and conclude with reminders and suggestions for how we can intentionally pursue holiness and integrity each day.

Common Battles for Preachers Today

While we strive for personal holiness and integrity, we also recognize our humanity and limitations. Pastors and preachers are people too. Pastors and preachers fight every sin and temptation known to humanity. We are not somehow above committing any sin, but sometimes the expectation or weight on our shoulders to never sin can cripple us. In *The Imperfect Pastor*, Zack Eswine pleads, "A pastor is a human being. *I believe that Christian life and ministry are an apprenticeship with Jesus toward recovering our humanity and, through his Spirit, helping our neighbors do the same.* . . . I also believe that the general absence of this recovery of our humanity within pastoral ministry is spiritually killing us."[8] The pressure of perfection may be causing many pastors to spiritually implode as hidden sins lurk in the shadows.

Ajith Fernando raises two common battles for every minister of Christ. He observes: "The first is our battle with our personal weaknesses. Under this we can include such weaknesses as gossip, a quick temper, lust, lack of planning and self-discipline, stubbornness, and wasting time online and in front of the TV" and "another battle we often face in ministry: the battle with those who oppose us. Many fine servants of God have lost their credibility and influence because of unwise responses to attacks or criticisms they have encountered. They act on impulse, and often that action is a foolish one."[9]

Since the title and role of pastor assumes spiritual health, we also forget to examine our spiritual well-being. Jim Cymbala helps us, as preachers,

6. Steve Norman, *The Preacher as Sermon: How Who You Are Shapes What They Hear* (Christianity Today, 2021), 18.

7. Tara Beth Leach, *Radiant Church: Restoring the Credibility of Our Witness* (IVP, 2021), 7.

8. Zack Eswine, *The Imperfect Pastor: Discovering Joy in Our Limitations Through a Daily Apprenticeship with Jesus* (Crossway, 2015), 35.

9. Ajith Fernando, *Joyful Perseverance: Staying Fresh Through the Ups and Downs of Ministry* (Crossway, 2024), 149–50.

explore our spiritual condition: "Are we filled with the Holy Spirit? Are we being controlled by the Holy Spirit? Have we humbled ourselves before the Lord and let him work in us? The hardest part of the sermon is what God has to do in us, so that we can go up and preach with moral authority and spiritual power. Three points and a conclusion is not hard to do; what's hard is having a message that penetrates and gets rid of the junk that God wants to deal with."[10] Acknowledging our propensity to sin—as the well-known hymn says, "prone to wander, Lord, I feel it"—we simultaneously hold tightly to the Holy Spirit and daily become filled by the Spirit.[11]

Reminders and Suggestions for Holy Living

I leave us with several reminders and practices to safeguard integrity as pastors, preachers, and disciples.

Confess Sins Regularly

The practice of confession has been relegated to an antiquated, bygone era. Since Christianity has become so privatized, we can have a strong aversion toward individual and corporate confession. Nehemiah 9:1–3 reads, "Now on the twenty-fourth day of this month the people of Israel were assembled with fasting and in sackcloth, and with earth on their heads. And the Israelites separated themselves from all foreigners and stood and confessed their sins and the iniquities of their fathers. And they stood up in their place and read from the Book of the Law of the Lord their God for a quarter of the day; for another quarter of it they made confession and worshiped the Lord their God" (ESV).

Are we accountable to anyone for our actions other than the Lord? Is there a trustworthy friend or board member we meet with regularly to confess? When pastors are above confession of sin, something is amiss. Not that we need to publicly broadcast our sins from the pulpit or at a church business meeting, but we do need consistent confession to a trusted friend(s) or ministry partner(s). A blaring alarm should sound in our minds when we no longer feel the need to confess sins. If there is a ministry-disqualifying sin in our lives, this must be confessed quickly.

10. Jim Cymbala, "What the Holy Spirit Can Do in Your Preaching," Preaching Today, accessed January 8, 2026, https://www.preachingtoday.com/preaching-guides/preaching-in-power-of-holy-spirit/holyspirit.html.

11. Robert Robinson, "Come, Thou Fount of Every Blessing," Hymnary.org, accessed January 8, 2026, https://hymnary.org/text/come_thou_fount_of_every_blessing.

Abide in Jesus

The old adage and warning states that pastors only read their Bibles when preparing their sermons. Jesus says in John 15:4–8,

> Abide in me, and I in you. As the branch cannot bear fruit by itself, unless it abides in the vine, neither can you, unless you abide in me. I am the vine; you are the branches. Whoever abides in me and I in him, he it is that bears much fruit, for apart from me you can do nothing. If anyone does not abide in me, he is thrown away like a branch and withers; and the branches are gathered, thrown into the fire, and burned. If you abide in me, and my words abide in you, ask whatever you wish, and it will be done for you. By this my Father is glorified, that you bear much fruit and so prove to be my disciples. (ESV)

Meditating on these verses, I'm reminded that the purpose of abiding in Christ is not for ministry results and for bearing fruit alone. The emphasis of the text is on bearing fruit, but I would submit to you that the intention of abiding in Jesus is simply to be with Jesus. When we are with Jesus, spending time with him, it's only natural that Jesus will rub off on us. When people see the living Christ living in us, Jesus becomes more attractive to everyone we interact with. When we spend time with Jesus, it transforms every aspect of our lives, including our pastoral leadership and preaching.

Refrain from Shortcuts

We are living in a shortcut-taking world. From pastors seeking shorter degrees to no degrees, from writing our own thoughts on paper to relying on artificial intelligence, from preaching our own sermons to "borrowing" someone else's sermon, from living in full obedience to God's Word to cutting corners on our sanctification, it seems every day that it's easier to rationalize away our integrity rather than to maintain it.[12]

At first glance, taking a shortcut seems rather innocent and innocuous. What's the big deal? We might ask, Why preach my own sermon when someone else has said it more eloquently? Why can't I make a false promise I don't intend to keep? Or why do I need to let my yes be yes and my no be no?

Taking shortcuts in life affects every part of life. With every seemingly minor slippage of our character, we normalize sin and stray from holiness. Yes,

12. See, e.g., Scott M. Gibson, *Should We Use Someone Else's Sermon? Preaching in a Cut and Paste World* (Zondervan, 2008); and Sean O'Callaghan and Paul A. Hoffman, *AI Shepherds and Electric Sheep: Leading and Teaching in the Age of Artificial Intelligence* (Baker Academic, 2025).

there is some element of wisdom in culture's platitudes like "Work smarter, not harder." In most cases, however, we are living in a culture that champions "getting away with doing less." In every moment of ministry, do the work with excellence and do it for the Lord. To be concrete, when we tell our church members we'll be there for their child's birthday party, show up. Keep promises. If we don't intend to keep them, don't say them.

Monitor Pride and Ambition

While moral failure bends toward sexual and financial sins, anecdotally one of the leading culprits of ministry failure relates to pride and its twin-sister-sin, ambition. There's a reason why God named pride one of the most heinous sins affecting his people. Proverbs 16:18 says, "Pride goes before destruction, a haughty spirit before a fall." Similarly, in the New Testament, James 4:6 reminds readers, "God opposes the proud but gives grace to the humble" (ESV).

Particularly for ministry leaders and preachers, pride seems to be a sin that plagues the masses. I wonder sometimes if it's because pastors and preachers live in alternate realities but conflate their everyday lives with their vocational callings. What I mean is that our identity as pastors often provides a buffer for how we live, as if the title of pastor gives a false sense of security and even a license to sin. We think that by having the title of pastor we are somehow above daily obedience and the pursuit of holiness and humility, that somehow being called Pastor Matt makes me better than my congregants and the people I am supposed to serve.

Monitor your pride daily. Ask yourself some hard questions: How do I feel when I'm asked or expected to serve, especially behind the scenes? Have I become too important to meet with people? Why am I doing pastoral ministry? Why do I want to preach? Who am I seeking to impress? How do I evaluate my preaching ministry? How do I feel when I receive critical comments regarding my pastoral and preaching ministries? Am I discontent in my current ministry role and context? If so, why? Do I have ulterior motives that I haven't vocalized to my elders? Is there a "dream" calling that I have not surrendered to the Lord?

Cultivate Humility and Surrender[13]

The older I get the more I struggle with humility. You would think that one would struggle with humility at earlier stages of life, when one possesses

13. It later dawned on me that Andrew Murray wrote a book titled *Humility and Absolute Surrender* (Hendrickson, 2005), which may have entered my mind subconsciously when writing this subheading.

optimal strength and energy to work and to live. Rather, I have found that the longer I live and the more I achieve the harder it is to be humble. Richard Foster, in *Learning Humility*, gives us an image to help us identify a humble person: "[Eugene Peterson's] 'down to earth with each other' is a helpful way to unpack humility. It brings to mind once again the most basic notion of humility as tied to the earth, *humus*."[14] Similarly, Andrew Murray, a Scottish pastor and missionary to South Africa, places stronger emphasis on the place of humility for the Christian: "Humility, the place of entire dependence on God, is, from the very nature of things, the first duty and the highest virtue of the creature, and the root of every virtue. And so pride, or the loss of this humility, is the root of every sin and evil."[15] Another way to consider humility is to ask yourself, "Am I approachable?" and "Do I talk to people?" Humble people are normal people. They strike a balance between not thinking too highly of themselves and not being overly down on themselves either.

Pride is birthed from many places, but pastors and preachers tend to struggle with humility or insecurity because of the comparison game. The cliché "the grass is always greener on the other side" exists because humans are never content with what we have or what we get to do. When we become discouraged by someone else's success in ministry, we quickly locate another who doesn't measure up to what we have accomplished to make us feel better. Cultivating humility and surrender as a preacher involves taking a posture of keeping our focus solely on Christ who, as the author of Hebrews tells us, is "the pioneer and perfecter of faith" (12:2). When I stare at Christ, I see myself for who I am: a sinner saved by grace, a child dependent on my Father, a disciple who needs the encouragement and power of the Spirit, a son or daughter who can't live another day without the outstretched arms of a Savior. If God has seemingly blessed someone else differently, perhaps in ways you want to be blessed, that's his prerogative. The apostle Paul in Romans 9:20 asks rather bluntly, "But who are you, a human being, to talk back to God? 'Shall what is formed say to the one who formed it, "Why did you make me like this?"'"

Though it's often challenging, surrender your heart and desires completely to the Lord. Don't play the comparison game. Don't put your significance in degrees or numbers or what people say or don't say about you or your ministry. When I became the senior pastor of a small church of thirty-five adults and

14. Richard Foster, *Learning Humility: A Year of Searching for a Vanishing Virtue* (IVP, 2022), 68.

15. Murray, *Humility and Absolute Surrender*, 6.

twenty kids, nobody invited me to preach at other churches. But I remember hearing the Lord tell me, "Just love them." Pursuing faithfulness became so freeing when I didn't compare myself with others. For our purposes, humility is staying close to the Lord, depending on the Lord, and surrendering our will and our wants to him. God has you in your current ministry station for a reason. As God said to me years ago, "Just love them." By loving them, we will look more like Christ, and the result will be that they will do the same for others.

Don't Stop Learning and Growing

Last, never grow tired of learning and growing in your life: spiritually, intellectually, emotionally, and relationally. It's easy to coast in ministry. We create, for the most part, our own schedules. We can study if we want, read if we want, exercise if we want, do nothing if we want. The lifestyle of a pastor is a double-edged sword. Either we become workaholics or we become lazy. Particularly, when we get in a groove, we begin to think, "I know what I'm doing" or "There's nothing more I have to learn."

On a monthly or quarterly basis, set regular goals for your learning and growth. How do you want to develop? Perhaps it's smaller goals like reading a book in a new genre to you, joining a weekly aerobics class, or auditing a seminary course in person or online. Consider bigger learning goals like continuing education, attending annual workshops or conferences, augmenting your preaching skills by taking courses toward an advanced seminary degree, or joining a pastor's accountability group. Let the pursuit and passion for learning and growing never end.

CONCLUSION

Holiness seems to be an impossible ask in a world where everything seems permissible—even for ministry leaders. We often live with the mindset of asking for forgiveness rather than asking for permission. God's tolerance toward sin hasn't changed from the beginning of time. He hates it! To be a preacher God can use, we also must hate sin.

Whether you are a college student, seminarian, or working pastor, take stock of your integrity, character, and desire for holiness in your life. Let nothing, particularly sin, disqualify you from serving the Lord. There is no foolproof formula leading to godliness, righteousness, and holiness, so we must be ruthless in our elimination of sin and disobedience.[16] In our next chapter, we will explore our prayer lives, which also play a significant part in our spiritual readiness for pastoral and preaching ministries.

QUESTIONS

1. What does holiness look like for you in this season?
2. Is holiness something you are actively pursuing in your life? Why or why not?
3. How do you need to grow in holiness and Christlikeness? What seems to get in the way of your integrity?
4. Where do you get tempted the most: money, sexual sin, power, politics, pride, or something else?

PRACTICES

1. In the ruthless elimination of sin in your life, list every single sin you are struggling with today. Who can you share this with? And how can you actively seek to overcome them?
2. Find an accountability partner (friend, spouse, ministry partner) with whom you can regularly share your sins and victories. Who will you confide in?

16. The phrase "the ruthless elimination of" I borrow from John Mark Comer's title, *The Ruthless Elimination of Hurry: How to Stay Emotionally Healthy and Spiritually Alive in the Chaos of the Modern World* (Waterbrook, 2019).

16

PRAYER

How Does Prayer Affect Our Preaching?

> I am the vine; you are the branches. If you remain in me and I in you, you will bear much fruit; apart from me you can do nothing.
>
> —John 15:5

When I was a candidate for my first full-time pastoral position, one of the assistant pastors at the church looked me up and down with his arms folded across his chest. It was an unnerving feeling as we were standing in the church's parking lot. He then pricked my conscience by asking this blunt question: "So, Matt, how many hours a day do you pray?"

My immediate reaction was one of scoffing on the inside. Excuse me? The nerve of this guy! Who does he think he is? However, to tell you the truth, the question stumped me. Good questions can sting the soul. I thought to myself, hours? I do not think in terms of hours. I think in terms of minutes. Instead of answering his question with a quantitative number, I embarrassingly just blurted out something generic. "Of course, I pray regularly." As I continued to search for that first pastorate, however, that question never escaped me: "So, Matt, how many hours a day do you pray?"

In asking this very pointed question, God was using this pastor to speak into my life. I was searching for a pastorate to shepherd others and to establish a preaching career, but I was not being shepherded by the True Shepherd. I did not have a vibrant prayer life or much of one at all. Three years in seminary and another three years pursuing a PhD left my spiritual life like a well gutted dry. On top of that, as a highly independent person, I often struggle with prayer. That same struggle followed me into my first call to ministry. If I am honest, prayer is still a constant battle.

Many preachers today would say, "Of course, prayer is an integral part of my preaching preparation." The question is, What correlation do we see between our prayer life and life transformation in our listeners? I am ashamed to say that it took me well over two years to figure out that prayer is an indispensable part of preaching. E. M. Bounds writes, "The little regard we give prayer is evident from the little time we spend on it."[1] Bounds further encourages us with these words, "Prayer, in the preacher's life, study, and pulpit, must be a conspicuous and all-impregnating force, an all-coloring ingredient. It must play no secondary role, be no mere coating."[2] Yes, I would pray here and there throughout the week for my upcoming sermon. I would pray for my sermon on Sunday morning and as I walked up to the pulpit. Yet did I really pray?

I once had a seminary colleague who jokingly and cleverly called prayer "Wasting time with God." Obviously, the statement is a form of sarcasm or irony. Time is never wasted when in the presence of the Lord. While our type A personalities and productivity meters are often annoyed by "wasting time" in prayer, prayer is the exact opposite. Prayer is productive. Prayer is foundational and essential for the Christian life, in general, and for pastors and preachers, in particular. Prayer only accelerates ministry work and efficiency because we are relying on God and not on ourselves.

Sermon Preparation Is Steeped in Prayer

R. Kent Hughes, who pastored College Church in Wheaton, Illinois, once had this to say about preaching: "My practice over the years has been to spend about 20 hours per week in sermon preparation. And I've said many times that sermon preparation is twenty hours of prayer, since it's 20 hours of asking the Father, Son, and Spirit to open the text as I struggle to grasp its place in the book, its thrust and symmetries, and its significance for my hearers. So sermon preparation is an ongoing conversation, 'Lord, help me; Spirit, help me.'"[3]

1. E. M. Bounds, *Power Through Prayer* (Whitaker House, 1982), 47.

2. Bounds, *Power Through Prayer*, 43.

3. R. Kent Hughes, "Preacher's Toolkit: How Do I Prepare My Heart to Preach?" February 10, 2016, The Gospel Coalition, https://www.thegospelcoalition.org/article/preachers-toolkit-how-do-i-prepare-my-heart-to-preach.

Twenty hours? How can we pray for twenty hours when we have so many things to do in ministry? God can use one-word prayers just as he can three-hour prayers. It's been said that the great leader of the Protestant Reformation, Martin Luther, started each day with three hours of prayer, saying: "I have so much to do that I shall spend the first three hours in prayer."[4] The Scottish preacher Robert Murray M'Cheyne taught pastors on the centrality of prayer: "Give yourselves to prayer and the ministry of the Word. If you do not pray, God will probably lay you aside from your ministry as He did me, to teach you to pray."[5]

What Hughes means, what Luther demonstrated through his practice of prayer, and what M'Cheyne learned the hard way is that prayer is invaluable in sermon preparation. Prayer is indispensable. We need to pray because we are engaged in a spiritual battle. The moment we walk into the pulpit we recognize that what we are doing is not something that just any communicator does. We are preaching Scripture, and the enemy doesn't want us to. The enemy doesn't want us to have power. He doesn't want us to display God's power through our sermon.

What we are doing is bathing our sermon in prayer. Bathing our sermon in prayer is acknowledging that every part of sermon preparation and proclamation requires it. We pray about which text to preach on (as covered in chap. 5). As we're going through the rigors of exegesis and determining what the author is talking about, we're constantly prayerful. What does it mean to pray in such a way that we're asking the Holy Spirit to guide us to understand the authorial intent of the passage? What does this mean for the people back in Bible times, and what does it mean for us today? I don't want to preach my own thoughts and my own ideas. I want to preach the Lord's thoughts and the Lord's ideas. Even in outlining or writing our manuscript, we are constantly soaking our sermon in prayer. We are praying through what it means to speak to people in such a way that God's Word comes alive in their midst. We are praying for God to open people's heart for growth, transformation, and greater discipleship and Christlikeness. Here are some specific prayer requests to make prayer a more foundational part of our preaching rhythms for our benefit and the benefit of those to whom we preach.

Pray for Holy Spirit Power

We have all experienced the mystery of prayer. It is not an exact science. Why do we need to pray as preachers? First, we acknowledge the need for

4. This quote is widely attributed to Martin Luther.

5. Robert Murray M'Cheyne, *The Works of the Late Rev. Robert Murray M'Cheyne: Containing His Life and Remains, Letters, Lectures, Songs of Zion* (1847; repr., HardPress, 2017), 68.

the power of the Spirit. Preaching in the power of the Holy Spirit recognizes that the Spirit works mysteriously and in powerful ways that we cannot fully comprehend or accomplish in our own strength.

I wonder if self-reliance occurs among God's preachers once we think we have this preaching thing down. Perhaps we pray a little less fervently today than when we first started. Perhaps we pray a little less urgently after we have found our "preaching voice." Perhaps we pray a little less regularly once we learn the ropes of building a "successful" church. Though we fail to recognize it, our preaching can be like a fully inflated tire that has been slowly leaking its Holy Spirit power.

Pray for the Holy Spirit's presence and power. The disciples eventually received the power of the Holy Spirit in Acts 2 at Pentecost, and their lives and ministries were transformed forever. Francis Chan writes, "[The disciples] were no longer timid or confused; they were bold and inspired and began to declare and live the gospel of Jesus through the power of the Holy Spirit."[6] If we are honest with ourselves, maybe we can admit that we have not been living in the power of the Holy Spirit, and as a result our preaching has suffered from spiritual anemia. Pray for the Spirit's power.

Pray for Transformed Lives

Second, pray for transformed lives through the working of the Holy Spirit. Ministry ebbs and flows through different seasons. After the initial honeymoon phase, pastors and parishioners commonly experience a lull in vitality. Our congregants' lives are messy. Sins abound. Illnesses spread. Cancer roars. Relationships fracture. Jobs are lost. Death snatches another victim. Depression and pain linger on. We minister in utter brokenness. It is a challenging time to be a pastor, as it always has been.

One of the ways we can pray, practically speaking, is through the church directory (although I recognize that some churches are bigger than others). Still, pray about your congregation's needs and struggles. You may not get to everyone every week but break it up into sizable groups. What is that family going through at this moment? What does it look like for this person who has lost her job to understand this sermon text? And as we do so, we slow down our preparation. We don't just rush through it to get the sermon finished. We don't just go through the exercise of exegesis. But we are prayerful about each moment of the sermon preparation process.

6. Francis Chan, *Forgotten God: Reversing Our Tragic Neglect of the Holy Spirit* (David C. Cook, 2009), 68.

Pray for life transformation in yourself and in your people. Remember Paul's words to the Christians in Rome: "Do not conform to the pattern of this world, but be transformed by the renewing of your mind" (Rom. 12:2). Pray for the Spirit to transform the church rather than have it cling to the lethal precipice of being corrupted by the world. We often see a lack of transformation in the lives of the people in our congregations, but if we use sober judgment, we might also see this transformational malaise in ourselves.

The Christian life was not meant to be like this! As pastoral leaders and preachers, we can change the world for Christ and his kingdom. We can pray for our congregants to live gospel-centered lives in their homes, workplaces, schools, and communities. We can pray for discipleship, sanctification, and holiness. We can pray for Jesus's love to shine through even the lives of tainted saints. Work your way through the church directory and pray, person by person, family by family, child by child. Pray for the Holy Spirit to transform God's people. Pray for transformed lives.

Pray for Congregational Intentionality

Third, pray for congregational intentionality. That is, what is your church's vision? Yes, every church has a vision statement or mission statement. Oftentimes they are very general statements like "Making Disciples" or "Loving God, Loving People." But are you aware of your church's contribution in reaching the lost in your communities?

What is your congregation intentional about? Being intentional is different than being reactionary. We can minister in reaction to something that happens to us personally or corporately. For example, if a group of homeless people begin to visit your church, you may react to the situation by writing up a church policy on how you will help these visitors. However, being intentional as a congregation means we will prayerfully become proactive participants in God's kingdom. We will intentionally learn about the needs in our community and find ways to meet those needs, whether they are financial, relational, emotional, cultural, or spiritual.

Preaching in the power of the Holy Spirit changes entire congregational visions. Remember the picture of the early church in the book of Acts; they devoted themselves to the apostles' teaching, breaking of bread, prayer, and fellowship (Acts 2:41–47). They gave to all in need. They were observant, intentional, communal, and sacrificial. They put others in front of themselves. They were hospitable, joyful, and praise filled. They were a vibrant expression of the in-breaking of the Holy Spirit's potency in their lives. Congregations today need intentional Spirit-led visions and not just reactionary impulses. Pray that the Holy Spirit will lead your congregation to intentionally live out your unique vision to make a ripple effect on your town, city, state, country, and world.

The Holy Spirit works in mysterious and powerful ways. There is much that we do not and will not understand about the Holy Spirit's person and deity. However, solicit the Holy Spirit's power in your life and in the lives of your church members. Pray for the Spirit to be present in your preaching and ministry efforts. Pray for the Spirit to transform your heart, which may suffer at times from discouragement and disappointment. Pray for the Spirit to invigorate your preaching with creativity and renewed passion. Pray for the Spirit to melt the hearts of your listeners who are regularly straddling the world and God's kingdom. Pray for the Spirit to bring back lapsed and wayward souls. Pray for the Spirit to use you and your ministry in ways you never envisioned. Preach in the power of the Holy Spirit. Be a preacher who is prayerful and Spirit led.

Pray for the Hurting

It took me years to figure out as a pastor that people in the congregation were hurting. People may hide their pain behind a smile, but there are always those in the church going through a difficult, challenging moment or season or even lifetime. They need a touch of God's grace as well as a touch of grace from their pastor. I confess that I used to get upset when people didn't seem happy or when the gospel didn't seem like enough in the Christian life. In my naivete, I thought: "Why isn't Jesus enough for them!" How wrong I was!

Jesus is enough, but sometimes the trials of life are excruciating and heart-breaking. I've gone through several seasons of trial in my life over the last couple of decades. I need grace just as much as my listeners do. Pray for the Holy Spirit to comfort those in your church who are weeping and hurting. Paul writes to the church in Rome: "In the same way, the Spirit helps us in our weakness. We do not know what we ought to pray for, but the Spirit himself intercedes for us through wordless groans. And he who searches our hearts knows the mind of the Spirit, because the Spirit intercedes for God's people in accordance with the will of God" (Rom. 8:26–27). Pray regularly for the hurting in your midst. Praying for our suffering listeners changes our hearts toward them just as it can bring healing to them through the active work of the Spirit. Only God can heal our wounds, even though the scars remain. Not only is prayer an integral part of extending our ministry to hurting people; it's also an opportunity to partner with our church members and ask them to pray for us.

Ask Others to Pray for You

Since preaching is dealing directly with the realm of the spiritual and engaging in spiritual warfare, it's only right that we regularly invite our congregation to pray for us and our preaching ministry. Using the apostle Paul as his example, Scott M. Gibson writes, "The Apostle Paul was a great cheerleader for prayer. When reading his letters written to the various churches as found in the New Testament, he regularly underscores the importance of prayer. . . . A powerful factor in preaching is having others pray for us as we preach. . . . Like Paul, we can enlist others to pray for us as we preach."[7] As Gibson suggests, we model our congregational prayer request after the apostle Paul's instructions in Colossians 4:4: "That I may make it clear, which is how I ought to speak" (ESV); "That I may make it manifest, as I ought to speak" (KJV); and "That I may make it clear in the way that I ought to proclaim it" (NASB). . . . "The 'it' to which Paul is referring is the gospel, the 'mystery of Christ' (Col. 4:3)."[8]

Asking the congregation to pray for us has a twofold benefit. It first helps the preacher. It reminds us that we, preachers, need the prayers of others. We enter the pulpit with a posture of humility. We are not above contradiction or correction. We need God's Word just as much as our listeners do. And it helps our preaching to be clear, as noted in the paragraph above.

Prayer also helps listeners. Perception is not a small element to throw away. Asking for prayer conveys to our congregation that the sermonic moment is not a one-person, one-directional performance. As noted, congregants become active participants in the preached Word. Now that they have prayed, they are hopefully invested. They've now asked God to open their hearts and minds for God's transformative work to take place. And in so doing, they become "doers of the Word" (James 1:22 ESV). Asking for prayer also reminds the church that we are a collective body to whom God is speaking and leading in the same direction.

Depend on God's Transformational Power

How are we doing with prayer lately and in general? This is not to make us feel guilty. It's an honest question that should never get old for any believer. Kyle Strobel and John Coe observe helpfully: "Unfortunately, most of us

7. Scott M. Gibson, "A Prayer for Preaching," Preaching Today, accessed December 2, 2025, https://www.preachingtoday.com/skills/2024/prayer-for-preaching.html.

8. Gibson, "Prayer for Preaching."

have never thought about where our journey of prayer has taken us. We are told where we should be and where we should go, but this isn't helpful until we can locate ourselves on the map. . . . Consider what kinds of adjectives describe your praying in each season. For some, words like exciting, loving, and joyful might be the first to come to mind. For others, words like lonely, abandoned, guilt-ridden, or boring come to the fore."[9] No matter where we find ourselves on this prayer journey, we can learn to depend more on God and on his transformational power. We can learn how to pray and pray more intentionally.

Can we change a life in our own strength and power? That's a rhetorical question. Let me answer that for us: No! It is humanly impossible to change or transform another person's life. No matter how eloquently we communicate and how impeccable our sermon's structure might be, only the triune God can save a life and transform it. For this reason, the only thing we can do is pray. We pray and depend on the Lord. So, with that challenge, will you dedicate yourself to praying for your preaching ministry? Make prayer your primary pursuit as a preacher and see what the Lord can do.

CONCLUSION

Prayer is the lifeblood of the sermon. Prayerless preaching results in impotent preaching. Without prayer, our sermons are empty words proclaimed by empty souls. Without prayer, our sermons lack transformative power. From beginning to end, the sermon is a prayer-filled, prayer-empowered opportunity to shepherd God's people through his very spoken Word. We are not too busy to pray. We pray, like Luther did, desperately and passionately because we are so busy. As we prepare to preach, as we enter the pulpit, as we share the meal that God has given us to feed ourselves and our flocks this week, pray. It's the only thing that can bring life transformation. Preaching devoid of prayer will produce people devoid of Christ's power. I often tell my students that of course I prayed as a pastor, but I always wish I had prayed more. Commit yourself to a preaching ministry marinated in prayer. You will never regret praying more for yourself and for your listeners, but you will regret prayerlessness.

9. Kyle Strobel and John Coe, *Where Prayer Becomes Real: How Honesty with God Transforms Your Soul* (Baker Books, 2021), 14.

QUESTIONS

1. Without being overly self-critical or legalistic, how are you doing in your personal prayer life?
2. Without being overly self-critical or legalistic, how are you doing in your prayer life in terms of your preaching ministry?
3. In what areas can you grow in your prayer life?
4. What may be some obstacles for developing your prayer life both personally and for the congregation?

PRACTICES

1. Spend time this week in prayer prior to selecting your text. How did praying intentionally shape your heart or mind this week in preparation for preaching?
2. Go through your membership directory and spend time each day praying for a group of listeners. Move sequentially through the list and pray for as many church members as you can.
3. As you pray for your congregation, ask them to also pray for you.

17

SPIRIT

What Role Does the Holy Spirit Play in Our Preaching?

> But you will receive power when the Holy Spirit comes on you; and you will be my witnesses in Jerusalem, and in all Judea and Samaria, and to the ends of the earth.
>
> —Acts 1:8

When I was in middle school and in the early years of high school, I had the privilege of playing basketball on my school's team. Back in the day, the cheerleaders memorized several different cheers to try their best to motivate the team and the spectators who were in attendance. One particular cheer comes to mind: "We've got spirit, yes we do. We've got spirit, how 'bout you?" It's an apt cheer in the sports world that applies to our preaching ministry as well. For pastors and preachers alike, here's a cheer for you: "We've got [the Holy] Spirit, yes we do. We've got [the Holy] Spirit, how 'bout you?"

The Holy Spirit is not an "it" or even a "ghost" as we sometimes like to refer to the Spirit.[1] Still, there is no shame in admitting the Holy Spirit is a mystery. What's not mysterious, however, is that the biggest X factor in the task of preaching is relying on the Holy Spirit for every part of the preaching process—from start to finish (including the postsermon sanctification work of the Spirit in us and in our hearers).

1. Donald Fairbairn, *The Trinity* (Union, 2024), 39–40.

The Bible is not silent on the Holy Spirit's personhood and work. According to Old Testament scholar John R. Levison, the Holy Spirit (Hebrew *ruakh*, Greek *pneuma*) is referenced nearly eight hundred times in Scripture.[2] The purpose of this chapter is twofold: to inform and remind us of not preaching in our own strength. We have the Holy Spirit readily at our disposal in our hearts and working in the hearts of our listeners. We've got the Spirit, yes we do, so let's rely solely on him.

The Person of the Spirit

As we've touched on in part 1, the Holy Spirit is a person and deity at the same time. The Spirit is the third member of the triune God. He is incomparably omnipotent and wholly omnipresent. At the same time, what's unique about the Holy Spirit is that the Spirit indwells every committed follower who has repented of sin and put their faith in Christ and is a disciple of the Lord Jesus Christ who seeks to obey his commands. As Romans 8:9 records, "However, you are not in the flesh but in the Spirit, if indeed the Spirit of God dwells in you" (NASB), and 1 Corinthians 6:19 underscores, "Or do you not know that your body is a temple of the Holy Spirit within you, whom you have from God, and that you are not your own?" (NASB). What a comfort and confidence afforded to those who are true believers and disciples to have the Holy Spirit dwelling inside of us.

Teaching on the person of the Holy Spirit has always been tricky. As a senior pastor, I preached children's sermons to our congregation once a month. If you can teach a complex theological concept or biblical truth to children effectively, you are doing something right and good. In seeking to do so, I have used well-written children's books for theological insights for children. In asking myself, "What can we learn about the Spirit from children's books?" I recently came across *Josey Johnson's Hair and the Holy Spirit*.

In his storybook, Esau McCaulley teaches on the person of the Holy Spirit through the medium of a children's story about his daughter's hair. The person of the Holy Spirit is described in McCaulley's book as a gift given at the event of Pentecost in Acts 2. Then, according to McCaulley's character, Josey's father explains the Spirit as appearing "as small flames above their heads—what the Bible calls 'tongues of fire.'"[3] The Spirit has no physical form.

2. John R. Levison, "The Spirit in the Christian Bible," St. Andrews Encyclopaedia of Theology, University of St. Andrews, February 15, 2024, https://www.saet.ac.uk/Christianity/TheSpiritintheChristianBible.

3. Esau McCaulley, *Josey Johnson's Hair and the Holy Spirit* (IVP Kids, 2022).

Yet isn't it interesting that even though the Spirit is a divine person, those who attempt to explain him incorporate visual images to represent what the Spirit is like? One of the most impressionable things we can do from the pulpit is to speak of the Holy Spirit as a distinct and divine person. Let's move on to what the Spirit does.

The Names and Works of the Spirit

For many in the pews, the Holy Spirit is not a personal, indwelling, known quantity in their lives. Rather, the Spirit is an abstract, amorphous unicorn mentioned every so often at church, who, according to Margaret Feinberg, may feel "more like a theological concept than a divine companion."[4] The Holy Spirit is primarily known, in Scripture, as the Great Helper. Jesus calls the Spirit the "Spirit of truth" (John 14:17) and "the Advocate" (v. 26), also translated in the ESV as "the Helper" (v. 26).

In another recent children's book I surveyed, Jessica Mireles similarly portrays the Holy Spirit to children primarily in the role of being our helper. For instance, in Mireles's *Holy Spirit Help Me*, the main character talks/prays regularly to the Spirit and requests the Spirit's help: "Holy Spirit can you help me today? Help me use kind and respectful words to everyone, no matter what they say!"[5] As the Great Helper, the Holy Spirit, as we've established in previous chapters, helps the preacher in many regards.

When it comes to the Spirit's work, perhaps we've felt as one writer put it: "Sometimes I felt that his [the Holy Spirit's] work is to give an occasional 'power boost,' for the purpose of bold evangelism, strong preaching, or passionate worship. Beyond this, I did not really understand the work of the Holy Spirit in our lives."[6] Developing a greater understanding and appreciation for the work of the Spirit only enhances our confidence in the Spirit and in the Spirit's profound role in shaping and transforming our lives.

The theological term for study on the Holy Spirit, as we know, is pneumatology. There are countless books written on the Holy Spirit that inform our understanding of pneumatology.[7] While I'm not able to provide

4. Margaret Feinberg, *The God You Need to Know Study Guide: 12 Practices to Awaken Your Relationship with the Holy Spirit* (HarperChristian Resources, 2025), 4.

5. Jessica Mireles, *Holy Spirit Help Me* (Jessica Mireles, 2025).

6. Arv B, "Enjoying the Work of the Holy Spirit," *The Gospel Coalition India*, June 27, 2022, https://in.thegospelcoalition.org/blogs/faith-not-sight/enjoying-the-work-of-the-holy-spirit.

7. Influential books on pneumatology include: Veli-Matti Karkkainen, *Pneumatology: The Holy Spirit in Ecumenical, International, and Contextual Perspective* (Baker Academic, 2018); Gordon T. Smith, *Welcome, Holy Spirit: A Theological and Experiential Introduction* (IVP

a comprehensive list of the works of the Spirit found in the entire canon of Scripture, allow me to borrow from the help of others here. As Margaret Feinberg explains, "The Spirit is the very presence of God, hovering over chaos, residing within us, guiding us, empowering us, and transforming us from the inside out."[8] Arv B, just mentioned above, notes: "The work of the Holy Spirit includes conviction of sin (John 16:8), regeneration (John 3:5–6), assurance of salvation (Rom. 8:16), enlightenment (John 16:13), transformation (2 Cor. 3:18), fruitfulness (Gal. 5:22–23), gifting (1 Cor. 12:7), and empowerment (Acts 1:8)."[9] In Patricia King's book *Spiritual Revolution*, she provides seventy functions of the Holy Spirit, of which I'll highlight some: The Holy Spirit anoints (Luke 4:18; Acts 10:38), the Holy Spirit ministers truth (John 14:17; 15:26; 16:13), the Holy Spirit washes, sanctifies, purifies, and justifies (Rom. 15:16, 1 Cor. 6:11; 2 Thess. 2:13; 1 Tim. 3:16; 1 Pet. 1:2, 22), the Holy Spirit invites us to walk with him (Rom. 8:4–5), the Holy Spirit gives access to the Father (Eph. 2:18), the Holy Spirit changes us into the image of Christ (2 Cor. 3:17), and the Holy Spirit convicts the world (John 16:8).[10] Now that we have a glimpse of the person of the Holy Spirit and the Spirit's works, how, then, does the Holy Spirit help us in our proclamation?

The Work of the Spirit in Preaching

In Greg Heisler's *Spirit-Led Preaching: The Holy Spirit's Role in Sermon Preparation and Delivery*, his analysis is spot-on when he says, "As preachers we are quick to confess the need for the Spirit's power in our preaching, but we fall short when it comes to explaining how to involve the Holy Spirit in our preaching. . . . My conviction is that we have failed to connect the discipline of homiletics with the doctrine of pneumatology, and as a result we find ourselves 'surprised by the Spirit' when he does move."[11] So, what's the solution?

Academic, 2021); Amos Yong, *Mission After Pentecost: The Witness of the Spirit from Genesis to Revelation* (Baker Academic, 2019); and Beth Felker Jones, *God the Spirit: Introducing Pneumatology in Wesleyan and Ecumenical Perspective* (Cascade Books, 2014).

8. Feinberg, *The God You Need to Know Study Guide*, 5.

9. Arv B, "Enjoying the Work of the Holy Spirit."

10. Patricia King, *Spiritual Revolution: Experience the Supernatural in Your Life Through Angelic Visitations, Prophetic Dreams, Visions, and Miracles* (Destiny Image, 2006), 118–22. While readers may not agree with all of Patricia King's premises, beliefs, arguments, and conclusions in *Spiritual Revolution*, the book still offers helpful information that lists the works of the Holy Spirit.

11. Greg Heisler, *Spirit-Led Preaching: The Holy Spirit's Role in Sermon Preparation and Delivery* (B&H Academic, 2018), introduction, Kindle.

Heisler contends that "the preachers who preach those sermons must become Spirit led and Spirit dependent in their preaching."[12] This section on the work of the Spirit in the preaching process will articulate how we can rely on the Spirit in our proclamation. My hope is that you will be able to exhale deeply as you learn to trust the Spirit's efficacious power to do what we cannot do.

The Holy Spirit Convicts

Oftentimes, preachers can get hung up on the false narrative that we need to muster up uber-eloquence and persuasiveness and twist the arms of our listeners to follow Jesus, to put their faith in him, and to become a disciple. It can be paralyzing to put the weight of that burden on our shoulders. No doubt, we are partially responsible to put together the most effective sermon that we can each time we preach. However, I have found that many preachers do not pray enough and trust the Spirit to work behind the scenes in the hearts and minds of our hearers.

The apostle Paul defuses this innate desire in preachers for pulpit eloquence. He says in 1 Corinthians 2:1, "And so it was with me, brothers and sisters. When I came to you, I did not come with eloquence or human wisdom as I proclaimed to you the testimony about God." In saying this, I don't believe Paul was telling the Corinthians that he didn't put forth any effort into his scriptural communication. Rather, eloquence and human wisdom were not a fascination or obsession for Paul. He wanted to explain the gospel and the Word simply and plainly for all to understand.

The Holy Spirit is not an add-on to the sermonic process. It is the Spirit who orchestrates the entire enterprise. As discussed throughout this work, we commit to praying to the Spirit before, during, and after the message because only the Spirit can convict our listeners of the truths being presented in God's Word. Do we fully believe in the Spirit's power to accomplish what we cannot? J. I. Packer explains this mysterious work of the Spirit: "Conversion is an exercise of divine sovereignty. Psychologically, the discernment and decision are ours, yet God turns us to himself by his own initiative and power. . . . In this act of almighty grace, the Holy Spirit is the direct agent. He illuminates, convinces, quickens, induces new birth, imparts repentance, and prompts the converted soul's confession, 'Jesus is Lord.'"[13] Pray that the Spirit works to convict the lost as well as those who have forgotten their identity as adopted

12. Heisler, *Spirit-Led Preaching*, introduction.

13. J. I. Packer, "The Work of the Holy Spirit in Conviction and Conversion," Lausanne Movement, May 5, 2018, https://lausanne.org/content/the-work-of-the-holy-spirit-in-conviction-and-conversion.

heirs who live and reign with Christ today and into an eternal inheritance. As you preach, remind your listeners of the Spirit's ability and power to transform them into disciples who obey God's truth in a culture that denies God's loving commands.

The Holy Spirit Applies

In addition to conviction and conversion, we can trust in the Holy Spirit's power to apply the Word in us and in our listeners. In Haddon W. Robinson's helpful definition of expository preaching, he is quick to magnify the Spirit's role in the work of sermonic application: "Not only does the Holy Spirit apply this truth to the personality and experience of the preacher, but according to our definition of expository preaching, he then applies that truth through the preacher to the hearers."[14] Whether it's instantaneous application or slow, steady, and deliberate, we can trust the Holy Spirit to nudge us or convict us to practice God's Word each moment of every day.

Application is both divine sovereignty and human responsibility. The sermon application needs to be communicated clearly by human preachers, but it is actualized, embodied, and lived out in the hearers by the Spirit. This has been my experience. There have been so many times where I've preached a message and a congregant shares her testimony with me after the service or even weeks later. In some inexplicable way, the Holy Spirit invited them to respond to the sermon in ways I didn't articulate. This is a profound mystery in the ministry of the Word that I will never fully comprehend. We cannot make anyone apply scriptural teaching on a Sunday afternoon or a Friday evening, but the Spirit can. In this way, only the triune God receives all the credit.

The Holy Spirit Transforms

Last, the Holy Spirit is the one and only primary agent who can transform preachers and the people listening in the pews. Our natural tendency is to live according to the desires of the flesh. Our propensity to sin is great, but the power of the Holy Spirit to transform is greater. We are commanded by Scripture to be "led by the Spirit" (Gal. 5:18) and to "keep in step with the Spirit" (v. 25). Thomas A. Tarrants clarifies, "The phrase *led by the Spirit* occurs only twice in the New Testament, and both instances

14. Haddon W. Robinson, *Biblical Preaching: The Development and Delivery of Expository Messages*, 4th ed. (Baker Academic, 2025), 9.

are frequently misused today. The first is in Romans 8:14, 'For all who are led by the Spirit of God are sons [and daughters] of God.' The immediate context is the believer's battle with the flesh through the empowerment of the Spirit. The second usage occurs in Galatians 5:18, 'But if you are led by the Spirit, you are not under the law.' Again, the immediate context is the believer's battle with sin. In both instances, the larger concern is to show us how to live joyful, obedient lives that produce the beauty of holiness and glorify God."[15]

A lifetime and lifestyle of spiritual transformation occurs as we become conformed to the image of Christ through the enablement of the Spirit. You and I cannot transform ourselves no matter how hard we try. It is the Spirit's work in us that facilitates the transformative process. Romans 8 is one biblical passage that most comprehensively articulates the Spirit's transformative presence and power in our lives: "Therefore, there is now no condemnation for those who are in Christ Jesus, because through Christ Jesus the law of the Spirit who gives life has set you free from the law of sin and death" (8:1–2). Here's the transformation the Spirit provides in verse 5, "Those who live according to the flesh have their minds set on what the flesh desires; but those who live in accordance with the Spirit have their minds set on what the Spirit desires." How does one know what the Spirit desires? By having a transformed mind and will that have been set free to live, walking in step with the Spirit.

It is paramount that in the preaching process we regularly encourage our listeners with preaching that is reliant on the Spirit. Help guide your listeners to walk in the Spirit each day of their lives. Transformation comes by the Spirit: "If by the Spirit you put to death the misdeeds of the body, you will live" (Rom. 8:13). Remind them of their true identity: "For those who are led by the Spirit of God are the children of God" (Rom. 8:14). Last, we proclaim this truth: "The Spirit himself testifies with our spirit that we are God's children. Now if we are children, then we are heirs—heirs of God and co-heirs with Christ, if indeed we share in his sufferings in order that we may also share in his glory" (Rom. 8:16–17). I'll end this section with Ingrid Faro's naming of how the triune God works in concert for our transformation: "Through our faith in following Jesus Christ, we become transformed into his image from one degree of glory to another degree of glory, as we cooperate with the Holy Spirit to renew our minds

15. Thomas A. Tarrants, "Being Led and Transformed by the Holy Spirit," C. S. Lewis Institute, December 5, 2016, https://www.cslewisinstitute.org/resources/being-led-and-transformed-by-the-holy-spirit.

and learn to think differently through God's Word (1 Cor. 3:17–18; 4:4–8; Rom. 12:1–2)."[16]

CONCLUSION

The greatest reassurance we have in our proclamation is that we are never alone in the pulpit. The fact that preaching is not dependent on me, my preparation, or my abilities alone is calming news. The mysterious, beautiful essence of preaching is that the Holy Spirit is with us and working in and through us and in spite of us, at all times, including during our preparation, proclamation, and postcommunication. Since preaching is not merely an intellectual or individual exercise, we do our best to depend on the Spirit, consult the Spirit, cry to the Spirit, pray to the Spirit, and expect the Spirit's power whenever we preach God's Word. Faithful preaching incurs spiritual warfare from the enemy. The work of preaching is entering into the front lines of spiritual warfare.[17] Remember, it is the Holy Spirit who convicts, applies, and transforms both the preacher and the hearers. Do your hermeneutical and homiletical best as you seek the Holy Spirit in your preaching. And then, give the rest and leave the rest to him.

QUESTIONS

1. What role does the Spirit play in your preparation, preaching, and postproclamation?
2. In your preaching thus far, how have you relied on the Holy Spirit?
3. How can you depend on the Holy Spirit more in your pastoring and preaching?
4. Have you explored the various ways the Holy Spirit works in your preaching?

16. Ingrid Faro, *Demystifying Evil: A Biblical and Personal Exploration* (IVP Academic, 2023), 113.

17. Siang-Yang Tan and Douglas H. Gregg, *Disciplines of the Holy Spirit: How to Connect to the Spirit's Power and Presence* (Zondervan, 1997), 74–76.

PRACTICES

1. For your next sermon, take inventory of how the Spirit is working in your particular text. Write down all the ways you see the Spirit's activity (written and unwritten) in your Scripture passage.
2. Incorporate in your upcoming sermon the Spirit's transformative power. Share this with your listeners and explain how they can rely on the Spirit for growing in spiritual maturity/Christlikeness.
3. Pray fervently for the Spirit to assist you in your preaching ministry during sermon preparation, proclamation, and postsermon application. Be a witness and testifier of how the Holy Spirit can accomplish more than we could ever do on our own.

PART 5

Communicationally Ready

This final part on communicational readiness puts everything we have read up to this point together. Since preaching is only one aspect of pastoral ministry, we want to explore the indispensable intersection between preaching and pastoring. Effective communicators embody the central characteristics of authenticity, passion, and empathy. In addition, with the ever-advancing and increasing use of technology, preachers would also benefit from considering the technological component to sermons. Finally, we seek to answer this question: What does effective communication and delivery look like today and going forward?

18

PRESENCE

Does Our Communication Embody Pastoral Presence?

> For I long to visit you so I can bring you some spiritual gift that will help you grow strong in the Lord.
>
> —Romans 1:11 (NLT)

Let's walk for a moment down memory lane. Which sermons do you remember hearing when you were little, or when you first became a Christian, or even in your lifetime? Which sermons do you remember preaching?

While I'm a big fan of the preaching enterprise (both preaching and hearing), I recognize, like many who have gone before me, that the sermonic moment is comparable to preparing and eating a meal. Preaching a sermon is much like preparing a meal, while hearing a sermon is much like eating a meal. Truthfully, there are very few sermons that I actually remember hearing and even fewer that I remember preaching. How many can you count for either one? Then, why do we bother to preach and listen to sermons?

The countless number of meals prepared or partaken in have nourished our bodies. Sermonic meals have similarly nourished our spiritual bodies. Though we often forget the sermons we've preached or heard, we do recall the times a pastor showed up for us in a moment of celebration or suffering, right? Your memory will not fail you in recalling every time your pastor gifted you with their presence, whether in times of rejoicing or hardship. Preaching is not just about what we communicate in the pulpit; it's primarily about being present with our people. Our presence, not just our preaching, is the greatest gift we can give to our congregants.

I'm saddened by the reality that there seems to be a growing number of seminarians and those seeking to enter pastoral ministry who want the spotlight on them from the stage but don't want to be stuck doing the behind-the-scenes, unglamorous acts of ministry service or the wearying task of listening to fractious souls. We want a platform to stand on but not a broom to push. My concern for those who only enjoy preaching but not pastoring is that preaching is only a slice of what ministers do. Preaching alone is not the comprehensive job description that God has called ministers to engage in. While admittedly taxing at times, the most wonderful part of being a pastor is knowing our people well and being with them in moments of laughter, sorrow, and everything in between.

Ian Pitt-Watson once observed: "Preaching divorced from pastoral concern is blind. It neither knows what it is talking about nor to whom it is talking."[1] I would second Pitt-Watson's claim that preaching and pastoring are inseparable. There is no substitute for being in the ministry trenches with the very people God has selected for us to shepherd. With this principle in mind, the question I'd like for us to consider in this chapter is: How do you pastor your people with your pastoral presence and pastoral communication in the pulpit? We are not simply bobblehead, armchair communicators who deliver a message from God. We are preachers of the Word who also minister to and shepherd God's people.

Keep the Main Thing the Main Thing

Historically, God has called only a select few people to be his messenger in the form of an itinerant, traveling preacher rather than a full-time vocational pastor in the local church. Only one name comes immediately to mind: Billy Graham. The hesitation to be a full-time pastor is understandable. I get it. Being a pastor is not easy.

Brian Croft and Ronnie Martin, in *The Unhurried Pastor*, express the sentiment of many toward their experiences in pastoral life and ministry: "There are the demands of 24/7 availability. The pressures of the workload. The mental toll of preparing several sermons or teachings every week. The emotional anguish that accompanies bearing the burdens of suffering people, while also carrying your own personal burdens. The financial compensation is commonly not adequate. Added to all this, pastors are trying to love and

1. Ian Pitt-Watson, *Preaching: A Kind of Folly* (Westminster, 1976), 58.

care for sinners—many are redeemed sinners, but they are still sinners. . . . The work of pastoral ministry is uniquely hard, and it always has been."[2] The last thing I want to do is to create additional burdens or expectations for your already full plate of pastoral responsibilities. Many of us already shepherd our people well. For those starting out in pastoral life, here are a few recommendations to illustrate what pastoral preaching, or preaching as one who pastors, involves.

Pastoral Preachers Love

Pastoral preachers and preachers who pastor foundationally and holistically love and shepherd their people. David A. Christensen defines pastoral preaching as "the building of a local community of faith in corporate worship by growing healthy disciples to become like Christ through biblical exposition empowered by the Holy Spirit while awaiting the return of Christ to the glory of God."[3] The work of pastoral preaching cannot be accomplished apart from a deep love for the flock. If we don't love our people, why are we pastors in the first place? As the apostle Paul framed it: "If I speak in the tongues of men or of angels, but do not have love, I am only a resounding gong or a clanging cymbal" (1 Cor. 13:1).

Love expresses itself differently according to one's culture. In Korean culture, the culture of my parents and ancestors, love is communicated through food. Whenever my grandmother asked us, "Did you eat yet?" or "Have you eaten?" she never had to verbalize the words, "I love you, Matt." Her love was conveyed clearly by asking whether I was hungry. It's not the food itself but the care behind the question that represents love. In other cultures, love is confirmed by time spent with the person or group. When a congregant says to their pastor, "I haven't seen you much at all lately," they're not saying they haven't visibly or physically seen your face in a room full of crowded people. What they are connoting indirectly is, "I haven't been able to spend time with you, and I'd like to (which is my way of showing love)."

Though cultural differences exist in expressing love, love through pastoral preaching is shown through one central, concrete way: patience. In our increasingly impatient culture, we find ourselves fleeing the scene any time we are expected to show patience. In 1 Corinthians 13, often referred to as the love passage, the apostle Paul commences this bountiful expression of pastoral

2. Brian Croft and Ronnie Martin, *The Unhurried Pastor: Redefining Productivity for a More Sustainable Ministry* (Good Book, 2024), 10.

3. David A. Christensen, *A Philosophy of Pastoral Preaching: Shepherding God's People with God's Word in One Place* (Wipf & Stock, 2023), 17.

love with these words, "Love is patient." It shouldn't be a surprise that Paul begins with equating love with patience because patience is one of the most unteachable traits. How does one teach patience? There is no simple answer! Patience is an attitude and a reflection of what's occurring in the heart. Signs of impatience include getting upset and frustrated, yelling, hurrying, bursts or fits of anger, stirring anxiety in the other person, and more. When it comes to pastoral ministry, patience is the most important and most challenging fruit to exhibit of all the fruit of the Spirit. That is why our default reaction to the demands of being a pastor is to want to leave or flee a congregation for another opportunity.

Pastoral Preachers Lead

The pastoral preaching moment is also a leadership moment. Every time we stand to proclaim God's Word to our congregation, it's another invitation to lead them closer to the triune God, align them closer to the triune God's mission and will, and lead them closer to Christ and to a life marked by Christian discipleship. Since preaching is such a strategic aspect of the life of the church, prayerfully consider how your preaching ministry leads and steers your people on the path to Christlikeness both collectively and as individual believers.

Thinking about herding sheep for a moment, the primary purpose of a shepherd's staff is not to hit or strike them. Rather, it's to goad, push, or lead them away from danger and onto the right path. When people in our congregations are living in unrepentant sin, drifting away from the Lord, disobeying God's Word, causing rifts and divisions, harming themselves, or displaying other signs of unrighteous behavior, the pastor's job is to lead them back to the Lord, back to the truth, back to safety, and back to unity. This leading happens in our preaching life and preaching ministry. We are fighting an uphill battle when it comes to preaching truth in an age of self-righteous defiance, and yet pastors never give up on their shepherding roles and responsibilities to lead.

Similarly, a pastor or preacher's leading is not only to remind listeners of God's truths but also to cast a vision for where the congregation is heading. This may be somewhat unfair, but part of the impetus behind the Israelites' misbehavior in the book of Exodus occurred because Moses neglected to cast a clear and compelling pastoral vision. Placing the Ten Commandments or rules to follow on a pedestal was not enough to engender biblical obedience. People grumble when they don't know what they're doing or where they're going. Every Sunday, we have a precious opportunity to lead our congregations with the guidance of Scripture, pointing them in the way they should go.

What is your vision for the church, articulated through your weekly proclamation? Where do you want this church to go? How does this church need to grow in discipleship, obedience, and Christlikeness? In what areas does your church need to repent and be transformed? What does this church need to do to build and expand God's kingdom, near and far? Preaching presence is leadership presence.

Pastoral Preachers Linger

Third, pastoral preaching is found in a preacher who lingers after the worship gathering. I want to sit under the teaching of a pastor who is not in such a hurry to get somewhere else—one who lingers or loiters (in the best sense of the word) and is approachable. A pastoral preacher makes each congregant feel seen and heard. Are we the type of pastor who makes others feel so treasured and vital in that way?

Over the years, I have benefited from being at churches where the preaching pastor was never too busy or too important to stand around and talk with people after the worship gathering. I've also been a part of churches where the pastor was always distracted and looking over my shoulder and not at me. The former is a beautiful image of pastoral presence, when the preacher is accessible and eager to speak with people. In many ways, preaching is an invitation to enter into community as we encounter the triune God together, a collection of individuals who are at the same time saints and sinners. When we linger, we make room for the very people God has called us to minister to and preach to. Lingering pastors get the best of both worlds: communicating but also pastoring, shepherding, or relation-ing (yep, just made that up) with those to whom one preaches God's Word. The second part of this chapter provides five additional characteristics that facilitate pastoral presence in preachers.

Characteristics of Pastoral Presence

A Worshiping and Worshipful Preacher

As pastors, it's easy for us to forget that our primary leadership role in the church is to be a worshiper of the triune God. Of course, pastors must focus their attention on any number of details to have a worship gathering go smoothly and without a hitch. Vision and execution of the plan are significant and necessary. The sermon is one embedded piece in the entire worship gathering or worship service. One of the most important leadership functions we can model for the congregation is to participate in singing to our awesome God with them.

I've been in a few worship settings, primarily when guest preaching at large churches, where the preacher does not sit in the worship space with the rest of the congregation. Rather, they sit tucked away in a "green room," perhaps for legitimate reasons: going over their message or resting before their "big sermonic moment." Yet this separation and isolation of the preacher from the worship gathering, to have alone time, is deeply troubling in terms of ecclesiology. If anything, the pastor/preacher is the lead worshiper in any ecclesial gathering. As a spirit of worship flows through the preacher, we emanate a worshipful disposition and will most likely preach a more worshipful sermon (i.e., a sermon preached with a heart of worship unto the Lord). Your presence in the pews worshiping with your local congregation matters just as much as if not more than your presence in the pulpit. There is a noticeable gap when the preacher is not worshiping alongside God's people, and this isolation is spiritually harmful for the pastor over the long haul of ministry.

An Authentic Preacher

I remember getting regularly frustrated during one season of my ministry as a senior pastor. It was just after the "honeymoon" phase, a few months into the second year of my pastorate. Some of my congregants' habits started to grate on me, like being consistently late to the worship service, their problematic and prevalent sins, and even the cliquishness of the church (which I believe stymied our growth). It seemed like people, in general, were being complacent and complaining more about what was or wasn't happening at church. I felt like I was often on the receiving end of those criticisms. As a result, and without me being aware of it, I started to show my annoyance and frustration (some may say anger) from the pulpit. One of the leaders approached me after one Sunday's sermon. He asked me if I was okay. When I responded, "Yes, I'm fine," he shot back, "Well, honestly, you seem frustrated and angry, and we can feel it in your preaching."

Authenticity seems like a trendy buzzword in our world today. What most people mean by *authentic* is to be real, honest, raw, unfiltered, not fake, genuine, and at times even crass. My example above illustrates that being authentic in the pulpit has boundaries. The preaching moment, standing in front of your congregation, is not the place for pastors to express anger or frustration. Of course, we can convey some inner feelings of discouragement or concern, but a preacher's more capricious forms of authenticity need not be on full display. In my case, I probably needed to be vulnerable and honest with our pastoral staff or lay leaders about how I was feeling in that season of ministry—outside of the pulpit.

The smell of authenticity does not present itself with either a grinning or frowning countenance. Authentic preaching shines through in being our best selves in the pulpit (I'll talk more about that in chap. 20). We're not always going to "feel like" preaching. In fact, you're probably going to "not feel like" preaching more than you "feel like" it.

People today want a pastor and preacher who is authentic and real. Authentic preaching means that listeners want to know that their pastor is honest and vulnerable about who they are. Some will perhaps want to know how their pastor is doing and whether they are living a life that's consistent with the gospel and what they're presenting in the pulpit.

A Relational Preacher

I wonder what it's like for any congregant to hear one sermon, let alone hundreds, from the same pastor/preacher with whom they've never experienced Christian fellowship either out for coffee or over a meal. Relationships are such an essential part of vocational ministry. During Jesus's three years of discipleship with his twelve disciples, I can only imagine how many meals they shared together talking about life, discipleship, and expanding the kingdom of God.

As an introvert by nature, I understand the exhaustion that settles in after a long day (Sunday) of pastoring, preaching, meeting, counseling, teaching, and leading (putting out fires and any number of stressors including unexpected ministry kerfuffles). Just the thought of additional meetings with people in the church during the week seems overwhelming. Yet, what about the people (regular attendees, church members, and even visitors) with whom you've never spoken beyond a courteous hello and an obligatory, "What's your name?" Granted, depending on the size of your church membership, it's not always feasible to have meals with every single person. You may want to consider opportunities where you could meet for coffee or lunch with three or four people at a time to build relationships with them.

It may seem sufficient to rely on your other pastoral staff or lay leaders to inform you of the happenings in congregational life, but nothing replaces a relational pulpit and pew. Remember, people in general are lonely. They are craving human, interpersonal interaction. That's why they've come to the worship gathering. They want to be known, loved, and feel a sense of belonging. Part of our role as pastoral shepherd is to get them there. As Shannan Martin notes in *Start with Hello*, "We can't claim to love what we don't know. We can't know what we don't see. We can't fully *see* anything if we don't put our bodies in places of tension and pain. There's a massive difference between loving people in theory and loving them in the moment—by name. It's up to us to choose."[4]

Just a quick anecdotal example: Over the course of my pastorate, there were several people in my congregation who were inattentive, to say it nicely, during the preaching of my sermons. However, once I met with them for coffee or bought them lunch or spent time with them participating in one of their hobbies, their countenance, demeanor, and sermonic attention began to alter noticeably and favorably. They began actively listening to the sermon each week. Those same people who seemed uninterested or disengaged were now smiling during the message, after I met with them (even just once). I could tell visibly that I now had relational "buy-in" from them because I invested time in building relational capital. Don't just take my word for it. Try it. You will, in my experience, never regret meeting with a congregant to gain relational trust.

A Warm and Friendly Preacher

Allow me to begin with a contrary example and then offer a positive one. A pastor from my past was known, at least in my world, as the "red-faced preacher." This nickname wasn't on account of his warm countenance and personality. Instead, it was because he was always red in the face from yelling at us. Even affectionate phrases like "Jesus loves you" were shouted with veins popping out of his neck. Though it seems like an exaggeration, this particular preacher failed to exhibit a warm, inviting presence. I wanted to give him the benefit of the doubt, but in all honesty, I was afraid of him. He was scary, and I was not the only one who felt that way toward him.

Pastoral warmth is a quality that cannot be assumed or taken for granted or feigned from the pulpit. Insincerity may fool a person once but never twice. Here's the honest truth: We may think we are warm (including in the pulpit), but that may not be what the popular opinion poll says about us. I think the "red-faced preacher" thought of himself as friendly and warm as well. We want to be known as a warm and friendly pastor and preacher.[5]

4. Shannan Martin, *Start with Hello (And Other Simple Ways to Live as Neighbors)* (Revell, 2022), 162.

5. To develop a warm, friendly, and welcoming presence, you might consider going to resources like Martin, *Start with Hello*; Laura Baghdassarian Murray, *Becoming a Person of Welcome: The Spiritual Practice of Hospitality* (IVP Formatio, 2025); and Matthew D. Kim, *Becoming a Friendlier Church: A Pathway to Genuine Community* (Baker Books, 2026).

Here are a few examples of warmth and friendliness in preaching: Simply smile appropriately, depending on what's being communicated in the sermon, such as when speaking on the love of Christ, grace, the gospel, or God's love (more on facial expressions in chapter 20), and use welcoming, inclusive language whenever possible, such as calling your church a family or saying out loud, "I'm so glad each of you is here!" While it may be temporarily painful, go back and watch a recent sermon you preached and honestly evaluate your warmth and friendliness. This might be a surprising experience for some.

An Unhurried, Nonanxious Preacher

The word "unhurried" is a double entendre of sorts. First, I mean unhurried in the communicational sense of one's rate of speech. Some preachers give the impression that they can't wait for the sermon to be over even before it starts. Everything about their preaching presence, mannerisms, words per minute, facial expressions, use of gestures, and body language conveys a stepping-on-the-gas, high-octane, frenetic preaching pace. The entire sermonic experience is hurried. The Scripture reading is rushed, as if there was no punctuation. There's no time to waste for pregnant pauses or any pauses. They might ask a brilliant question but leave no room for listeners to ponder it. Unhurried preachers take their time even though they still have a time limit.[6]

Being unhurried can also contribute toward becoming a nonanxious presence, which has become popularized in our culture. For a preacher to be a nonanxious presence entails a preacher recognizing that there is already enough in our world to be anxious about. Without knowing it, we can create undue stress and anxiety for our listeners in our manner of speech and in our word choice. We don't need to fan the flames of anxiety and worry by preaching in an anxious manner. What does anxious or anxiety-producing preaching look like?

Some preachers exude anxiety when they preach: Hearing every sermon feels like I'm experiencing a guilt trip. Anxious preachers communicate a sense of insufficiency or inadequacy in their hearers: Somehow we are not enough, we are not doing enough, we are not being enough, we are not giving enough, we are not happy or joyful enough, or we are not fill-in-the-blank enough! They use weighty or heavy-handed words that intentionally or unintentionally shame or guilt the listener (e.g., "should," "must," "need to," "have to," "ought to"),

6. Several unhurried pastors/preachers come to mind who seemed to take their time, never seeming to be in any hurry: Alistair Begg, Timothy Keller, Jim Cymbala, Fred Craddock, Haddon Robinson, and more recent unhurried preachers stand out like Tara Beth Leach, Patricia Batten, Mary Hulst, Francis Chan, David Platt, Jay Kim, Glenn Packiam, Rich Villodas, and others. See Croft and Martin, *The Unhurried Pastor*.

when a simple indicative statement or a well-timed or well-asked question may suffice. Rather than using guilt-inducing words, we can shift to encouraging, inspiring, or motivational words like "we want to" or "we desire to" or "we seek to." Because the Holy Spirit is the one who convicts and corrects, the last thing I want from my pastor/preacher is to feel more anxious as a result of hearing their sermons. Our world could benefit from more unhurried, nonanxious preaching and preachers.

CONCLUSION

As Jesus became incarnational, Immanuel, God with us, we, too, would be best served to don the ministry model of Christ and be with our congregants regularly and as often as possible. We are never above people just as Christ was never too important for even the least of these. We enter into the joys and pains of our listeners. That's what pastoral preaching is all about. In *Lament-Driven Preaching*, Eliana Ah-Rum Ku helpfully uses the term "pastoral consciousness," which nicely summarizes this chapter: "[Pastoral consciousness] in preaching places an emphasis on the congregation's needs, especially the concrete problems of suffering, or the challenges of human life."[7]

When pastors become "too big for their britches" (yes, I'm a transplant to Texas), we've lost sight of the true meaning of the pastoral vocation and office. We are not just preachers, communicators, and pulpiteers. We are God's messengers embodied within a local church body, a community filled with sinners who are saints. Don't neglect your pastoral presence in view of a call to preach. Preaching is only a small portion of what we are called to do as pastors—even if it is a significant portion. You are both a preacher and a pastor, never just a preacher. In the next chapter, we'll continue this conversation on pastoral presence by exploring the world of empathy in preaching.

QUESTIONS

1. How have you practiced pastoral presence in your ministry and preaching?
2. Is your natural inclination to love, lead, and linger? If not, what prevents you from doing so?

7. Eliana Ah-Rum Ku, *Lament-Driven Preaching: Proclaiming Hope amid Suffering* (Pickwick, 2024), 133.

3. How warm and friendly are you and how can you grow your heart for others?
4. What are some ways you can increase your pastoral presence in the lives of your listeners?

PRACTICES

1. Take out your weekly calendar and count the number of times you'll be meeting with people (groups and individuals).
2. If our default mode is not to meet with our congregants during the week, try to include at least one meeting each week with someone new to you in your church (especially from a different cultural or subcultural background from you) for coffee, a meal, or to participate in their hobby.

19

EMPATHY

Does Our Communication Demonstrate Empathy?

> Jesus went through all the towns and villages, teaching in their synagogues, proclaiming the good news of the kingdom and healing every disease and sickness. When he saw the crowds, he had compassion on them, because they were harassed and helpless, like sheep without a shepherd. Then he said to his disciples, "The harvest is plentiful but the workers are few. Ask the Lord of the harvest, therefore, to send out workers into his harvest field."
>
> —Matthew 9:35–38

During my years of pastoring and preaching weekly, as a senior pastor and as a youth pastor, I acknowledged my lack of empathy for people at times. Perhaps, for good reason, I didn't appreciate those select individuals who conveniently designated my Sunday preaching moment as a weekly nap time. Patience grew thin, particularly when eyeballs wandered to the back of some listeners' skulls. (As soon as I entered the pulpit, I could count on six of them to fall asleep like clockwork.) Internal voices would escalate in my head: "Don't you know how hard I worked on this sermon?!" "Why can't 'you people' change?" Sometimes, in my most unholy moments in ministry, I prayed what I call "unholy prayers," such as, "Lord, would you please make this difficult person go away and find another church?" I lament my secretly abysmal attitude toward some of the people in my flock. In short, I lacked the heart of the Great Shepherd. I lacked a spirit of love, empathy, and compassion.

Whenever I think of what being a pastoral shepherd truly entails, I'm reminded of Jesus's words above in Matthew 9:35–38. In the previous chapter, I hope to have convinced you of the importance of the inseparable bond between pastoring and preaching. Pastors may preach, but not every preacher pastors their flock, to the chagrin and detriment of Christian ministry and churches. For a holistic sense of what pastors and thus preachers do, this chapter articulates a vision for preaching with an empathetic heart toward our people. When Jesus looked at the crowds, Matthew records, "he had compassion on them" (v. 36). The word translated as "compassion" here is *esplanchnisthē* (verb, aorist, indicative, passive), meaning to "have pity, feel sympathy," but the noun form *splanchnon* is graphically rendered "inward parts."[1] In other words, the Lord Jesus had a visceral, inward, guttural reaction to the sheep being without a shepherd or in today's vernacular, "people without a pastor." Do we have this type of empathy for people? I know I haven't always. Yet thankfully my empathy and compassion for others have increased over time.

As pastoral shepherds and preachers, we are called to follow Jesus's example in enhancing our love, compassion, and empathy for congregants and hearers. While empathy has not come naturally to me or perhaps to everyone, the good news is empathy can be learned and developed.[2] What does preaching with empathy look like? We'll address this question in this chapter and conclude with some intentional practices on how to cultivate empathy in our preaching.

Empathy, What's That?

Empathy is quite literally *em*, meaning "put in or into, bring to a certain state,"[3] and *pathy*, meaning "feeling or suffering."[4] In other words, empathy is entering into the feeling or suffering of another person. Empathy has always had a positive connotation for me. It's a trait that Christians are expected to demonstrate toward others, much like "putting yourself in someone else's

1. Frederick W. Danker, Walter Bauer, William F. Arndt, and F. Wilbur Gingrich, *Greek-English Lexicon of the New Testament and Other Early Christian Literature*, 3rd ed. (University of Chicago Press, 2000), 1628, under "σπλάγχνον."

2. The work of empathy in preaching is so significant that I'm working on a full-length treatment on the subject tentatively titled *Preaching with Emotional Intelligence* (Baker Academic, forthcoming).

3. Etymonline, https://www.etymonline.com/word/em.

4. *Merriam-Webster Dictionary*, "-pathy," accessed January 8, 2026, https://www.merriam-webster.com/dictionary/-pathy.

shoes." More strongly, as demonstrated in Matthew 9:35–38, Jesus demonstrates empathy through his gut-wrenching compassion when seeing the crowds without a shepherd.

However, for some, fighting the Christian culture wars has relegated empathy to something pejorative, undesirable, even sinful. Joe Rigney points out in *The Sin of Empathy*, "Given the prevalence of appeals to empathy in our society, it's vital that we learn to distinguish good from bad, healthy from toxic, the virtue of compassion from the sin of empathy."[5] Empathy has become a polarizing issue, and people on both sides of the debate (whether pro-empathy or against it) seem to be demonizing those on the other side. The divisiveness of empathy transfixes us on absolute empathy or focuses us on one's feelings alone to the exclusion of truth (primarily biblical and theological truth).[6]

Where we have gone wrong when manufacturing "empathy" into a binary term is that the word has lost its ability to be nuanced. Any concept that fails to maintain biblical fidelity is a term gone astray. Empathy, I would contend, is a necessary trait of any disciple of Jesus, especially for those serving in Christian ministry, including pastors and preachers. Preaching devoid of empathy is merely a sterile, academic speech or lecture. How can we preach without showing empathy through greater love, compassion, and understanding? In *Deeply Loved*, Bill and Kristi Gaultiere write, "Empathy is an expression of God's grace. The God of the universe with empathy and love sent his son Jesus to enter our human experience, co-suffering with us to meet us on our level. . . . Jesus' empathy finds you whenever you get lost. Your Savior understands your needs, forgives your sins, heals your hearts, gives you flourishing life, and teaches you the great blessing of loving others as he loves you."[7] Summarizing their words, to know God is to know and experience his empathy.

Incarnational ministry is what Jesus embodied and exemplified in his earthly life and ministry. The Scriptures tell us so. For instance, John 1:14 says, "And the Word became flesh and dwelt among us, and we have seen his glory, glory as of the only Son from the Father, full of grace and truth" (ESV),

5. Joe Rigney, *The Sin of Empathy: Compassion and Its Counterfeits* (Canon, 2025), 1. In addition, see Joe Rigney, "The Enticing Sin of Empathy: How Satan Corrupts Through Compassion," Desiring God, https://www.desiringgod.org/articles/the-enticing-sin-of-empathy, where Rigney warns against the extremes of empathy such as, "Empathy demands, 'Feel what I feel. In fact, lose yourself in my feelings.'"

6. I would agree that empathy absent of biblical truth puts us in danger of biblical and theological error and possible sin. However, empathy in general is a positive characteristic for any Christian disciple.

7. Bill Gaultiere and Kristi Gaultiere, *Deeply Loved: Receiving and Reflecting God's Great Empathy for You* (Revell, 2025), 17.

and 1 Timothy 1:15–16 reads, "The saying is trustworthy and deserving of full acceptance, that Christ Jesus came into the world to save sinners, of whom I am the foremost. But I received mercy for this reason, that in me, as the foremost, Jesus Christ might display his perfect patience as an example to those who were to believe in him for eternal life" (ESV). Notice, particularly in the 1 Timothy passage, that through Jesus's incarnation we are given mercy and an example of "perfect patience" in the model of how Christ himself lived. In our self-important, impatient world, we have little tolerance for showing mercy to others and don't know how to overlook an offense. We are quick to judge, criticize, and dehumanize others for believing differently. While we sometimes exhibit little patience for others, we expect others to show patience as a first response. How sad the state of the world has become, even among Christian pastors.

The Spectrum of Empathy

Sandi McGeough explains that everyone is somewhere on the "spectrum of empathy." She contends that people develop empathy along a continuum of four stages (see the diagram below):

- from pity, "a passive response that often distances us from others' struggles"
- to sympathy, "acknowledging others' pain while maintaining a degree of emotional distance"
- to empathy, "stepping into another's shoes, fully immersing ourselves in their emotions, and understanding their perspective"
- to compassion, "a profound expression of empathy in action. Compassion moves beyond understanding to tangible acts of support and kindness."[8]

I would start this spectrum at apathy (having no feeling) and progress to pity and so on. The Y (vertical) axis on the diagram shows that in order to grow in understanding and engagement (X, or horizontal, axis) to the level of compassion, it will take intentional effort on our part (see fig. 19.1). Where do you find yourself along this empathic continuum? Also, how much do you desire compassion as your normative response to others and their concerns, in this case, as it relates to your pastoring and preaching?

8. See Sandi McGeough, "Exploring the Spectrum of Empathy," https://www.linkedin.com/posts/sandimcgeough_mindyourbeing-livelifeonpurpose-empathy-activity-7179085277531918336-OS4D.

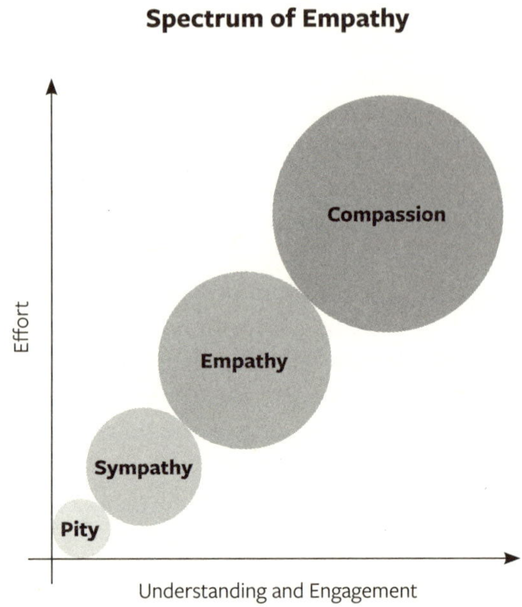

Image by Sandi McGeough, Mind Your Being LLC. Used by permission.

Figure 19.1. The spectrum of empathy

In the previous chapter, we spent time reminding ourselves that preaching cannot be separated from pastoring and being present with our people. Here, as we dive deeply into empathy, let's first explore what a lack of empathy looks like in the pulpit; next we'll consider what empathy in preaching looks like; and finally, we'll name some practices to become more empathetic preachers.

A Lack of Empathy in the Pulpit

If preaching with empathy means to enter into the feeling and suffering of another, then naturally preaching devoid of empathy does not enter into the feeling and suffering of others. Four areas that frequently demonstrate a lack of empathy in our preaching include demonizing people who hold contrary perspectives, ignoring who's there, failing to acknowledge those who are hurting, and projecting hyperempathy.

Demonizing People Who Hold Contrary Perspectives

It is good and right for pastors and preachers to maintain historically biblical boundaries and perspectives. In our attempt to maintain biblical and theological orthodoxy, however, preachers are tempted to fight theological battles in the pulpit with perceived or imaginary adversaries or with an argument of silence, as though we have *the* one, true, proper doctrinal perspective on nonessential doctrines and ministry philosophies. Demonizing those who hold contrary nonessential perspectives is a common way to destroy empathy in the pulpit. When preachers say things like: "You cannot believe _______ and still be a faithful Christian," we have crossed the line.[9]

Ignoring Who's There

On a recent vacation to South Korea with my extended family, my in-laws, who are in their eighties and nineties, were left standing on a sightseeing train. While they were holding on to a metal bar, four late-teen or early twentysomethings right beside them were sitting comfortably. I am certain these young people were cognizant that elderly people were standing nearby. The proper etiquette, at least in Korean culture, would be for the young people to get up and give their seats to the elderly persons. Instead, they sat there talking, laughing, and enjoying the view, as if my nonagenarian father-in-law and octogenarian mother-in-law didn't exist. They simply chose to ignore them for the sake of their own comfort.

As preachers, we can similarly fall into the trap of ignoring certain individuals or groups who are present in the worship gathering. Reflecting again on cultural preparedness (see part 3), there can be various cultures and subcultures represented in any given congregation. Preaching comes with regular and irregular catch-22 moments where we identify people (or perhaps shouldn't) according to life stages or specific backgrounds—for instance, married couples to the exclusion of singles, those with children to the exclusion of families who have difficulty conceiving or those who have experienced a miscarriage or those who simply choose not to have children, those with a college education to the exclusion of those without, and so on. People, at their core, want to be seen, appreciated, and valued in any setting, including in the church context. Preachers who show empathy will intentionally let their listeners know they see them through the questions they raise, the illustrations they offer, and the applications that are tethered to their lives.

9. The definition of a nonessential doctrine, for me, is a doctrine where one's salvation is not at stake. Essential doctrines would include the full deity and humanity of Christ, the sinlessness of Christ, the core gospel of the sacrificial life, death, burial, resurrection, and ascension of Christ, and other central doctrines articulated in the Apostles' Creed and Nicene Creed. We can have differing opinions about many theological and ministerial concepts and still be part of the family of God.

Failing to Acknowledge Those Who Are Hurting

Countless reasons could be given for the development of an apathetic society and even an apathetic Christian culture. Lenny Luchetti has taken notice: "Apathetic disengagement has become normative in Western [and I would add Eastern] society. The human capacity for empathic understanding, feeling, and responding appears to be diminishing. Societal apathy has been mounting for decades and, according to research, is at its peak."[10] For Christians, apathy is the spiritual malady of not caring about others or feeling numb toward another person. When someone tells you they've had a bad day, for instance, we might immediately come up with a pressing reason to walk away or give no reason at all. Apathy is ubiquitous in our day. It's even prevalent in many pulpits.

Whether it's tragic news in our local community or in national/international news coverage, many preachers preach as if nothing has happened and express this through their silence. Preachers commonly or conveniently fail to acknowledge those who are hurting in their congregations.[11] We are so committed to preaching our sermon outline and manuscript that empathy cannot be squeezed into that airtight message. Not that those who are going through emotional hardship or immediate suffering need or want to be acknowledged from the pulpit per se, but preaching happy-go-lucky sermons most or all of the time is what we might call "tone-deaf" homiletics. Such messages show that the preacher cannot gauge the emotional or spiritual climate in the room.

Regardless of what we have prepared for this particular Sunday's message, a concerted acknowledgment that there are or might be people hurting in the congregation because of recent events, situations, or circumstances goes a long way. People in the pews want to know that their pastor cares about them and about what's happening in the broader world. This is not an indictment of any specific preacher or their sermons. As a general practice, we can briefly acknowledge the hurt and make people feel seen and loved.

Projecting Hyperempathy

Last, preachers can project a sense of hyperempathy, where we almost exaggerate the level of connection with our listeners by saying the following:

10. Lenny Luchetti, *Preaching with Empathy: Crafting Sermons in a Callous Culture* (Abingdon, 2018), 1.

11. See, e.g., Matthew D. Kim, *Preaching to People in Pain: How Suffering Can Shape Your Sermons and Connect with Your Congregation* (Baker Academic, 2021).

- "I know exactly what you're going through!"
- "You're going to be stronger because of this!"
- "See, this person overcame the same situation, so you will too!"

In our attempt to console or create a stronger bond with hearers, we overstate our case. Hyperempathy, though well-intended, has several unintended consequences. First, it can minimize what another person is going through in this moment or season. Second, hyperempathy can feel disingenuous and inauthentic. Third, hyperempathy fails to truly personalize a person's pain or suffering because it assumes we know how people are feeling. With these three common demonstrations of lack of empathy, what can preachers do to show meaningful homiletical empathy in their messages?

Practices for Cultivating Homiletical Empathy

Let's conclude this chapter with four practices for cultivating our homiletical empathy: Allow people to sit in their pain, use sensitive words, verbalize love for your congregation, and give invitations to respond to God's Word.

Allowing People to Sit in Their Pain

Lament is a biblical concept that is not often addressed by preachers. Many stories in the Bible are stories of lament. Several books of the Bible convey teachings of people who are hurting in some tangible and relatable ways. In fact, I don't know if there is a single book of the sixty-six books of the Bible that does not include some element of pain and suffering. For this reason, it's important for preachers to allow people to sit in their pain. If we're being honest, most preachers like to see smiling faces on Sunday, not frowning ones. This innate desire for happy congregations discourages listeners from being authentic and honest about their posture in coming to worship the Lord.

Instead, what if preachers were to provide space in the worship gathering to give people permission to breathe, exhale, cry, vent, be raw and real, show frustration or even anger (without getting violent), and lament to God (who can take all of it)? Yes, the goal of the worship gathering is ultimately to point people to the hope and joy and freedom that is offered in the triune God, namely in the person of Jesus Christ. Sometimes, though, people need freedom to just be themselves and show plainly their true spiritual colors before a loving and merciful God. Church is not for keeping the appearance of tidiness but experiencing empathic community for those experiencing profound losses and needs. These are tacit but palpable ways we can encourage empathy and compassion for our hearers.

Using Sensitive Words

Being careful with our words and instruction is a challenge for all preachers. When listeners misunderstand us or when we preach insensitively, we expect listeners to show us grace. However, that's not how communication works (all the time). Depending on one's culture or background, the words we speak from the pulpit can be heartening or disheartening, empathetic or hurtful.

I tend to be blunt and direct in my speech (for good and sometimes for ill). A helpful practice over the years has been to have someone from a different cultural or subcultural background read over or listen to my manuscript prior to preaching it (especially if I'm feeling uncertain about what I'm about to communicate). I ask them how they think these words will land if I were to preach them this Sunday. Am I being insensitive with these comments? Am I using the right and proper words for the cultural or subcultural context? While this practice cannot preclude every listener from remaining unscathed with our word choice, being conscientious about using sensitive words is a beneficial practice for all communicators.

Verbalizing Love for Your Congregation

I'm not sure where we got the notion that the apostle Paul was a grumpy curmudgeon of a pastoral leader. If anything, his letters project a spirit of love and a loving disposition toward the people worshiping in his church plants, regularly giving thanks for them. As Megan Hill notes,

> One of the constant features of Paul's epistles is thanksgiving for the churches. In nearly every letter, he gives thanks to God for the congregations to which he writes. He thanks God for their public profession of faith (Rom. 1:8), for their gifts and graces (1 Cor. 1:4–7), for their prayers (2 Cor. 1:11), for their love for other Christians (Eph. 1:15–16; Col. 1:3–4), for their partnership with him in the gospel (Phil. 1:3–5), for their steadfastness (1 Thess. 1:2–3), and for their growth in the faith (2 Thess. 1:3). We can imagine him looking for things to rejoice over and delighting in the chance to give public gratitude to God.[12]

12. Megan Hill, "4 Ways Paul Encourages Us to Love the Church (Even When It's Hard)," Crossway, May 16, 2020, https://www.crossway.org/articles/4-ways-paul-encourages-us-to-love-the-church-even-when-its-hard.

Referring to the church as a family is a nice metaphor. For some, their family of origin is anything but familial and loving. That does not negate the fact that God's family, the church, is intended to be a nurturing, love-generating community. I know a pastor who verbally communicates to his congregation every Sunday that he loves them. Pastoral love and expressions of love are not rocket science. While at first he didn't know how it would be received, it has now become a staple of every Sunday gathering to convey to the church his love for them. If the words are empty of meaning, there's no reason to fake it. There is no unspoken rule that says a pastor must speak the words "I love you" publicly. However, we are pastoral shepherds called by God to love the sheep, and our people would benefit from hearing such words of love and appreciation on a regular basis from their pastor.

Giving Invitations to Respond to God's Word

A final way that empathy and compassion can be offered to God's people is through giving regular invitations to respond to God's Word. Similar to the first recommendation, people need to know they can be free, without judgment, to respond to the Lord in whatever way they feel at a given moment. Perhaps on this particular Sunday, the best way listeners can respond to God is simply to sit in silence, to weep, to ponder, to reflect, to sing, to worship, to surrender, to raise their hands, to fall to their knees, to lie prostrate on the ground, to stand, to come to the altar, to receive prayer from others, or to just be still. For others, the best way to encourage them might be to invite participation by taking concrete action steps and putting into practice the sermon's applications. There is no wrong way to respond to God's Word, at least in principle, but a habitual lack of response is spiritually deadly over time. Empathy from the preacher enables listeners to be who they are and respond how they will, and it creates space for preachers to walk alongside their people in this marathon journey called the Christian life.

In a sermon delivered by Pastor Jim Cymbala at Brooklyn Tabernacle, he openly confessed a moving story about a homeless individual named David who approached him after an Easter Sunday sermon. Thinking David wanted money from him, Cymbala pulled out his wallet to give him some cash. David, whose body odor was palpable, responded, "I don't want your money. I want this Jesus, the one you were talking about, because I'm not going to make it. I'm going to die on the street." David eventually went on to receive Jesus as Lord, and he became a pastor at a nearby congregation. Cymbala challenged his congregation to see others as Jesus saw them. He concludes, "And I was so close to saying, 'Here, take this [cash]; I'm a busy preacher.' We can get so full of ourselves."[13] Cymbala accompanied these words by applying the message. He encouraged the congregation to actively find ways to love and embrace others who are different from them for the sake of Christ.

CONCLUSION

Empathy is the ability to come alongside another and enter into their feelings and experiences of pain and suffering (to the best of our ability). Compassion takes empathy to the level of acting and participating by entering into another's hardships or circumstances with them. In Matthew 9:35–38, Jesus was literally in pain while witnessing his people who were without a spiritual leader. Similarly, I want to be the type of pastor whose heart breaks for those who are hurting and I want to come alongside them in their suffering. Empathy and compassion are traits that can be learned and developed as we interact with our congregants, one person at a time. Empathetic and compassionate pastors make for empathetic and compassionate preachers. Will you prayerfully ask the Lord to show you personally and congregationally how you can exhibit empathy and compassion today?

QUESTIONS

1. What is your definition of "empathy" and "compassion"?
2. Where would you rate yourself on the spectrum of empathy provided earlier? Are there particular people for whom offering empathy and compassion is more challenging? Name those people and confess that to the Lord.
3. How is your congregation doing in terms of empathy and compassion toward others?
4. What are some ways you've attempted to cultivate empathy and compassion in your pastoring and preaching?

13. I watched Jim Cymbala's sermon clip years ago. This transcription from Jim Martin, "Jim Cymbala's Easter Story," *From a Pastor's Heart* (blog), April 5, 2013, https://pastorjimmartin.blogspot.com/2013/04/jim-cymbalas-easter-story-true-story.html, maintains the essential message of the original sermon video.

PRACTICES

1. Talk about empathy with your church leadership. How do they feel about empathy being expressed in the church today?
2. Practice empathy and compassion in your church's weekly rhythms. Who needs more empathy and compassion in your congregation today? Schedule a time in your calendar to meet with someone who needs your empathy and compassion.
3. Cultivate the four practices offered at the end of this chapter. Write down your observations on how the church is growing in this area of empathy and compassion over the next several weeks and months.

20

COMMUNICATION

Does Our Communication Speak to a Variety of Listeners?

> But when he, the Spirit of truth, comes, he will guide you into all the truth. He will not speak on his own; he will speak only what he hears, and he will tell you what is yet to come.
>
> —John 16:13

Thank you for going on this journey with me through all nineteen chapters to get to this point. I want to take a moment to celebrate with you! I know it was a lot to digest. Please exhale, we're almost through! Hopefully by now either you've learned some new things about preaching or at least you've been reminded of them. In this final chapter, let's try to put the things you've learned and processed together. All that we've covered so far leads to the main event: communicating and delivering the sermon to God's people!

The root word of communication is to "commune" or to be with others primarily in the form of Christian fellowship. We often don't think of the preaching moment as fellowship, but that's what it really is. By definition, "fellowship" is a "community of interest, activity, feeling, or experience."[1] Granted, not every listener necessarily wants to hear a sermon today, but, in general, preachers and listeners share a common interest in wanting to know what God has to say to us in his holy Word.

1. *Merriam-Webster Dictionary*, "fellowship," accessed January 8, 2026, https://www.merriam-webster.com/dictionary/fellowship.

Though in many ways the sermon is monodirectional, true preaching does not take place if there is no give-and-take, back-and-forth, preacher-listener interaction and engagement. Ultimately, a central goal in preaching is that we are traveling in unison and growing in our faith collectively as God's children—both preacher and hearers alike.

In my opinion, there's nothing quite like delivering a sermon and communicating with our listeners. Observing the congregation walk through a passage of Scripture is mind blowing just as it is mysterious—this sacred moment called preaching the sermon. Thankfully, we can rest in the promise that the triune God is at work in the ministry of preaching the Word. By God's design, Christian preaching cannot happen effectively apart from him. So, what is our part in the communication process and how can our communication include a variety of delivery skills to most effectively convey God's message to the people?

Choose to Communicate

Let's start with the elephant in the room. The first thing to name about public speaking is that it's scary and even terrifying for most people. In doing research for *A Little Book for New Preachers*, I found that the majority of people (approximately 75 percent) fear public speaking more than they fear death itself.[2] You may find yourself among the 75 percent mentioned in the previous sentence. This is why some of my seminary students wait until the last semester to take their preaching course.

Take heart! For worse or better (hopefully the latter), God has called you into this significant leadership role in being a pastor and preacher. Yes, God chose you. We don't get to choose to be pastors and preachers. The Lord is the one who calls! And he has found it fit in his infinite, sovereign wisdom to include you in this magnificent calling and ministry of being a pastor/preacher!

Instead of trying to dodge your calling, like Moses, Jonah, and others, choose today to embrace it. So, first, be courageous, very courageous, like Joshua entering the promised land, and choose to preach! Kenton C. Anderson emboldens starting preachers with these words: "You have to choose to preach. The world conspires to keep us quiet. Inertia stills our tongues. It takes a concerted effort of the will to choose to tell the truth despite the trouble it entails. Proclamation is a choice. You have to choose the road less traveled."[3]

2. Matthew D. Kim, *A Little Book for New Preachers: Why and How to Study Homiletics* (IVP Academic, 2020), 22.

3. Kenton C. Anderson, *Choosing to Preach: A Comprehensive Introduction to Sermon Options and Structures* (Zondervan, 2006), 22.

The nonbelieving world doesn't appreciate preachers who properly, correctly, accurately, and forthrightly communicate God's truth to them. It's our job description, as biblical preachers, to preach the Bible and tell the people what God is saying to them without mincing his words. One thing I always tell my students in the introduction to preaching course is to enjoy the preaching moment. In secular terms, own the moment, take ownership! If we don't enjoy the experience, then neither will our listeners. People sitting in the pews can see right through our discomfort, nervousness, pacing, jittery hands and feet, uncertainty, displeasure, and general awkwardness. How will they be comfortable listening if we are not comfortable preaching? This requires the common hurdle of accepting who we are.

Become Comfortable in Your Own Skin

To get to a place where we are comfortable and even enjoy preaching involves a significant first step (that can take time): becoming comfortable in your own skin. Now, I have met the occasional (rare) person who cannot get over how incredible they are, but most of us fall into the second category, where we need to give ourselves a pep talk. We may not like something about our appearance, the sound of our speaking voice, or another feature that we can't change about ourselves, but let's stop the defeatist, negative self-talk. You are the exact person God created in his own image. You are beloved, and God wants to use you! What a privilege and a joy!

One of the most common and natural mistakes young preachers make is to idolize and thereby mimic their favorite preachers and their preaching styles (particularly their voice and mannerisms). Who is that person for you? Now, I get it. There are many talented preachers out there. We all have preachers we gravitate toward. One favorite preacher blesses you when they stand to proclaim and deliver God's Word. That preacher seems to have received a double portion of the Spirit in how they exegete the Word or the way they deliver the message. It resonates with our soul. In some cases, we sit under someone else's preaching ministry so long that it becomes ingrained in us. Like a newborn infant, we look at mom and dad and begin to replicate what we hear and see.

In my introduction to preaching classes, I begin the semester by telling the students to preach out of who they are but also to try and bring their best selves to the pulpit (as I mentioned in chap. 18). Who are you in your best moments, when you feel comfortable with your present company, when your natural demeanor is jovial and positive, and when you're speaking with people you love and enjoy hanging around with? Be that person in the pulpit. Be the best version of yourself when you stand to preach. I know that's easier said than done. Pray and ask the Holy Spirit to help you be your best self every opportunity you have to preach God's Word.

Since I teach preaching, people often like to ask, "So, who are your favorite preachers?" Frankly, I have never responded well to this question because I don't have a favorite or a plurality of favorites. One way to prevent being a copycat of your favorite preacher is to listen to a plethora of different effective preachers instead of only hearing one preaching voice and observing one style. Listen to men and to women, from different denominations and those who hold a different theological or ministerial perspective. Listen to people with larger-than-life personalities and those who are more demure or less charismatic. Learn from preachers who almost teach like a lecturer and those who enjoy humor and telling stories.

Over time, you will discover what your preaching persona and path will be. A key takeaway in this entire chapter on communication is to be natural. Don't fake, imitate, mimic, or impersonate some other preacher. Be yourself and be genuine! Be comfortable in your skin because it is God who calls and equips you to be his messenger. God never asked you to be anyone else or like anyone else. He asked you to be yourself!

What's the "Secret Sauce" of Sermons?

Imagine a scenario where two different preachers are preaching from an identical manuscript. Though the content is the same, one preacher is easy on the ears, while the other is hard to hear. What gives? As Haddon W. Robinson once asked himself as a novice preacher, "Some people preach for an hour, and it seems like twenty minutes. Others preach for twenty minutes, and it seems like an hour. I wonder what the difference is?"[4]

In today's language, people want to know: What is the secret sauce of sermons? The correct answer is not "some people have it, and others don't!" How discouraging would that be? No, what makes a sermon and therefore a preacher either boring or engaging comes down to two primary factors: one's energy (which we'll cover in a moment) and one's delivery (verbal and nonverbal). These are ingredients in the secret sauce of communication that generate greater sermonic efficacy. Thankfully, both of these forms of communication can be learned and improved. Even though I've been preaching for decades, and think myself to be a competent preacher, I mean it when I say, "I'm always a student of preaching and of other preachers. I always want to

4. Steve Smith, "Truth Poured Through Personality: Dr. Haddon W. Robinson," DTS Voice, https://voice.dts.edu/article/truth-poured-through-personality-smith-steve.

learn from others and get tips on how to improve my craft." So, let's unpack the two main ingredients in our sauce, beginning with energy and moving to verbal and nonverbal communication.

High Energy

If I were to boil down what can make the difference between a mediocre sermon and an outstanding sermon (content aside), it would be the preacher's energy level. As a preaching professor, I've instructed and coached well over a thousand different student preachers. Here's one common lesson I've picked up: When a preacher exhibits high energy or at least moderate levels of energy, the enthusiasm in the room for Scripture and listeners' attention escalate. This simple principle of a preacher's energy can assist the entire preaching moment for everyone involved.

What I mean by high energy is not being flamboyant or dancing, prancing, shouting, or jumping up and down, per se, or other over-the-top mannerisms. Listeners can immediately sniff out a person's aura, whether a preacher is energized by God's Word and energized to speak to them or the preacher would rather be somewhere else. High energy radiates from the preacher through how one walks confidently up to the podium, pulpit, or music stand, and through eye contact, posture, presence, vocal volume, tone, rate of speech, body language, facial cues, and the ability to interact and engage with the listeners—the entire package.

If you are a lower-energy person or possess a naturally shy disposition, you don't have to gulp an energy drink immediately before you preach. We can work toward something tangible now to boost your pulpit energy. Think with me about the times when you get most excited in life. Perhaps it's when you're rooting and cheering for your favorite sports team or music artist. Don't tell me you're slouching, watching indifferently while sitting on the couch. Quite the opposite, you're probably highly focused, at times laughing, smiling, screaming, celebrating, yelling, clapping, heartbroken, and even making unusual noises as you root for your team! Tone it down a notch and voila, you have your high-energy preaching presence. Bring that high-energy person into the pulpit every time you preach God's Word. If we are not energetic to preach God's Word, why would anyone be energetic to receive and apply it?

Verbal Communication

Verbal communication, at its core, comes down to four primary elements: word choice, tone, volume, and variety. A quick word now about each of these four factors in verbal communication.

WORD CHOICE

When we speak from the pulpit, our words matter. Depending on which words we select, they will communicate in a binary fashion: kind or mean, encouraging or discouraging, hopeful or negative. The ultimate difference maker is our word choice. For this reason, it is critical to review our manuscripts and choose words carefully so that they will motivate and inspire our listeners toward greater discipleship and transformation and not the reverse. Off-putting, critical words can be a spiritual and emotional downer in any sermon.

TONE

You've probably heard someone say or said yourself, "It's not what you said but how you said it," when explaining one's hurt feelings from another's comments. Another way of considering a preacher's tone is attitude. We can express words in such a manner that people receive them well or they are perceived as snarky or derogatory based on our tone. Tone is easier to pick up in spoken language than in written words on a page. Practice your tone before you preach. If there are words that might be misconstrued or misunderstood, take a mulligan and find another one.

VOLUME

There's no reason to shout from the pulpit, but we want to be loud enough to be heard clearly. While every sermon should have a standard, middle-of-the-road volume level, in times of greater emphasis, we can get louder or softer to make a point pop. Here's a case where microphone levels, of course, need to be properly measured. Yet some preachers forget how loud or soft they can be. Vocal projection and enunciation are powerful tools for clear communication. A common faux pas, especially for beginning preachers, is to mumble or trail off at the end of sentences and questions. Stay the course! Make sure that the beginning, middle, and ending of a sentence can be heard.

VARIETY

Have you ever worshiped next to a tone-deaf singer? I have many times. I apologize for calling you out now, since I know it cannot be helped. However, tone-deaf or monotone speaking is more painful to listen to when it's from the pulpit. Some preachers don't recognize that they are speaking in a monotone fashion. What does it sound like? I wish I could play a clip for you, but let's try to describe its sound even on this printed page. I can't emphasize enough the importance of working on our vocal variety throughout a sermon. We don't want to sound like we're practicing musical scales from the pulpit. However, we also don't want our voices to be so static and drone-like that our listeners literally tune us out.

I would be remiss not to mention timely and effective pausing for variety. Particularly when we're dealing with nerves or feel the pressure of a ticking clock, we forget to pause and provide space for listeners to ponder any part of the message. For instance, we might ask a provocative question but immediately start speaking again, answering that question for them. Pausing is vital for effective communication because we speak more quickly than people can hear and process. Have you ever told a joke and wondered why there wasn't an immediate uproar? Wait for it! Laughter takes time because our brains need space to hear and process information. Vocal variety can be practiced and improved. Verbal communication is a conscious effort toward developing our word choice, tone, volume, and variety.

IMPROVE YOUR STORYTELLING

It's not hard for me to confess that my wife is an excellent storyteller. Everyone knows she has this skill. Whenever she tells a story, everyone, I mean everyone, is listening. She captivates a room with her flair for telling a good story. Me, thanks for asking, not so much. This is an element of preaching where I am constantly seeking to develop my craft.

Lee Eclov shares some characteristics of effective storytellers: "Good storytellers take their time. They never hurry. They pause for listeners to catch up. They don't have to tell us the point of the story. Preaching may be somewhat different, but most people get the point without the preacher hammering it down. Think how often in Scripture we're told a story where the writer expects us to see the point without being told."[5]

Much like preaching, effective storytelling is a combination of content and delivery. My wife provides the right amount of details, just enough vocal animation and variety, just enough suspense through pauses, eye contact, humor, sound effects, gestures, just enough of just about everything to make for a gripping storyteller. It's been a privilege to learn how to tell a story from her as I seek to improve my knack for story.[6] Moreover, to improve our

5. Lee Eclov, "Mirrors, Windows, and Pictures: How to Use Sermon Illustrations," Preaching Today, accessed December 2, 2025, https://www.preachingtoday.com/skills/2023/mirrors-windows-and-pictures.html.

6. We can learn a thing or two about effective storytelling from authors who are adept at their craft, such as Meg Bowles, Catherine Burns, Jenifer Hixson, Sarah Austin Jenness, and Kate Tellers, *How to Tell a Story: The Essential Guide to Memorable Storytelling from the*

storytelling abilities, read widely, read fiction, read nonfiction, read short stories, read magazine articles and columns, read the newspaper—plain and simple, just read.

SHARE A PART OF YOURSELF

Though the sermon is never about one person, preaching is still dispensed through the vessel and medium of the human messenger. I don't want my listeners to leave the worship gathering saying, "Wow, Pastor Matt is my hero" or "Pastor Matt talks about himself way too much." I shout a hearty "Amen" that the hero of every sermon is the triune God. There's no question that the primary agent and character of every sermon is God!

Simultaneously, however, a preacher who never shares anything about herself or himself can also create a peculiar disconnect. We don't have to linger long in talking about ourselves, but perhaps it would be worthwhile to share a bit of ourselves in the pulpit in every sermon: a quick example, a quick story, a personal anecdote, a question you've been pondering, a pastoral vision, or any sort of testimony. Preachers will have differing opinions on this point, but I believe, by nature, people want to connect with their pastor/preacher. Humanize yourself by including a bit of your story, identity, passions, questions, or discipleship journey to resonate with your listeners.

BORROWING RHETORIC AND USING HUMOR

Before moving on to nonverbal communication, what can preachers learn from rhetoric, and how does humor fit into the preaching moment? On the *Bible and Theology Matters* podcast, Abraham Kuruvilla defines homiletics with this thoughtful equation. Kuruvilla says, "Homiletics (the science and art of preaching) = Hermeneutics (which is the science and art of interpreting texts of Scripture) + Rhetoric (which is the science and art of communicating)."[7]

Since we've covered homiletics and hermeneutics in some depth, what can we learn and borrow from rhetoric? In his book *A Manual for Preaching*,

---

Moth (Crown, 2023); Will Storr, *The Science of Storytelling: Why Stories Make Us Human and How to Tell Them Better* (Harry N. Abrams, 2021); Annette Simmons, *The Story Factor: Inspiration, Influence, and Persuasion Through the Art of Storytelling*, 3rd ed. (Basic Books, 2019); Han Kang, *The Vegetarian: A Novel* (Hogarth, 2016); and Malcolm Gladwell, *What the Dog Saw: And Other Adventures* (Little, Brown, 2009). Another approach would be to watch and learn from "clean" comedians!

7. Abraham Kuruvilla, interview by Samuel Allen, guest host, *Bible and Theology Matters*, podcast, episode 108, "Homiletics and Hermeneutics w/ Dr. Abraham Kuruvilla," April 11, 2024, https://www.bibleandtheologymatters.com, also available at https://youtu.be/Fus5QTumRRk.

Kuruvilla explains that "preaching came to be seen as an argument made by the preacher to influence and persuade listeners."[8] A major rhetorical strategy to bolster one's ability to "influence and persuade listeners," promoted by Kuruvilla, "is founded on a hermeneutic that sees authors *doing* things (the pragmatics) with what they say (the semantics)."[9] Not only do listeners need a clear explanation of what is being communicated in Scripture, Kuruvilla submits that listeners need to understand "what the author is *doing*" with what is being said.[10]

Furthermore, the art of rhetoric is communicating with an aim toward persuasion. We persuade others using rhetorical principles, such as Aristotle's triumvirate, in connection with the preacher's ethos (ethics, character, or morality), pathos (emotional connection, empathy, or passion), and logos (clarity, organization, and logical development of one's argument). Mark Buchanan simplifies this tripart rhetorical construction as: "*Logos* is Greek for logic. . . . *Pathos* is Greek for passion. . . . *Ethos* is Greek for ethics."[11] In practically every sermon we preach, listeners are on a vast spectrum of requiring little to much convincing from evidence, proof, or persuasion to believe that God's Word is trustworthy, that God's ways and plans and commands are higher and better than their own, and that they need to live in accordance with the Scriptures. In essence, in every sermon, we are trying to answer the question on many listeners' minds: Why? Using this rhetorical paradigm of appealing to logos, pathos, and ethos in our sermons can be fruitful in attempting to persuade our listeners to follow and obey Christ and to pursue Christlikeness.

With regard to humor in the pulpit, I would submit that humor is our friend.[12] I can say with confidence that humans like to laugh. By no means do I suggest that we should aspire to be pulpit comedians. That would be an utter travesty and mockery of our sacred preaching task. However, the palpable weight felt by listeners in bone-dry preaching cannot be overstated. It's no wonder that some people refer to the sermon as a lecture!

Humor in preaching is not resorting to mere joke telling, nor should we try to go out of our way to be funny. Rather, pulpit humor shines through

8. Abraham Kuruvilla, *A Manual for Preaching: The Journey from Text to Sermon* (Baker Academic, 2019), 269.

9. Kuruvilla, *A Manual for Preaching*, 270–71.

10. Kuruvilla, *A Manual for Preaching*, 272.

11. Mark Buchanan, "Good Talking: Preaching and Rhetoric," Preaching Today, accessed December 2, 2025, https://www.preachingtoday.com/skills/2024/good-talking-preaching-rhetoric.html.

12. For works on preaching and humor, you might consult Alyce M. McKenzie and Owen Hanley Lynch, *Humor Us! Preaching and the Power of the Comic Spirit* (Westminster John Knox, 2023); and Karl N. Jacobson and Rolf A. Jacobson, *Divine Laughter: Preaching and the Serious Business of Humor* (Fortress, 2022).

in doing careful cultural exegesis in constructing our manuscripts. Humor can be expressed in how we say things or how we spin a story. Humor is a natural response when we make an unplanned mistake in our sermon or when something funny happens in the worship space. Humor is good and fruitful when it is well-timed and appropriate.

We can find humor scattered throughout Scripture itself. Isn't it interesting or funny that God would include humor in the Bible? For example, one of the first instances of laughing in Scripture can be found in Genesis 18:9–15, where Sarah laughs out loud in disbelief over the news of having a son in a year's time. I also find it rather odd and comical that there is an unnamed naked man running and making an entrance at the time of Jesus's arrest in Mark's Gospel (Mark 14:51–52). Who is he and what is he doing there? While it does not need to be scripted, humor is an ally of the preacher. Let's not laugh at another's expense, laugh at someone and their culture, or be cruel through unhealthy sarcasm. We can use humor appropriately, intermittently, organically, and culturally responsibly, which will go a long way in our overall preaching ministry and efficacy. Here's a pro tip: Make sure what you think is funny is funny to everyone!

Nonverbal Communication

There's a preaching cartoon making the rounds that shows a scared-to-death minister white-knuckling the apex of the gargantuan pulpit, as the caption reads, "My theme for today is effective communication." For many aspiring and experienced preachers, present author included, we wish we could preach hidden from our hearers behind a colossal podium. Unfortunately, that's not how the medium and mode of preaching work. Preaching is oral and aural communication in full view and in full hearing of the people to whom we are speaking. Thus enters . . . drum roll . . . the critical preaching emphasis on nonverbal communication.

In this digital age, it's easy for preachers to video record our messages for quick feedback on our nonverbal communication. Nonverbal communication is expressed primarily through our facial cues, physical/hand gestures, and movement. To this point, we've been focusing on our verbal communication, the words we speak, the outline of the sermon, the manuscript we've crafted. This is foundational for effective communication. At the same time, Joy E. A. Qualls puts her finger on the pulse of a disconnect that can occur between a preacher and her message: "For all the time and effort that go into sermon preparation, preachers often overlook how the message is coming across. Many fail to realize nonverbal cues can speak louder than words."[13] She identifies some of these cues: "tone, volume, timing, movement, gestures, facial expressions, eye contact, and even personal appearance."[14] In what follows, we'll consider nonverbal communication, which is as equally salient to the preaching task as verbal communication.

FACIAL EXPRESSIONS

A facial expression is "how you move your face to communicate emotions, thoughts, or desires nonverbally. Often, these expressions are involuntary. Other times, they are purposeful."[15] Did you know that humans can emote over ten thousand different facial expressions using forty-three separate facial muscles?[16] These ten thousand facial expressions, also known as micro-expressions, can be distilled down to seven major emotive expressions, including surprise, sadness, anger, disgust, fear, contempt, and happiness.[17]

When preaching, we want to match the words being spoken with the expression presented on our faces. Have you ever seen a pastor/preacher grinning widely throughout a funeral ceremony or a pastor/preacher frowning during a wedding ceremony? It's an eerie feeling that can produce cognitive dissonance in our listeners.

Figure 20.1 contains sketches for what I submit are the four most common facial expressions we emote when we preach. As a visual learner, I've often found this chart helpful.

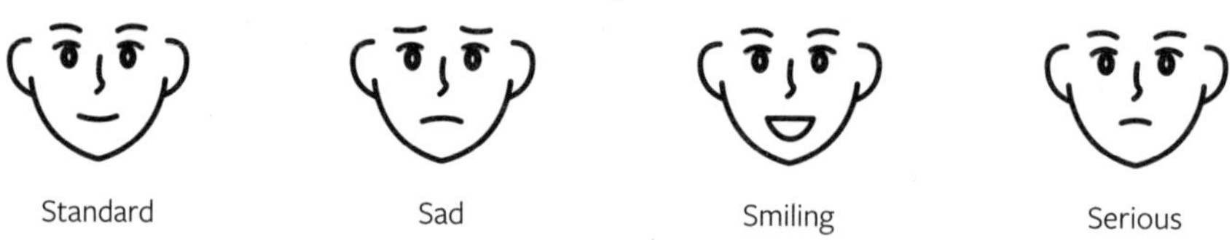

Figure 20.1. Four facial expressions

Most of the time, we will be preaching with a standard face or a smiling face. At times, when the preaching text and sermonic content warrant it, we'll shift to a sad or serious face. Getting comfortable with these four preaching

13. Joy E. A. Qualls, "Louder Than Words: Nonverbal Communication Can Help or Hinder Preaching," *Influence Magazine* (Spring 2025): 86.

14. Qualls, "Louder Than Words," 86.

15. "The Seven 'Universal' Facial Expressions," BetterHelp, updated December 1, 2025, https://www.betterhelp.com/advice/body-language/7-universal-facial-expressions-what-do-they-mean.

16. "Seven 'Universal' Facial Expressions."

17. "Seven 'Universal' Facial Expressions."

facial expressions is our goal as we learn to preach while reading the room. This might seem silly or unnecessary, but practice them by standing in front of a mirror before the next time you preach. Work on your facial expressions as you rehearse your manuscript or outline. Facial expressions, especially those matched to the sermonic content, are of substantial benefit.

EYE CONTACT

Depending on your cultural background, eye contact has varying degrees of importance for communication. In Western cultures, eye contact is highly significant in interpersonal communication. In Eastern or collectivist cultures, eye contact still has its place in the preaching moment but to a lesser extent than in Western ones. Eye contact serves various purposes in the preaching task. In general, in interpersonal communication, people want to know they've been seen, and this happens through eye contact. Eye contact creates warmth, personalization, and connection with our people. Eye contact is also one of those fine-line topics where people want just enough eye contact but not too much. Too short feels disingenuous, while too long feels creepy. Eye contact is crucial when we are addressing a topic directly or seeking to apply the text concretely for our listeners. So, make direct eye contact with individuals and not just fleeting contact.

A pet peeve of mine (and most likely for you as well) is when I'm standing in a circle or sitting around a table and a person chooses to make eye contact with everyone *but me*. The lack of eye contact is noticeable and—perhaps I'm being overly sensitive—it can be hurtful. That's how significant and meaningful eye contact can be! If you are preaching to a smaller group of listeners (less than one hundred), it is possible to make eye contact with everyone or almost everyone in the worship space during the length of a regular sermon. For larger worship spaces, here are two tips: First, think of the worship space as four quadrants. Without making a circular motion with your head, zero in on each of these quadrants throughout your message. Remember, people in the back of the room and on the sides need our love and attention too. A second tip is to focus your attention on three people at a time. Maintain eye contact with the person in the center and all three people will feel like you've made eye contact with them. Of course, the ability to maintain eye contact with our listeners throughout the sermon depends on how prepared we are to preach. If I'm heavily dependent on my notes or manuscript, then this will inhibit me from regularly looking at my hearers and making eye contact with them. The more comfortable we are with our sermon, the more we can prioritize eye contact. This can be cultivated as well with intentionality and better preparation.

GESTURES

While it seems unnecessary to write on the use of gestures, consider with me watching and hearing a sermon where the preacher glues their hands to their sides without any movement. How strange and unnatural that would be to witness! Hand gestures are part and parcel of the communication task. They have potential to serve a few different functions in interpersonal communication as long as they are not distracting.

With gestures, we can emphasize the point we are making. Using gestures helps us to be more demonstrative with our words. For instance, we can illustrate with hand motions something's size (small or big), speed (slow or fast), height (short or tall), and so on. In general, using gestures makes the overall preaching moment more interesting for the listener, since we won't seem like a stiff, robotic bobblehead. A quick, technical hint about gestures.[18] Try to gesture from the listeners' perspective. For example, when we are referring to the sequence of past, present, and future, or numbers such as one, two, and three, we tend to gesture from our vantage point of left to right. The problem is that the listener is seeing your gesture from right to left. Next time you watch a home plate umpire give the hitting count at a baseball game, you'll immediately notice what gesturing in the wrong direction will do for those observing it. I don't know how many 1–3 counts I've seen from a home plate umpire when they actually mean three balls, one strike. Gesture according to your listeners' point of view. Practice in daily conversation to make it a regular part of your speaking routine.

MOVEMENT

Here's the point about movement: Be strategic. Have you ever watched a preacher constantly move back and forth, or pace incessantly from left to right and right to left, in the pulpit? It's extremely taxing and even dizzying. You have to refrain yourself from yelling: Preacher, stop moving! Movement, while appropriate, should not be uncalculated. We can physically move our feet and stand in a different place each time we present a new preaching "move" (discussed in chap. 10). Therefore, a preacher might relocate themselves two to four times during a sermon. The best approach might be to physically move to another part of the stage or platform during a transition to the next sermonic move. Refrain from pacing back and forth, and limit your overall movement in order not to be a distraction for your hearers. Remember the adage, "Less is more."

18. Much of what I'm sharing in these sections on the use of gestures and movement comes directly from Scott M. Gibson in a course titled Preaching for Modern Listeners at Gordon-Conwell Theological Seminary.

Multisensory Communication

With the understanding we have today of varied learning styles, we might incorporate multisensory communication in our preaching ministry. The five senses that God created for us to use and enjoy can be beneficial to accommodate learning differences. For visual, sight-oriented learners, having artwork projected on a screen or providing an object lesson once in a while or showing a brief video clip can be a worthy exercise to increase attention, learning, and application of your message. For those who learn aurally, or through sound, we might have light instrumental music playing in the background at certain points of the sermon to give emphasis. Taste is seldom used in preaching other than when participating in Communion. Are there ways that we can incorporate the sense of taste in our messages such as tasting a grain of salt or a lick of honey when speaking about biblical images? Smell is another sense that rarely gets attention in our sermons. If appropriate, we might burn a candle in the sanctuary or bring in freshly baked loaves of bread for the Lord's Supper. An expert on multisensory preaching, Rick Blackwood speaks highly of its rewards: "Instead of engaging only the ears of your congregation, multi-sensory communication enables you to engage their ears, eyes and hands; and it brings more of the whole person into the learning process."[19]

Culturally Sensitive Communication

Next, here are two comments about culturally sensitive communication. First, every culture uses idioms or phrases that don't make sense unless you grew up hearing them. As native English speakers, we forget that many idioms don't make sense to non-native English speakers. When we use culturally normative phrases, like "close, but no cigar" or "your ears must be burning," we are disconnecting with non-native listeners who are not familiar with such idioms. I was reminded of this recently in real time while watching the US Open Grand Slam tennis tournament on television, where the non-American player being interviewed didn't know a cultural idiom and replied, "I'm sorry?" because the comment didn't register. We don't have to call attention to them, but we can create a list of who the non-native English speakers in your church might be and consider how we might limit or at least explain the idioms we use in our message.

19. Rick Blackwood, "The Power of Multi-Sensory Preaching," Preaching.com, accessed December 2, 2025, https://www.preaching.com/articles/the-power-of-multi-sensory-preaching. For a full treatment on the topic, see Rick Blackwood, *The Power of Multi-Sensory Preaching and Teaching* (Zondervan, 2008).

Second, as a bicultural person, I've had to learn the hard way that not all gestures are universally transferable. Gestures have different meanings depending on one's culture. For instance, when we gesture for someone to come over to us, we, in America, show our palms up as we wave our fingers collectively forward and back. In certain Asian cultures, however, that same motion is derogatory and reserved only for dogs and animals. Now, this is not to make us paranoid or paralyzed because we don't always know or see who's out there listening. Yet, it is something you should be aware of. If we don't know what's culturally sensitive, all it takes is the courage to ask someone from a different culture if we are missing the mark or have unintentionally offended them.

Practice and Rehearse the Sermon

You'll never regret practicing and rehearsing your message for Sunday, but you probably will regret failing to do so. Just as a wedding rehearsal is a moment to practice what will soon take place in real time, so rehearsing the sermon prepares the preacher. Here are a few principles for getting the message into your head, or what some have called internalization.

During my time as a senior pastor, I made it a Saturday evening and Sunday morning ritual to read over the manuscript several times. Typically, I would read through the script two or three times out loud on Saturday night. Then, on Sunday morning I would practice again out loud (but this time softly since everyone was asleep) using my condensed one-half-sheet version of the outline. There is something powerful that happens with regard to memory when you read over and rehearse the manuscript the night before you preach. During those hours of evening respite, the message becomes lodged into your brain cells.

Here are a couple of tips for preaching without notes or with minimal notes (such as a half sheet of paper). Most people are terrified of preaching without notes (also known as our safety blanket). I understand their concern. Having preached without notes and with notes, I definitely feel less stressed with the notes sitting directly on my Bible and under my eyes. The reason for preaching without notes is clarity. If our sermon is clear, we don't need to rely on our notes. The other rationale for no-notes preaching is that it helps us maintain eye contact and direct communication.

In any event, I'd like you to try something. Take out your sermon manuscript/outline. Try to write out from memory each of your main moves in full sentences. Try to remember which corresponding verses in your Scripture text align with those moves. Next, under each of the subordinate paragraphs which explain, illustrate, or apply, attempt condensing the entire paragraph into one primary word that summarizes your move and submove. Don't peek back at your sermon manuscript or outline. See how much of the sermon you can recall using the one-word method. You will be surprised at just how much of the sermon you can remember on Sunday morning after waking up.

Here's where your next step of faith is queued. While it's perfectly acceptable to bring your entire 2,500–4,000-word sermon manuscript (probably five to eight pages, single-spaced) up with you to the pulpit, attempt to preach with only a half sheet of paper listing and highlighting your main moves and subpoints. After employing this method for an entire sermon series, preach with only a 3×3 inch Post-it Note. From there, you might be emboldened enough to preach without *any* notes. Essentially, this process will wean you from being tied to your sermon manuscript, outline, and notes. The most important thing is that you are comfortable with whichever approach you choose. In general, I would advocate for less notes than more notes.

Final Thoughts on Delivery

Preaching in a Digital Age

In spring of 2020, COVID-19 forced most, if not all, preachers to broadcast their sermons online. Nobody was prepared for this jolting moment, which caused stress and perhaps trauma for many pastors and congregations. Post-COVID, most congregations have continued to video record and share their sermons online for congregants who cannot be there in person or as an attempt to reach a wider audience. While I'm not a complete Luddite or against all modes of digital communication, a sobering word of caution needs to be mentioned as we preach in this digital age.

Here's some basic ecclesiology: Preaching is intended for the local church. Our primary mission is to preach to the flesh-and-blood people sitting in the room with us and not for an "imaginary audience" somewhere out there. It has become acceptable and normative for churches to broadcast their sermons. Everyone's doing it, we like to say. But sometimes, preachers become so hyper-focused on "imaginary" listeners that they forget to communicate and deliver messages to their real listeners, not to mention that the financial investment required to produce decent or high-quality video streaming each week can eat up a sizable portion of a church's annual budget (both equipment and personnel). If we cater to the digital world, the cost may be the neglect of our most important ministry—the people who are physically present and before us.

Another possible challenge of preaching in our digital age is distraction or preachers feeling like they are competing with phones. As Stephen Stallard observes and wonders in his book *Missional Preaching*, "In our secular age, distraction is rampant. Our phones have changed us. A generation that lives in the perpetual glow of a tiny screen inevitably forgets how to engage with truths presented in a sermon. In the digital world, if you get bored, you keep scrolling or you open a streaming app. . . . Preachers stand behind the sacred desk and open something incredibly old-fashioned—a book. . . . Our listeners are distracted. How do we get through to them?"[20] I want to encourage you to preach whenever possible from a physical Bible rather than a tablet or computer. You might respond, "Well, that's not convenient," or "Get with the times!" There's something unspeakably powerful when a preacher reads from or raises a physical Bible in the pulpit rather than a device. Encourage your listeners to bring a physical copy of the Bible to church. The more we can decrease screen time even during a worship service, the more we may increase our listeners' ability to concentrate on the living and active Word of God.

Preaching and Artificial Intelligence (AI)

A final consideration in communication that we must address is preaching and artificial intelligence. AI is now part of the atmosphere and the air we breathe. We can try to deny the fact that AI is here to stay, but that would be naive. Due to space limitations and the fact that entire dissertations are being written on the topic, here are some thoughts and observations as we navigate this world of preaching and AI. First of all, instead of condemning the use of AI outright, let's consider a couple of benefits. Most users of AI would confess that the primary reason why they choose to partake of AI is speed. If pressed, they would blame AI use on personal laziness.

When prompting an AI overview on Google, I recently typed "Preaching and AI" and received the following response: "AI can assist in sermon preparation by brainstorming, providing research, summarizing commentaries, generating content like social media posts or graphics, and helping refine arguments and structure. However, it should be used as a tool, not a substitute for spiritual discernment and personal connection to God's Word, with pastors providing rigorous oversight, theological editing, and ensuring the final sermon reflects their personal voice and conviction."

The first half of this response is somewhat acceptable. We can probably benefit from some brainstorming ideas or even gathering research information for our sermons. The rest, however, is highly problematic. AI assumes that

20. Stephen Stallard, *Missional Preaching: Communicating the Gospel in an Age of Unbelief* (B&H Academic, 2025), 6.

the preacher herself or himself will fail to do their due diligence and merely edit a prewritten sermon for them. A sermon not written by one's own mind and effort is pulpit plagiarism.[21] Pulpit plagiarism is a moral and ethical issue and addresses a pastor's integrity. The congregation expects us to write our own sermons, and they compensate us for doing so. Failing to write our own sermons betrays the church's trust and involves more than one form of cheating. In short, be careful in how you use AI (if you choose to do so). Write your own sermons and share the credit, and cite your sources, even if AI helped you find a resource or two to include in your message.[22]

Let's go back to the basics: The sermon is a God-given calling and responsibility to those whom he calls to preach. As Karen Swallow Prior writes, "This is the first calling of every human being: to bear witness to the God who created the world. We are all called to this work. God's original design for humanity remains even today. Everything we do re-presents God, whether ill or well."[23] For preachers, this means we, in our calling as God's messengers, "re-present God" to both the congregation and the wider world "whether ill or well." Preaching that is partially or wholly reliant on AI puts into severe question whether we are fulfilling our calling as preachers of the Word. A preacher's use of AI puts our work ethic and integrity in peril since we are not giving our best effort to pray, think, and rely on the Spirit's work in and through us to communicate a contextualized sermon for the Lord's people. As you can tell, I'm discouraging us from using AI, apart from the occasional research aids that it might possibly provide. Give your congregation your undivided attention and effort in the task of preaching because you love them and they deserve as much. A robot will never touch their hearts as well as their own pastor can. Nota bene: AI information is not without its errors!

CONCLUSION

Now that we've laid the groundwork for what becomes a bona fide sermon, the preached Word, here are some final words of encouragement regarding communication. Remember to communicate! The word "communication" derives from "commune" or to be with and connect with others. Christian

21. See Scott M. Gibson, *Should We Use Someone Else's Sermon? Preaching in a Cut-and-Paste World* (Zondervan, 2008).

22. See Sean O'Callaghan and Paul A. Hoffman, *AI Shepherds and Electric Sheep: Leading and Teaching in the Age of Artificial Intelligence* (Baker Academic, 2025).

23. Karen Swallow Prior, *You Have a Calling: Finding Your Vocation in the True, Good, and Beautiful* (Brazos, 2025), 5–6.

preaching is a form of Christian fellowship. Effective sermon delivery relies on two distinct parts: high energy and verbal/nonverbal communication. If we can be intentional about each, this will automatically augment the experience for us preachers and our listeners, those sitting in the worship gathering. In addition, be your best self in the pulpit. Draw attention to the greatness of our triune God rather than allowing our feelings and emotions to detract from the message as a whole. Be creative and willing to experiment with different communication styles, including multisensory preaching, that will most tangibly benefit your listeners. Seek to be intentional about communicating cross-culturally and contextually as congregations today are not monolithic and monocultural. Most significantly, pray that God would allow your communication to work both visibly and behind the scenes in ways that we could never expect. Just ask the triune God, who is our greatest equipper and encourager!

QUESTIONS

1. How would you describe your communication style? In what areas has this chapter helped you widen your definition or practice of communication in preaching?
2. What comes more naturally to you in the areas of energy, verbal and nonverbal communication, and variety?
3. Who are the people in your congregation that may need more intentional consideration regarding sermonic delivery?
4. What is your attitude toward and practice concerning the use of artificial intelligence in preaching?

PRACTICES

1. Work on practicing your sermon this week and consider how you might depend less on your sermon manuscript/outline.
2. Try to practice and video record your sermon in front of your phone. What is your energy level like? What does your tone sound like? And how effective is your use of gestures?
3. Write the names of all your congregants with whom you are not very familiar. What are their ethnic, racial, cultural, and subcultural

backgrounds? How can you develop a relationship with them so that your preaching can be more contextualized for their discipleship growth?

4. Think about some natural ways to enhance your use of multisensory delivery forms and try one this week. What did you learn? What went well and what could have been done differently?

CONCLUSION

> At the name of Jesus every knee should bow, of those in heaven,
> and of those on earth, and of those under the earth,
> and that every tongue should confess that Jesus Christ is Lord,
> to the glory of God the Father.
>
> —Philippians 2:10–11 (NKJV)

Do you feel ready to preach? Of course, I say this tongue in cheek. Nobody is ever unequivocally prepared to preach. Yet, hopefully by now you will verify some level of greater confidence in your preparation. Since I don't particularly enjoy long-winded conclusions, let's drive home a few final points that I hope will stick.

As you've worked your way through these pages, it probably dawned on you several times how complex the task of preaching is. The sheer number of variables is beyond limit. We can technically organize and write an orthodox, clear, theologically sound, and inspiring message only to witness it falter between the pulpit and the pew. Even if we systematically work through each of these ten sermonic steps, there is no 100 percent money-back guarantee that your sermon will effectively transform listeners. Nevertheless, week in and week out, we put our most noble human effort into the message. Why? We pray and trust the triune God to divinely transform our listeners in mysterious and surprising ways. Like the little boy who is memorialized because he offered Jesus his modest lunch, the triune God can exponentially accomplish what we cannot with our sermonic meals. In God's sovereignty, he still wants you to sacrifice and offer your weekly lunch to him, as a symbol of obedience, worship, and love, trusting in *him* to feed and nourish others according to his plan.

Instead of summarizing the contents of this book, I want to conclude by tugging on a motivational string. Who is your primary audience when you preach God's Word? What or who is driving your preaching ministry? The apostle Paul's cautionary and sobering words in Philippians 2:10–11 declare who our ultimate audience is in the task and work of preaching. We preach in view of the day when everyone will bow their knees and worship King Jesus, to the Father's glory! While we do prepare our sermons for individual people and for the congregations we shepherd, ultimately we preach for the triune God alone. Preach in such a winsome way that you help lead and shepherd the congregation toward greater worship and growth in Christlikeness as they bow their knees daily before Christ Jesus the King, through the power of the Holy Spirit, and to the glory of God the Father.

Why bring up motivation at the end? I want your preaching ministry to endure as long as God wills. After a while, preaching can easily fall into the realm of the mundane and become mere habit. I've experienced the roller-coaster ride and the doldrums of being driven by people's comments. People's words land more strongly when we are overly concerned about our own names rather than being consumed with the name of Jesus. Taking to heart too deeply people's praise or criticism is a recipe for a short-lived preaching ministry. Listeners are capricious in their opinions about your messages. Some weeks, on the drive home, you will feel like the greatest orator on planet Earth. Other weeks you will want to hide yourself like a snail in a shell.

For this reason, "be strong and courageous" (Josh. 1:9) as you fulfill your preaching call. With love and forthrightness, preach with a backbone and tell them what God told you. Don't fall into the trap of preaching to please people, telling them "what their itching ears want to hear" (2 Tim. 4:3). As Taylor Combs warns, "But fear of man [and woman] is kryptonite for ministry faithfulness. We are not speaking from humans or for humans; we are speaking from God and for God."[1] If we preach for the triune God alone, we will preach with a spirit and posture of love, humility, surrender, obedience, and dependence on this great God for the work that only this God can do to accomplish what this God desires.

As we bring this work to a close, I want to share with you, pastors and preachers, a word of appreciation. Thank you for reading this book and most importantly for listening and following God's calling on your life to be a

1. Taylor Combs, "Why We Venerate and Vilify Christian Leaders," *Leadership Journal* 38 (2025): 26.

pastor and preacher of the Word. Much like the enthusiastic announcement offered over the intercom by flight attendants when they say, "We know you have a choice in air travel so we thank you for choosing to fly with us today," I similarly say to you, "I know you had a choice of homiletics books to read and I thank you for choosing to read this preaching textbook. I don't take your reading for granted. Thank you very much!"

Finally, I officially leave you with Haddon W. Robinson's words of wisdom, which I hope will extend to you a profound sense of peace, mitigate anxiety, and impart greater confidence in the call to preach: "There are no great preachers, only a great Christ." To expand and fit the theme of this trinitarian book, we might add: There are no great preachers, only a great triune God. Therefore, as you get ready to preach, "preach for the love of people and the joy of life transformation, preach with the transformative power of the Holy Spirit, preach for the sake of Christ and the glorious gospel, and preach for the glory of God the Father! Amen."[2]

2. Matthew D. Kim, *A Little Book for New Preachers: Why and How to Study Homiletics* (IVP Academic, 2020), 122.

FURTHER READING

Theologically Ready

Anizor, Uche. *How to Read Theology: Engaging Doctrine Critically and Charitably*. Baker Academic, 2018.

Butner, D. Glenn. *Trinitarian Dogmatics: Exploring the Grammar of the Christian Doctrine of God*. Baker Academic, 2022.

Emerson, Matthew Y., and Brandon D. Smith. *Beholding the Triune God: The Inseparable Work of Father, Son, and Spirit*. Crossway, 2024.

Gannett, Amy. *Fix Your Eyes: How Our Study of God Shapes Our Worship of Him*. B&H, 2021.

Holmes, Stephen R., Paul D. Molnar, Thomas H. McCall, Paul S. Fiddes, and Jason S. Sexton. *Two Views on the Doctrine of the Trinity*. Zondervan, 2014.

Jones, Beth Felker. *Practicing Christian Doctrine: An Introduction to Thinking and Living Theologically*. Baker Academic, 2014.

Koessler, John. *Folly, Grace, and Power: The Mysterious Act of Preaching*. Zondervan, 2011.

Kuhn, Chase R., and Paul Grimmond, eds. *Theology Is for Preaching: Biblical Foundations, Method, and Practice*. Lexham, 2021.

Lee, Ahmi. *Preaching God's Grand Drama: A Biblical-Theological Approach*. Baker Academic, 2019.

Lischer, Richard. *A Theology of Preaching: The Dynamics of the Gospel*. Wipf & Stock, 2001.

Meyer, Jason C. *Preaching: A Biblical Theology*. Crossway, 2013.

Reeves, Michael. *Delighting in the Trinity: An Introduction to the Christian Faith*. IVP Academic, 2012.

Sanders, Fred. *The Triune God*. Zondervan, 2016.

Smith, Robert Jr. *Doctrine That Dances: Bringing Doctrinal Preaching and Teaching to Life*. B&H Academic, 2008.

Vidu, Adonis. *The Same God Who Works All Things: Inseparable Operations in Trinitarian Theology*. Eerdmans, 2021.

Biblically Ready

Arthurs, Jeffrey D. *Preaching with Variety: How to Re-Create the Dynamics of Biblical Genres*. Kregel, 2007.

Gupta, Nijay K. *A Beginner's Guide to New Testament Studies: Understanding Key Debates*. Baker Academic, 2020.

Kaminski, Carol M. *Casket Empty: God's Plans of Redemption Through History, Old Testament Study Guide*. Casket Empty Media, 2012.

Klein, William W., Craig L. Blomberg, and Robert L. Hubbard Jr. *Introduction to Biblical Interpretation*. 3rd ed. Zondervan Academic, 2017.

Kuruvilla, Abraham. *Privilege the Text! A Theological Hermeneutic for Preaching*. Moody, 2013.

McCaulley, Esau, Janette H. Ok, Osvaldo Padilla, and Amy Peeler, eds. *The New Testament in Color: A Multiethnic Bible Commentary*. IVP Academic, 2024.

Merkle, Benjamin L. *Exegetical Gems from Biblical Greek: A Refreshing Guide to Grammar and Interpretation*. Baker Academic, 2019.

Mounce, William D. *Greek for the Rest of Us: Using Greek Tools without Mastering Biblical Languages*. Zondervan, 2007.

Palmer, David L. *Casket Empty: God's Plan of Redemption Through History, New Testament Study Guide*. Casket Empty Media, 2016.

Platt, David. *How to Read the Bible: A Simple Guide to Deeper Intimacy with God*. Thomas Nelson, 2025.

Redmond, Eric C. *Stories on the Way to the Kingdom: Interpreting and Applying Biblical Narratives*. Baker Academic, 2025.

Spencer, Aída Besançon. *The Exegetical Process: How to Write a New Testament Exegesis Paper Step-by-Step*. Kregel Academic, 2025.

Stuart, Douglas K. *Old Testament Exegesis: A Handbook for Students and Pastors*, 5th ed. Westminster John Knox, 2022.

Virkler, Henry A., and Karelynne Gerber Ayayo. *Hermeneutics: Principles and Processes of Biblical Interpretation*. 2nd ed. Baker Academic, 2023.

Culturally Ready

Bailey, Justin Ariel. *Interpreting Your World: Five Lenses for Engaging Theology and Cultures*. Baker Academic, 2022.

Blackwood, Rick. *The Power of Multisensory Preaching and Teaching: Increase Attention, Comprehension, and Retention*. Zondervan, 2008.

Bock, Darrell L. *Cultural Intelligence: Living for God in a Diverse, Pluralistic World*. B&H Academic, 2020.

Campbell, Heidi A., and John Dyer. *Ecclesiology for a Digital Church: Theological Reflections on a New Normal*. SCM, 2022.

Chatraw, Joshua D., and Karen Swallow Prior, eds. *Cultural Engagement: A Crash Course in Contemporary Issues*. Zondervan, 2019.

Feldhahn, Shaunti, and James N. Sells. *When Hurting People Come to Church: How People of Faith Can Help Solve the Mental Health Crisis*. Tyndale Refresh, 2025.

Gaventa, Bill. *Preaching Disability: A Resource for Pastors*. Eerdmans, 2026.

Glenn, Mike. *Preaching in a Post-Truth World: Recentering the Pulpit in a Chaotic World*. B&H, 2025.

Haidt, Jonathan. *The Anxious Generation: How the Great Rewiring of Childhood Is Causing an Epidemic of Mental Illness*. Penguin, 2024.

Inazu, John. *Learning to Disagree: The Surprising Path to Navigating Differences with Empathy and Respect*. Zondervan, 2024.

Kalas, J. Ellsworth. *Preaching in an Age of Distraction*. InterVarsity, 2014.

Kim, Matthew D. *Preaching to People in Pain: How Suffering Can Shape Your Sermons and Connect with Your Congregation*. Baker Academic, 2021.

Kim, Matthew D. *Preaching with Cultural Intelligence: Understanding the People Who Hear Our Sermons*. Baker Academic, 2017.

Kim, Matthew D., and Paul A. Hoffman. *Preaching to a Divided Nation: A Seven-Step Model for Promoting Reconciliation and Unity*. Baker Academic, 2022.

Muehlhoff, Tim, and Richard Langer. *Winsome Persuasion: Christian Influence in a Post-Christian World*. IVP Academic, 2017.

O'Callaghan, Sean, and Paul A. Hoffman. *AI Shepherds and Electric Sheep: Leading and Teaching in the Age of Artificial Intelligence*. Baker Academic, 2025.

Rhodes, Michael J. *Reimagining Biblical Politics: What Scripture Says About Public Life and Why It Matters*. Baker Academic, 2026.

Root, Andrew. *The Pastor in a Secular Age: Ministry to People Who No Longer Need a God*. Baker Academic, 2019.

Spiritually Ready

Bailey, Justin Ariel. *Discipling the Diseased Imagination: Spiritual Formation and the Healing of Our Hearts*. Baker Academic, 2026.

Bounds, E. M. *Pastor and Prayer: Why and How Pastors Ought to Pray*. Aneko, 2018.

Heisler, Greg. *Spirit-Led Preaching: The Holy Spirit's Role in Sermon Preparation and Delivery*. B&H, 2018.

Kaemingk, Matthew, and Kathryn Roelofs. *Leading Worship for Workers: How to Design Liturgies for All of Life*. Baker Academic, 2026.

Leach, Tara Beth. *The GREAT Morning Revolution: Daily Spiritual Practices for Meaningful Moments with God*. Zondervan Reflective, 2025.

Reed, Rick. *The Heart of the Preacher: Preparing Your Soul to Proclaim the Word*. Lexham, 2025.

Sanders, J. Oswald. *Spiritual Leadership: Principles of Excellence for Every Believer*. Moody, 2017.

Taylor, Barbara Brown. *The Preaching Life: Living Out Your Vocation*. Canterbury, 2013.

Villodas, Rich. *The Deeply Formed Life: Five Transformative Values to Root Us in the Way of Jesus*. Waterbrook, 2021.

Vines, Jerry, and Jim Shaddix. *Power in the Pulpit: How to Prepare and Deliver Expository Sermons*. Moody, 2017.

Ward, David B. *Practicing the Preaching Life*. Abingdon, 2019.

Warren, Tish Harrison. *Prayer in the Night: For Those Who Work or Watch or Weep*. IVP, 2021.

Communicationally Ready

Arthurs, Jeffrey D. *Preaching as Reminding: Stirring Memory in an Age of Forgetfulness*. IVP Academic, 2017.

Lybrand, Fred R. *Preaching on Your Feet: Connecting God and the Audience in the Preachable Moment*. B&H, 2008.

Mathews, Alice P. *Preaching That Speaks to Women*. Baker Academic, 2003.

McKenzie, Alyce M. *Making a Scene in the Pulpit: Vivid Preaching for Visual Learners*. Westminster John Knox, 2018.

Muehlhoff, Tim, and Todd V. Lewis. *Authentic Communication: Christian Speech Engaging Culture*. IVP Academic, 2010.

Robinson, Haddon W., and Craig Brian Larson. *The Art and Craft of Biblical Preaching: A Comprehensive Resource for Today's Communicators*. Zondervan Academic, 2023.

Schultze, Quentin J. *Communicating with Grace and Virtue: Learning to Listen, Speak, Text, and Interact as a Christian*. Baker Academic, 2020.

Stallard, Stephen. *Missional Preaching: Communicating the Gospel in an Age of Unbelief*. B&H Academic, 2025.

Tice, Rico. *Honest Evangelism: How to Talk About Jesus Even When It's Tough*. Good Book, 2015.

Wilson, Jim L. *Illustrating Well: Preaching Sermons that Connect*. Lexham, 2022.

Introductory Preaching Textbooks

Anderson, Kenton C. *Choosing to Preach: A Comprehensive Introduction to Sermon Options and Structures*. Zondervan, 2006.

Baxter, Wayne. *Preparing Sermons from the Page to the Pulpit: Exegesis to Exposition in Seven Steps*. Lexham, 2023.

Carter, Terry G., J. Scott Duvall, and J. Daniel Hays, *Preaching God's Word: A Hands-On Approach to Preparing, Developing, and Delivering the Sermon*. 2nd ed. Zondervan, 2018.

Chapell, Bryan. *Christ-Centered Preaching: Redeeming the Expository Sermon*. 3rd ed. Baker Academic, 2018.

Glanville, Mark R. *Preaching in a New Key: Crafting Expository Sermons in Post-Christian Communities*. IVP Academic, 2025.

Helm, David. *Expositional Preaching: How We Speak God's Word Today*. Crossway, 2014.

Keller, Timothy. *Preaching: Communicating Faith in an Age of Skepticism*. Viking, 2015.

Kim, Julius J. *Preaching the Whole Counsel of God: Design and Deliver Gospel-Centered Sermons*. Zondervan, 2015.

Kim, Matthew D. *A Little Book for New Preachers: Why and How to Study Homiletics*. IVP Academic, 2020.

Kuruvilla, Abraham. *A Manual for Preaching: The Journey from Text to Sermon*. Baker Academic, 2019.

Lowry, Eugene. *The Homiletical Plot: The Sermon as Narrative Art Form*. Westminster John Knox, 2000.

McDill, Wayne. *12 Essential Skills for Great Preaching*. B&H Academic, 2018.

O'Donnell, Douglas Sean, and Philip Ryken. *The Beauty and Power of Biblical Exposition: Preaching the Literary Artistry and Genres of the Bible*. Crossway, 2022.

Robinson, Haddon W. *Biblical Preaching: The Development and Delivery of Expository Messages*. 4th ed. Baker Academic, 2025.

Scharf, Greg. *Prepared to Preach: God's Work and Ours in Proclaiming His Word*. Christian Focus, 2007.

Sunukjian, Donald R. *Invitation to Biblical Preaching: Proclaiming Truth with Clarity and Relevance*. Kregel, 2007.

Webster, Douglas D. *More than a Sermon: The Purpose and Practice of Christian Preaching*. Lexham, 2024.

Wilson, Paul Scott. *The Four Pages of the Sermon: A Guide to Biblical Preaching*. Abingdon, 2018.

Genre-Sensitive Preaching

Alcántara, Jared E. *How to Preach Proverbs*. Fontes, 2022.

Arthurs, Jeffrey D. *How to Preach Narrative*. Fontes, 2022.

Boys, Ryan. *How to Preach Apocalyptic*. Fontes, 2024.

Langley, Kenneth J. *How to Preach the Psalms*. Fontes, 2021.

Long, Thomas G. *Preaching and the Literary Forms of the Bible*. Fortress, 1989.

Long, Thomas G. *Proclaiming the Parables: Preaching and Teaching the Kingdom of God*. Westminster John Knox, 2024.

Mathewson, Steven D. *The Art of Preaching Old Testament Narrative*. Baker Academic, 2021.

Mathewson, Steven D. *The Art of Preaching Old Testament Poetry*. Baker Academic, 2024.

Thompson, Andrew C. *How to Preach the Prophets*. Fontes, 2023.

Other Useful Resources for Preaching

Alcántara, Jared E. *The Practices of Christian Preaching: Essentials for Effective Proclamation*. Baker Academic, 2019.

Bargerhuff, Eric J., and Matthew D. Kim. *What's God Saying Here? How to Navigate Awkward, Troubling, and Bizarre Passages We Would Rather Skip*. Zondervan Reflective, 2025.

Begg, Alistair. *Preaching for God's Glory*. Crossway, 2011.

Bullmore, Mike. *The Heart of Preaching: The Functional Centrality of the Gospel in the Life and Work of the Preacher*. Crossway, 2026.

Carty, Austin. *Some of the Words Are Theirs: The Art of Writing and Living a Sermon*. Eerdmans, 2025.

Chan, Sam, and Malcolm Gill. *Topical Preaching in a Complex World: How to Proclaim Truth and Relevance at the Same Time*. Zondervan, 2021.

Currie, David A. *The Big Idea of Biblical Worship: The Development and Leadership of Expository Services*. Hendrickson, 2017.

Duduit, Michael. *Handbook of Contemporary Preaching: A Wealth of Counsel for Creative and Effective Proclamation*. 2nd ed. B&H Academic, 2024.

Edwards, O. C., Jr. *A History of Preaching*. Abingdon, 2004.

Gardner, Tyshawn. *Social Crisis Preaching: Biblical Proclamation for Troubled Times*. B&H Academic, 2023.

Gibson, Scott M. *Preaching for Special Services*. Baker Books, 2001.

Gibson, Scott M. *Preaching Points: 55 Tips for Improving Your Pulpit Ministry*. Weaver, 2016.

Gibson, Scott M. *Preaching with a Plan: Sermon Strategies for Growing Mature Believers*. Baker Books, 2012.

Gibson, Scott M., and Matthew D. Kim. *Homiletics and Hermeneutics: Four Views on Preaching Today*. Baker Academic, 2018.

Hulst, Mary S. *A Little Handbook for Preachers: Ten Practical Ways to a Better Sermon by Sunday*. IVP Books, 2016.

Kim, Matthew D., and Scott M. Gibson. *The Big Idea Companion for Preaching and Teaching: A Guide from Genesis to Revelation*. Baker Academic, 2021.

Kim, Matthew D., and Daniel L. Wong. *Finding Our Voice: A Vision for Asian North American Preaching*. Lexham, 2020.

Kuruvilla, Abraham. *A Vision for Preaching: Understanding the Heart of Pastoral Ministry*. Baker Academic, 2015.

LaRue, Cleophus J., and Luiz C. Nascimento. *The Future Shape of Christian Proclamation: What the Global South Can Teach Us About Preaching*. Cascade Books, 2020.

Lewis, Karoline M. *A Lay Preacher's Guide: How to Craft a Faithful Sermon*. Fortress, 2020.

Luchetti, Lenny. *Preaching with Empathy: Crafting Sermons in a Callous Culture*. Abingdon, 2018.

Merida, Tony. *Faithful Preaching: Declaring Scripture with Responsibility, Passion, and Authenticity*. B&H, 2009.

Mitchell, Henry H. *Celebration and Experience in Preaching*. Abingdon, 2008.

Pennington, Jonathan T. *Small Preaching: 25 Little Things You Can Do Now to Make You a Better Preacher*. Lexham, 2021.

Plantinga, Cornelius. *Reading for Preaching: The Preacher in Conversation with Storytellers, Biographers, Poets, and Journalists*. Eerdmans, 2013.

Powery, Luke A. *Spirit Speech: Lament and Celebration in Preaching*. Abingdon, 2009.

Quicke, Michael J. *Preaching as Worship: An Integrative Approach to Formation in Your Church*. Baker Books, 2011.

Redmond, Eric C. *Say It! Celebrating Expository Preaching in the African American Tradition*. Moody, 2020.

Rutledge, Fleming. *By the Word Worked: Encountering the Power of Biblical Preaching*. Baylor University Press, 2024.

Shaddix, Jim. *The Passion-Driven Sermon: Changing the Way Pastors Preach and Congregations Listen*. B&H Academic, 2003.

Stott, John. *Between Two Worlds: The Challenge of Preaching Today*. Eerdmans, 2017.

Tisdale, Leonora Tubbs. *Preaching as Local Theology and Folk Art*. Fortress, 1996.

Wiersbe, Warren W., and David Wiersbe. *The Elements of Preaching: The Art of Biblical Preaching—Clearly and Simply Presented*. Tyndale, 1986.

Willimon, William H. *Leading with the Sermon: Preaching as Leadership*. Fortress, 2020.

Wright, Christopher J. H. *How to Preach and Teach the Old Testament for All Its Worth*. Zondervan, 2016.

INDEX